D0149238

Re-Creating the Corporation

Re-Creating the Corporation

A Design of Organizations
for the 21st Century

Russell L. Ackoff

New York   Oxford
Oxford University Press
1999

Oxford University Press

Oxford   New York
Athens   Auckland   Bangkok   Bogotá   Buenos Aires
Calcutta   Cape Town   Chennai   Dar es Salaam   Delhi
Florence   Hong Kong   Istanbul   Karachi   Kuala Lumpur
Madrid   Melbourne   Mexico City   Mumbai
Nairobi   Paris   São Paulo   Singapore
Taipei   Tokyo   Toronto   Warsaw

and associated companies in
Berlin   Ibadan

Copyright © 1999 by Oxford University Press, Inc.

Published by Oxford University Press, Inc.
198 Madison Avenue, New York, New York 10016

Library of Congress Cataloging-in-Publication Data
Ackoff, Russell Lincoln, 1919–
Re-creating the corporation : a design of organizations for the 21st century
p.   cm.
Includes bibliographical references and index.
ISBN 0-19-512387-5
1. Management. 2. Industrial organization.
3. System theory. 4. Organizational change. 5. Business planning. I. Title.
HD31.A284   1999   658—dc21   99-13605

1 3 5 7 9 8 6 4 2
Printed in the United States of America
on acid-free paper

To "THE GUYS"
who keep my mind from falling asleep

Herb Addison
Bill Altier
Dick Clelland
Jamshid Gharajedaghi
Norm Gross
Aron Katsenelinboigen
Bijan Khorram
Jay Minas
Louis Padulo
Shel Rovin
Iraj Zandi

No century in recorded history has experienced so many social transformations and such radical ones as the twentieth century. They, I submit, may turn out to be the most significant events of this, our century, and its lasting legacy. In the developed free-market countries—which contain less than a fifth of the earth's population but are a model for the rest—work and work force, society and polity, are all, in the last decade of this century, *qualitatively* and *quantitatively* different not only from what they were in the first years of this century but also from what has existed at any time in history: in their configurations, in their processes, in their problems, and in their structures.

Peter F. Drucker
"The Age of Social Transformation,"
Atlantic Monthly

Contents

Preface

My learning, both theoretical and practical, has come primarily from practice and discussions with my three principal teachers: Edgar A. Singer, Jr.; Thomas A. Cowan; and C. West Churchman. I was originally educated to be an architect. One does not learn architecture in classrooms or libraries as much as one does by doing it and reflecting on the outcomes and their effects on others. My work on systems, organizations, and management has been no different.

My graduate work was done in the philosophy of science. I was dismissed from my first professorial appointment in the philosophy department of what was then Wayne University in Detroit because I wanted to create a Center for Applied Philosophy and I dared put on a conference on Philosophy and City Planning. In this conference, I wanted to marry two types of practice.

Once I changed my academic affiliation from philosophy to operations research, I was allowed to practice the kind of thinking I learned in philosophy and the kind of design I learned in architecture. My migration from operations research into systems was an evolution brought about by changing times and the different demands it created in practice.

I put a great deal of what I had learned in practice into my earlier book, *Creating the Corporate Future* (Wiley, 1981). I subsequently expanded and extended some parts of it in *The Democratic Corporation* (Oxford, 1994). I recorded most of my new thinking about the subjects covered in these books in a number of articles published in widely dispersed journals. It seemed to me to be time to pull it all together in one place. This is it.

This is not a collection of previous publications, but a new presentation of ideas put forth in a number of articles and books. Here

I have updated some of the ideas that needed it, expanded others, and integrated all of them into what I hope is a cohesive whole, a system of ideas.

I hope the readers have as much pleasure in taking this book apart as I have had in putting it together.

I have had a great deal of help in doing this from Pat Brandt, who provides a great deal of help in all my work, and from her daughter, Tina Fellerbaum. They play a large part in making the work fun as well as possible.

Philadelphia   Russell L. Ackoff
October 1998

Part I

BACKGROUND

1

The Nature of Systems

Introduction

Without changing our patterns of thought, we will not be
able to solve the problems we created with our current patterns of thought.

—Albert Einstein

Over time, every way of thinking generates important problems
that it cannot solve. Nevertheless, Albert Einstein's simple but
profound thought is not widely appreciated or acted on. As a result,
our society, its institutions, and the organizations operating within it
continue to try to solve their critical problems in old ways, but succeed
only in exacerbating them.

For example: the United States has the highest percentage of its
population in prison of any country in the world, yet has the highest
crime rate. It spends more per capita on health than any other country
in the world, yet ranks seventh in the results obtained and is the only
developed country without universal coverage. It pours money into
education, yet has the highest rate of illiteracy in the developed world,
and that rate is increasing. It adds highways and expressways while
increasing congestion and air pollution. It has a larger percentage of
eligible voters not voting than any developed country. And perhaps

most important, it has a distribution of wealth that is continually getting worse. According to a study by the U.S. Department of Agriculture that was released on September 15, 1997, 11 million people a year in this country go hungry. What irony—the richest country in the world has a higher percentage of its population living in poverty than any other developed country.

And what about corporations? According to Arie de Geus (1997):

By 1983, one-third of the 1970 Fortune 500 companies had been acquired or broken into pieces, or had merged with other companies. (51)

The high corporate mortality rate seems unnatural. No living species suffers from such a discrepancy between its maximum life expectancy and the average span it realizes. (52)

we [have] found that across the Northern Hemisphere, average corporate life expectancy [is] well below 20 years. (53)

Something is fundamentally wrong!

Although Toffler (1971) and many others who have followed him have made us aware of fundamental changes that are taking place, only a handful (like Drucker, 1994) have tried to explain them. Many know that changes in our way of thinking have begun to take place, but few understand the nature of these changes and their implications.

Every culture has a shared pattern of thinking. It is the cement that holds a culture together, gives it unity. A culture's characteristic way of thinking is imbedded in its concept of the nature of reality, its *world view*. A change of world view not only brings about profound cultural changes, but also is responsible for what historians call a "change of age." An age is a period of time in which the prevailing world view has remained relatively unchanged. Today, our world view is changing in fundamental ways; therefore, we are involved in a change of age.

Such changes do not occur often. The last one, the Renaissance, took place in the fourteenth and fifteenth centuries. The Machine or Modern Age it ushered in has begun to pass and a new age has begun to emerge. It still has a long way to go. It is not at all clear that the United States will lead the nations of the West in this change. It is not even apparent that it will follow.

Few individuals within a culture can articulate its prevailing world view and its imbedded way of thinking because most absorb them unconsciously, by osmosis, while growing up. Resistance to adopting a new pattern of thought is widespread; most people treat their knowledge of the old pattern as an investment that has not yet been fully exploited. Those who have benefited most from the old pattern of thought are comfortable with it and have a high tolerance of the problems it has created and leaves unsolved. The educational system is among the principal beneficiaries of such an old pattern and therefore is a major force in maintaining it. Those who suffer most because of an old pattern generally do not have the knowledge and understanding required to replace it. We suffer not only from a maldistribution of wealth, but also from a maldistribution of knowledge and understanding.

Emergence of the new world view was stimulated to a large extent by a growing awareness of the nature of *systems* and the implications of their nature to effective organization and management. There is no one source of the emerging world view, but the work of von Bertalanffy (1968) was certainly one of its major stimuli. "Although von Bertalanffy first presented his idea of a 'General System Theory' in a philosophy seminar at the University of Chicago in 1937, it was only after World War II that his first publications appeared on this subject" (Laszlo and Laszlo, 1997, 7). By the 1960s, the "systems movement" was well on its way.

To understand the emerging way of thinking, it is necessary to understand the nature of systems.

The Nature of Systems

This book is a product of applying systems thinking to the management and organization of enterprises. Therefore, an understanding of the nature of systems and systems thinking is essential for understanding what this book is about.

Although most people can identify many different systems, few know precisely what a system is. Without such knowledge, one cannot understand them, and without such an understanding, one cannot be aware of their implications for their management and organization and for treatment of the most important problems that currently face them.

There are many different definitions of "system" in the literature, but they are more alike than different. The one that follows tries to capture their core of agreement.

A system is a whole consisting of two or more parts that satisfies the following five conditions:

1. The whole has one or more defining properties or functions.

For example, a defining function of an automobile is to transport people on land; one of the defining functions of a corporation is to produce and distribute wealth; the defining function of a hospital is to provide care for the sick and disabled. Note that the fact that a system has one or more functions implies that it may be a part of one or more larger (containing) systems, its functions being the roles it plays in these larger systems.

2. Each part in the set can affect the behavior or properties of the whole.

For example, the behavior of such parts of the human body as the heart, lungs, stomach, brain, and lungs can affect the performance and properties of the whole. On the other hand, the (vermiform) appendix, which is not known to have any effect on the whole, is not a part of the system but is an add-on or attachment to it, as its name implies. (If the appendix is ever found to have a function in the body, its name will have to be changed.) The manuals, maps, and tools usually found in the glove compartment of a car are examples of appendices rather than parts of the car. They are not essential for performance of its defining function.

3. There is a subset of parts that is sufficient in one or more environments for carrying out the defining function of the whole; each of these parts is necessary but insufficient for carrying out this defining function.

These parts are *essential* parts of the system; without any one of them, the system cannot carry out its defining function. An automobile's engine, fuel injector, steering wheel, and battery are essential—without them the automobile cannot transport people. Each type of medically trained participant in a hospital's care system—doctors, nurses, technicians, and so on—affect the care provided. They are essential, but the television rental agents and attendants in the gift shops are not.

Most systems also contain *nonessential* parts that affect its functioning but not its defining function. An automobile's radio, ashtray, floor mats, and clock are nonessential, but they do affect automobile users and usage in other ways, for example, by entertaining or informing passengers while they are in transit.

A corporation is a system some of whose parts are essential—for example, finance, purchasing, production, and marketing—and some of whose parts may not be—for example, public and employee relations. A corporation may also have appendices, for example, a corporate foundation or a tenant in a building it owns and occupies. Note that suppliers, wholesalers, retailers, and customers who are parts of a corporation's environment may also be essential to it.

A system that requires certain environmental conditions in order to carry out its defining function is an *open* system. This is why the set of parts that form an open system cannot be sufficient for performing its function in every environment. A system that could carry out its function in every environment would be completely independent of its environment and, therefore, be *closed*. A hermetically sealed clock is a relatively closed system since it can perform in most environments in which it might be placed.

The *environment* of a system consists of those things that can affect the properties and performance of that system, but over which it has no control. That part of its environment that a system can influence, but not control, is said to be *transactional*. Consumers and suppliers, for example, are part of a corporation's transactional environment. That part of a system's environment that can neither be influenced nor controlled is said to be *contextual*, for example, the weather and other natural events, such as floods and earthquakes, and, in the case of a corporation, at least some competitive behavior.

4. The way that each essential part of a system affects its behavior or properties depends on (the behavior or properties of) at least one other essential part of the system.

Put another way, the essential parts of a system form a connected set, that is, a path can be found between any two parts. No essential part of a system has an independent effect on the system of which it is a part. For example, the way the heart affects the body depends on what the lungs are doing, and the way the lungs affect the body depend on what the heart, brain, and other parts are doing. The way that a manufacturing department affects a corporation's performance depends on the behavior of its marketing department; the behavior and properties of the marketing department are affected by the behavior and properties of the production and engineering department; and so on.

The essential parts of a system necessarily interact, either directly or indirectly. Therefore, a collection of automobiles, even if owned by one person, does not constitute a system because the automobiles do not interact. On the other hand, the motor and brakes of an automobile are essential and they do interact.

5. The effect of any subset of essential parts on the system as a
    whole depends on the behavior of at least one other such
    subset.

Like the individual parts of a system, no subset of the parts of a system
has an independent effect on it. The effect of the metabolic subsystem on
the human body depends on the behavior of the nervous subsystem, the
effect of the nervous subsystem depends on the behavior of the motor
subsystem, and so on.

If the parts of an entity do not interact, they form an aggregation,
not a system. A crowd, as distinct from an organization, is a familiar
example. Many holding companies and conglomerates are aggrega-
tions, not systems; the only thing their parts have in common is their
ownership. They do not interact.

It follows from the definition of a system that its properties derive
from the *interactions* of its parts, not their actions taken separately.
Therefore, when a system is disassembled, it loses its defining function
and so do its parts. When an automobile is disassembled, it is no longer
an automobile, even when all of its parts are held within one room.
The automobile, like every system, is a product of the interactions of
its parts, not their sum. The same is true of a person: when disassembled (say, by surgery) the person no longer lives.

Furthermore, when a system is disassembled its essential parts lose
their defining properties or functions. For example, if the motor that is
essential for the functioning of an automobile is removed, it can move
nothing, not even itself. A hand removed from a person's arm cannot
point, write, or pick up anything. Persons see, not their eyes; persons
think, not their brains. The eye and brain removed from the head see
and think nothing. A manufacturing department cannot function without purchasing, marketing, finance.

A system is a whole whose essential properties, its defining functions, are *not* shared by any of its parts. For example, no part of an automobile by itself can transport a person from one place to another, nor
can any part of a person live when separated from him or her.

Summarizing and oversimplifying:

A system is a whole that cannot be divided into independent parts
    without loss of its essential properties or functions.

This hardly seems revolutionary, but its implications are. Consider
some of them that relate to the organization and management of corporations.

System Performance: Whole-ing the Parts

Because the properties of a system derive from the interactions of its parts rather than their actions taken separately,

> when the performances of the parts of a system, considered separately, are improved, the performance of the whole may not be (and usually is not) improved.

In fact, the system involved may be destroyed or made to function less well. For example, suppose we were to bring together one each of every automobile currently available and, for each essential part, determine which automobile had the best one. We might find that the Rolls Royce had the best motor, the Mercedes the best transmission, the Buick the best brakes, and so on. Then suppose we removed these parts from the automobiles of which they were part and tried to assemble them into an automobile that would consist of all the best available parts. We would not even get an automobile, let alone the best one, because *the parts don't fit together.* The performance of a system depends on how its parts interact, not on how they act taken separately. (This principle has considerable significance when considering benchmarking, as we will see in Chapter 12.) If we try to put a Rolls Royce motor in a Hyundai, we do not get a better automobile. Chances are we could not get it in, and if we did, the car would not operate well.

Despite all this, most systems are managed in a contradictory way: they are focused on improving the parts taken separately. This perspective is induced by management education. Most business schools teach each of the functions of a corporation separately—production, marketing, finance, personnel, and so on—and never or inadequately deal with the way they interact.

Clearly, if an essential part of a system fails, the system as a whole may do so, for example, when the motor of an automobile freezes. Therefore, the way each essential part of a system performs is critical to the performance of a system as a whole, but only as it affects the whole. No part of a system should be changed without understanding its effect on the whole and determining that this effect is beneficial.

It follows that a fundamental function of management is to manage (1) the interactions of those units and individuals for whom they are responsible, (2) the interactions of their units with other units within the organization, and (3) the interactions of their units with other organizations or their units in each one's environment.

We need a type of organization that facilitates such management.

The conventional autocratic hierarchy found in most corporations does not do so. What is required is the subject of the remainder of this book.

Righting the Wrongs

The performance of any system has two dimensions: the *efficiency* with which it does whatever it does (doing things right) and the *effectiveness* of what it does (doing the right thing, its value). These should be taken together because *the righter we do the wrong thing, the wronger we become.* It is better to do the right thing wrong than to do the wrong thing right. When we do the right thing wrong, we make a mistake that can be corrected; hence, we learn how to be more effective. Put another way: it is better to aim at and miss the right thing than aim at and hit the wrong thing.

Consider our so-called health care system. The fact is that it is not a health care system. Its servers are compensated for taking care of sickness and disabilities; it is a sickness-and-disability-care system. If it succeeded in eliminating sickness and disabilities, the system would no longer exist and the servers within it would be without employment. Therefore, whatever the intentions of the individual servers, the system is so operated as to make sure there are people who require the "care" they provide. It is well known in medical circles that a significant percentage of those in hospitals are there because of "errors" the hospital made on their last or current visit, that unnecessary tests and surgery are frequently carried out, and that pharmaceuticals prescribed either separately or in combination are responsible for a great deal of the illness and disabilities requiring treatment.

Improvement of the automobile is an excellent example of doing the wrong thing right. The concept of an automobile has not changed significantly since early in this century. However effective the automobile may have been then, it has become increasingly dysfunctional since. Today it is justly referred to as a "menace." Congestion continues to mount, making automotive travel in many cities increasingly time- and nerve-consuming, as in Mexico City, Santiago, Caracas, London, and New York. In some cities, legislation now limits the use of automobiles to designated days of the week; others have prohibited use of automobiles in specified areas—restricting traffic there to pedestrians and, sometimes, public transportation.

Furthermore, pollution produced by automobiles continues to get worse. In Mexico City, children are kept from school when it is unhealthy for them to venture out of the house because of pollution.

The average number of people in automobiles in most cities of the world is less than two and about 80 percent of them carry no more than two. These automobiles move at considerably lower speeds than those of which they are capable. In short, they are too big, too fast, and too polluting for effective urban use during the work week.

Renault has started to produce small two-passenger urban automobiles, but are selling them at a price that precludes their widespread use. Nevertheless, this is a move in the right direction. They are doing the right thing wrong. Other manufacturers have announced that they are following suit.

Corporate efforts to improve the quality of their products is obviously the right thing to be doing, but as discussed in Chapter 12, since most of these efforts have not met expectations, corporations have gone about it in the wrong way. On the other hand, as I will try to show in the same chapter, downsizing is a case of doing the wrong thing, no matter how efficiently it is done.

Systems Analysis and Synthesis

The predisposition to take systems apart and treat the parts separately is a consequence of *analytic* thinking. Unfortunately, "analysis" and "thought" are frequently treated as synonyms, but analysis is only one way of thinking; *synthesis* is another. Both involve three steps.

1. In analysis, something that we want to understand is first taken apart. In synthesis, that which we want to understand is first identified as a part of one or more larger systems.

In the first step of analysis, a corporation might be taken apart into purchasing, manufacturing, marketing, and so on. In the first step of synthesis, a corporation is taken to be a part of a larger system, for example, an industry or society.

2. In the second step of analysis, an effort is made to understand the behavior of each part of a system taken separately. In the second step of synthesis, an effort is made to understand the function of the larger system(s) of which the whole is a part.

In analysis of a corporation, an effort would be made to understand each of the functions within it. In synthesis, the effort would be to identify the defining function(s) of the larger system(s) containing the corporation. The function of society might be identified as providing its members with the opportunity to pursue their objectives efficiently.

3. In analysis, the understanding of the parts of the system to be understood is then aggregated in an effort to explain the behavior or properties of the whole. In synthesis, the understanding of the larger containing system is then disaggregated to identify the role or function of the system to be understood.

Analysis of a system reveals its structure and how it works. It provides the knowledge required to make it work efficiently and to repair it when it stops working. Its product is know-how, knowledge, not understanding. To enable a system to perform effectively we must understand it—we must be able to explain its behavior—and this requires being aware of its functions in the larger systems of which it is a part. The behavior of a corporation is not explained by describing its parts, how they work, and the effect of their interactions, such as the production and marketing of a specified type of product. The behavior of a corporation can only be understood by being aware of its functions in society, for example, the production and distribution of wealth.

Although analysis cannot yield an explanation of the behavior or properties of the whole, it can explain the behavior of the parts by revealing their role or function in the whole, how they contribute to the functioning of the whole. No amount of analysis of American and English automobiles can explain why they are driven from different sides on different sides of the road. Nor will any amount of analysis of American cars explain why most of them were built for 6 passengers until recently. They were built that way because they were intended to carry the average American family, which consisted of 5.6 people at the time. It is now 3.2, hence the cars are becoming smaller.

Perhaps the most costly disassembly in which our culture has been engaged is the disaggregation of life itself into work, play, learning, and inspiration. Each of these aspects of life has been separated from the others by creating institutions for engaging in only one at a time, excluding the other three as much as possible. Businesses are designed for work, not play, learning, or inspiration. Country clubs, theaters, and sports stadiums are designed for play, not work, learning or inspiration. Schools are designed for learning, not work, play, or inspiration. Museums and churches are designed for inspiration, not work, play, or learning. However, one of the most important products of systems thinking is the realization that the effectiveness with which any of these four functions can be carried out depends on the extent to which they are carried out together, in an integrated way.

We will succeed in continuously improving our standard of living and quality of life only to the extent that we erase the distinctions between work, play, learning, and inspiration, and the institutions that facilitate them. Their interaction is another interaction that management must come to manage effectively.

Messing Up Problems

One of the most damaging misconceptions plaguing most people, including managers, is that problems are objects of direct experience. Not so; they are abstractions extracted from experience by analysis. Problems are related to experience as atoms are to tables. Tables are experienced directly, not atoms. We are almost never confronted with separable problems but with situations that consist of complex systems of strongly interacting problems. I call such systems of problems *messes*.

Therefore, the behavior of a mess depends more on how its parts interact than on how they act independently of each other. However, it is standard practice to reduce messes to lists of problems: to prioritize and treat them separately, as self-contained entities. Most people, including managers, do not generally know how to deal effectively with messes, with reality taken as a whole.

Effective management requires *dissolving* messes, not solving or resolving problems.

Ways of Treating Problems and Messes

There are four very different ways of dealing with problems and messes in the "real" world.

> *Absolution:* to ignore a problem or mess and hope it will take care of itself and go away of its own accord.

More problems are treated this way than most of us would care to admit. To manage this way is to manage by default. This is attractive to many managers because it is much more difficult to attribute responsibility for not doing something that should have been done than for doing something that should not have been done. The fact is that "letting well enough alone" sometimes works well.

> *Resolution:* to do something that yields an outcome that's good enough, that "satisfices."

Resolution involves a clinical approach to problems or messes, one that relies heavily on past experience, trial and error, qualitative judgment, and so-called common sense. It focuses more on the uniqueness of a problem or mess than on what it has in common with other problems.

> *Solution:* to do something that yields or comes as close as possible to the best possible outcome, something that optimizes.

This involves a research approach to problems or messes, one that relies heavily on experimentation, quantitative analysis, and uncommon sense. It focuses more on the general aspects of a problem or mess than its uniqueness. Problem solving is a major occupation of the management sciences, which emerged in the military during World War II and whose use became the principal thrust of management in the 1950s and 1960s. Unfortunately, it turned out that many of the problems that emerged in the late 1960s and 1970s did not lend themselves to solution. This stimulated development of the systems sciences, which focuses on ways of dissolving problems and messes. (See Ackoff, 1979.)

> *Dissolution:* to redesign either the entity that has the problem or mess, or its environment, in such a way as to eliminate the problem or mess and enable the system involved to do better in the future than the best it can do today, in a word, to idealize.

Dissolution focuses equally on the generality and uniqueness of a problem or mess, and it employs whatever techniques, tools, and methods—clinical or scientific—that can assist in the design process.

The difference between solutions and dissolutions is illustrated by the following very simple example. Placing the instruction "Close Cover Before Striking" on the front of old paper matchbook covers, to prevent a flying spark from igniting the matches it contained, constituted a solution to the problem. When the abrasive was placed on the back of the matchbook rather than the front, the problem was dissolved.

The differences between the four types of treatment are illustrated by the following relatively simple example.

> Back in the 1950s, General Electric's Appliance Division was confronted with a problem involving refrigerators. Two versions of every model had to be produced, one with doors hinged on the left and the other with doors hinged on the right. The proportion of sales of each varied substantially by market and within markets over time. This resulted in seri-

ous inventory problems, the inability to meet demand some of the time and a resulting loss of sales, and excess stock at other times and places. Most customers were not willing to wait while the right- or left-handed refrigerator was ordered for them; they were more inclined to switch brands to get the door they wanted.

This problem was ignored (absolution) for many years, during which time it became worse. Salesmen were then enlisted in producing forecasts of sales of each version of each model by market areas (resolution). Their forecasts were often significantly wrong and the average error increased with increases in sales. Management science (solution) was then invoked, and it produced statistically based forecasts that were an improvement over judgmental forecasts but still not good enough.

The problem was eventually dissolved by developing refrigerators with doors that could be mounted on either side of a refrigerator and thus be made to open either way. This not only eliminated the inventory-mix problem, but was an attractive marketing feature: when the owner of a refrigerator moved and the move required a change in direction of their refrigerator's door opening, the refrigerator did not need replacement. The door could be mounted on the other side.

Problems and Disciplines

One of the greatest disservices of formal education lies in the fact that students are induced to believe that every problem can be placed in an academic discipline such as the physical, chemical, biological, psychological, sociological, political, and ethical. In business schools, problems are placed in such categories as financial, personnel, public relations, production, marketing, distribution, and purchasing. However, the world is not organized like universities, colleges, and schools, by disciplines. Disciplinary categories reveal nothing about either the nature of the problems placed in them or the best way to deal with them, but they do tell us something about the nature of those who categorize them.

There is a classic case in which the tenants of a large office building complained about the increasingly poor elevator service. A consulting firm specializing in elevator-related problems was employed to deal with the situation. It first established that average waiting time for elevators was too long. It then evaluated the possibilities of adding elevators, replacing existing elevators with faster ones, and introducing computer controls to improve utilization of elevators. For various reasons, none of these turned out to be satisfactory. The engineers declared the problem to be unsolvable.

When exposed to the problem, a young psychologist employed in the building's personnel department made a simple suggestion that dissolved the problem. Unlike the engineers who saw the service as too slow, he saw the problem as one deriving from the boredom of those waiting for an elevator. So he decided they should be given something to do. He suggested putting mirrors in the elevator lobbies to occupy those waiting by enabling them to look at themselves and others without appearing to do so. The mirrors were put up and complaints stopped. In fact, some of the previously complaining tenants congratulated management on improvement of the elevator service.

It is not uncommon for problems to be best solved in domains other than the one in which they were first identified. Headaches are a simple example. They are not usually treated by performing brain surgery, but by putting a pill in the stomach. Understanding the way the parts of a system interact enables one to find a better place to enter the system.

The effect of categorizing problems by disciplines is that they then tend to be dealt with only by people in that discipline. When, for example, a problem is categorized as "marketing," it tends to be retained within the marketing department. However, it is important for managers to know that the best place to treat a problem is not necessarily where it appears.

Consider the following example:

A vice president of production of a large paper-producing company noted that one of the company's plants was suffering from a continuing reduction of output over a five-year period. He conducted analyses that showed it was not due to decreased productivity of the equipment involved nor to increased downtime for maintenance. He then identified the cause. The company had added a large number of new papers to its product line in the last five years, and this required more and shorter production runs. Therefore, significantly more time was required to set up these production runs. Such setup time was not productive.

Therefore, the vice president engaged a research group to find a way of sequencing production runs to minimize setup time. In the early stages of its work, the research group found that most of the products produced and sold by the company were not profitable. Since the problem resulted from an increased number of production runs, it suggested cutting back on the product line, eliminating unprofitable products. Control of the product line was a responsibility of the marketing department. When the vice president of marketing was approached with the problem and the proposed solution, he rejected it because, he said, every unprofitable product was purchased by heavy users of profitable products. When asked how he knew this, he said he didn't but was not willing to risk losing profitable sales by conducting the research required to find out whether he was right.

The research group then reconsidered the formulation of the problem, which had been formulated as the need to reduce the number of products offered for sale in order to reduce the number that had to be produced. The group realized that the number of products produced could be reduced another way: by reducing the number of products sold in the product line without reducing the product line. Therefore, an incentive system was designed in which salesmen would receive a commission proportional to the profitability of their sales, not their dollar volume, as was the case at the time. The commission for profitable sales was set so that if the same amount of profitable products were sold next year as had been sold last year, the salesmen's income would remain unchanged. They were to receive no commission for unprofitable sales.

The compensation system was installed on a trial basis in one of the five regional sales areas. During the trial period, more than half the products in the product line were not sold, and salesmen earnings and company profit increased significantly. The system was then adopted nationally. The originally formulated production problem was more than

solved because the number of production runs were reduced
below the number involved before the decline of production
output had begun.

Not all ways of viewing a problem are equally productive, but the
one that is most productive is seldom obvious. Therefore, problems
should be viewed from as many different perspectives as possible
before a way of treating them is selected. The best way often involves
collaboration of multiple points of view. Unfortunately, universities
and colleges discourage interactions between disciplinary departments,
and they frequently penalize faculty members who try to interact.
Students get a message from this that is both strong and wrong.
Corporations do much the same thing when they create "silos" that are
difficult to penetrate and to make interact. This situation can be corrected by means of a type of organization discussed in Chapter 9.

Conclusion

The discussion in this chapter has not by any means exhausted either
the nature of systems and systems thinking or their implications to
management and the organization of enterprises. More of each of
these topics is dealt with in the remainder of Part I. In Chapter 2, I
consider different types of systems and their effects on organizations
and the way they are managed. In Chapter 3, I consider the basic types
of traditional management and planning and their deficiencies and discuss a new, systems-oriented type of management and planning, an
interactive one.

In Part II, Chapters 4 to 8, each of the five aspects of interactive
planning is treated in a separate chapter.

In Part III, three major types of managerial and organizational
transformations are described and explained: democratization of what
are normally autocratically structured and managed organizations
(Chapter 9); substitution of a market economy within organizations for
one that is centrally planned and controlled (Chapter 10); and a multidimensional organizational design that eliminates the need to restruc-
ture when internal or external changes require adaptation (Chapter
11).

In Part IV, I examine currently popular panaceas and the reasons
they fail to fulfill their promises in most cases (Chapter 12). Finally, in
Chapter 13, I consider what a systems-oriented transformation of an

organization consists of and requires, and what leadership of such a transformation consists of and requires.

A set of suggested systems-oriented readings is provided in Appendix A. This list is intended to provide exposure to the diversity of thinking in the field, not to reinforce what I present in this book. Appendix B contains a description of an application of interactive planning (such as is described in Part II) of a major activity in DuPont, one that is responsible for safety, health, and the environment.

2

Types of Systems and Models

Introduction

> Social progress makes the well-being of all more and more
> the business of each.
>
> —Henry George

Whatever one considers systems to be, there are obviously different ways of classifying them. They can be classified in many different ways, for example, by size, by discipline (physical, chemical, biological, psychological, and so on), by location, and by function. The
choice of a classification scheme depends on how one intends to use it.
For my purposes—examining the consequences of mismatching systems and the way we think about them—the critical classifying variable
is *purpose*, and purpose can only exist where there is *choice*, and choice is
of either means or ends, that is, desired outcomes.

An entity is purposeful if it can select both means and ends in two
  or more environments.

Although the ability to make choices is necessary for purposefulness,
it is not sufficient. An entity that can behave differently (select different
means) but produce only one outcome in any one of a set of different

environments is *goal seeking*, not purposeful. Servomechanisms are goal seeking. For example, automatic pilots on ships and airplanes and thermostats for heating systems have a desired outcome programmed into them; they do not choose them. The destination of a ship or airplane on automatic pilot is programmed into it, as is the temperature to be maintained by a thermostat. In contrast, people can pursue different outcomes in the same and in different environments and therefore are obviously purposeful; so are certain types of social groups. Some entities can seek different outcomes in different environments but have no choice as to which outcome they seek; it is externally determined, not a matter of choice. An automatic pilot can be set for different destinations at different times. The outcome of purposeful behavior is never completely determined externally. It is at least partially determined by the choice made and therefore by the one making the choice.

The typology of systems used here depends on whether or not the parts of a system and the system as a whole are purposeful. Using this criterion, there are four different types of systems and four different types of system models. (These are shown in Table 2.1.)

1. *Deterministic*, systems and models in which neither the parts nor the whole are purposeful.
2. *Animated*, systems and models in which the whole is purposeful but the parts are not.
3. *Social*, systems and models in which both the parts and the whole are purposeful.
4. *Ecological*, systems and models in which some parts are purposeful but as a whole have no purposes of their own.

These four types of systems form a sort of hierarchy. Animated systems have deterministic systems as their parts: humans, for example, are animate, but their organs are deterministic. In addition, some animate systems, like people, can create and use deterministic systems such as machines, but deterministic systems cannot create animate systems. Social systems have animated systems as their parts, but animate

Table 2.1 Types of Systems and Models

Systems and Models	Parts	Whole
Deterministic	Not purposeful	Not purposeful
Animated	Not puposeful	Purposeful
Social	Purposeful	Purposeful
Ecological	Purposeful	Not purposeful

systems do not have social systems as their parts. All three types of systems are contained in ecological systems, some of whose parts are purposeful but not the whole. For example, the planet Earth is an ecological system that has no purpose of its own; however, it contains social and animate systems that do and deterministic systems that don't.

Consider each of these types of systems in more detail.

Deterministic Systems

Systems that have no purpose of their own and whose parts do not either are systems whose behavior is determined. They are exemplified by mechanisms, for example, automobiles, fans, and clocks. Although deterministic systems, including mechanisms, have no purposes of their own, they frequently serve the purpose or purposes of one or more entities external to them—their creators, controllers, or users. Provision of that service is their function. Therefore, the function of an automobile is to transport its driver and passengers to a desired location. Although the parts of a mechanistic system do not have purposes of their own, they do have functions serving the function of the whole: the motor of an automobile has the function of moving the body and its contents. Therefore, all the subsystems of a deterministic system are also deterministic systems whose function it is to serve the function of the whole.

If the behavior or properties of a deterministic system are affected by its environment, it is an *open* system. If it is not affected by its environment, it is *closed*. Even closed deterministic systems have a function: to serve either the purposes of an external entity or the function of a larger system of which they are a part. For example, Descartes and Newton conceptualized the universe as a closed mechanistic system, as a hermetically sealed clock, and they believed that this system had been created by God to serve His purposes and to do His work. This was its function. Although such commonplace open deterministic systems as automobiles, generators, and computers have no purposes of their own, they serve either the purposes of their producers and users or the function or functions of the system that contains them.

Mechanisms are not the only deterministic systems; plants are also mechanistic even though they are alive. Neither they nor their parts can display choice; neither they nor their parts have purposes of their own. It follows that the defining characteristic of life is not purposefulness. Computers that play chess choose means but not ends. The outcome they produce is completely determined by the information and program put into them by external sources. Instructions programmed into a computer are its causal laws. These, together with its internal structure and externally provided inputs, completely determine its behavior.

Deterministic systems can be differentiated by the number of functions they have. An ordinary clock has one function, to tell time. On the other hand, an alarm clock is multifunctional since it also has a wake-up function. Some clocks have additional functions, for example, they can measure lapsed time and reveal the temperature. Which functions clocks have are determined by an external entity, as when a person sets or unsets the alarm on a clock.

Animated Systems

Animated systems have purposes of their own, but their parts don't. The most familiar examples are, of course, animals, including human beings. All animated systems are *organisms*—they are living—but not all organisms are animated systems. Life is currently defined in terms of *autopoiesis*, which is defined as the "maintenance of units and wholeness, while components themselves are being continuously or periodically disassembled and rebuilt, created and decimated, produced and consumed" (Zeleny, 1981, 5). Living systems are self-organizing and self-maintaining. It follows from this definition that social and ecological systems are also living systems.

Plants do not have purposes, but like all living things have survival either as a goal or purpose. Plants *react* to changing external conditions in such ways as to make their survival possible, but their reactions are determined, not matters of choice. Humans, on the other hand, make choices whose intended outcome is survival.

For animals in general, survival is *a*, if not *the*, most important purpose. They are purposeful organisms whose parts (some of which are called "organs") have functions but no purposes of their own. The behavior of an organism's parts is determined by its structure and the organism's state and activity. An animal's heart, lungs, brain, and so on, have no purposes of their own, but their functions are necessary for the survival and pursuit of the purposes of the whole.

Historically, animated systems have often been treated as though they were nothing but complicated mechanisms. Mechanistic biology dominated the study of living things for centuries. For example, the biomechanist Roux was said to have taken the position that "biology admits of exact formulation because matter alone exists; there is no ground for a fundamental distinction between the living and non-living. The animate, appearing as cells with nuclei, developed from the inanimate by the operation of mechanical laws, and is governed by them" (E. F. Flower, 1942, 72). Opposition to a mechanistic conception of animate systems surfaced in the mechanist-vitalist controversy, which arose out of mechanists' inability to account adequately for the nature of life. Today, when life tends to be defined in terms of self-organization and self-renewal (autopoiesis), it is apparent that essential aspects of organisms are not included in mechanistic models of them.

On the other hand, mechanistic entities have seldom been conceptualized as organisms. The only exceptions I can find occur among primitive people whose beliefs are said to have been "animatistic," which according to the *Encyclopedia Britannica* (1911) is "the doctrine that a great part, if not the whole, of the inanimate kingdom, as well as all animated beings, are endowed with reason, intelligence, and volition, identical with that of man."

Social Systems

Social systems—for example, corporations, universities, societies—have purposes of their own, contain parts (other social systems and animated organisms) that have purposes of their own, and are usually parts of larger social systems that contain other social systems (corporations and nations; exceptions are some primitive societies that have lived in complete isolation, hence not part of a larger social system). I am not aware of anyone trying to model organisms or mechanical systems as social systems, but social systems have often been modeled organismically and even mechanically (e.g., Jay Forrester, 1961 and 1971). The sociologist Sorokin (1928) summarized the mechanistic interpretations of two prominent social physicists, Haret and Barcelo, as follows:

> In their works the translation of the nonmechanistic language of social science into that of mechanics goes on in the following way: The individual is transformed into a material point, and his social environment into a "field of forces." . . . As soon as this is done, there is no difficulty in applying the formulas of mechanics to social phenomena; all that is necessary is to copy these formulas, inserting the word individual instead of material point, and the term social group instead of physical system or a field of forces.

"An increase in the kinetic energy of an individual is equivalent to a decrease in his potential energy." "The total energy of an individual in his field of forces remains constant throughout all its modifications . . . and so on." (17–18)

In addition, Sorokin wrote:

H. C. Carey's *Principles of Social Science* is one of the most conspicuous attempts in the second half of the nineteenth century at a physical interpretation of social phenomena. (13)

Carey applied such laws as those of gravitation to social phenomena. For example, if an individual is taken as a molecule and the social group as a body, then the attraction between any two bodies is in direct proportion to their masses (the number of individuals per unit volume) and inversely proportionate to the square of the distance between them. In addition, Carey took centralization and decentralization of populations to be the same as centripetal and centrifugal forces.

Herbert Spencer, the nineteenth-century evolutionary philosopher, provides a excellent example of biological modeling of social systems. His position was summarized by A. M. Hussong (1931):

Spencer himself groups together under four heads these comparisons of life and society which result in showing three phenomena well known to characterize *life*, to be no less characteristic of anything to be called a *society*. They are: (1) growth; with which life is associated, (2) increasing differentiation of structure, and (3) increasing differentiation of function. (23)

Consider the first of Spencer's points to help clarify his position:

In both biological and social organisms, growth is evidenced by the same phenomena. In both, there are increases in mass—in the biological individual, an expansion from germ to adult form; in the social, an expansion from small wandering hordes to great nations. In both, aggregates of different classes reach various sizes—among biological organisms, the Protozoa rarely increase beyond a microscopic size; among social organisms the primitive Tasmanian seldom form large groups, while the empires of civilization include millions of people. In both, increases by simple multiplication of units is followed by union of groups and unions of groups of groups. In both, finally, a multiplication of individuals goes on within each group of units. (23)

Organismic models do not take the purposes of the parts of a social system into account. However, they are useful in dealing with social systems in which the purposes of the parts are very limited or not relevant, for example, in organizations that are managed or ruled autocratically. The more autocratic an organization, the more appropriate is the application of an organismic model to it.

Autocratic control of a social system runs into trouble with (1) increasing education of its members, (2) increasing technology that they must master to do the tasks assigned to them, and (3) increasing variety of demands made on them. The better those who are managed, governed, or ruled learn how to carry out their function, the less effective autocratic control by those who manage, govern, or rule them. A democratic organization, one in which the members have considerable freedom and opportunity to make choices, can't be adequately modeled organismically precisely because such modeling misses the ability of its parts to make choices. This inadequacy is particularly apparent where problem solving is involved.

Consider the use of *case studies* in management education. I recently asked managers in an executive development program who had just completed working on a case what would happen if they presented their proposed solution to the senior management of the relevant corporation. The class members said that these managers would probably find a number of reasons for not accepting it, but that if they accepted the solution, it would probably not be implemented as intended because of opposition to it by those who would be responsible for its implementation. The point is that *the managers and the implementers were part of the problem, not external to it.* In the organismic model of the corporation that the class had unconsciously used, the purposes of those who had to approve of any proposed action, let alone those who had to carry it out, were not taken into account. Had the class used a social systemic model, they would have treated acceptance and implementation of its solution to the problem in the case as part of the problem, not as separate from it.

In the political arena, finding what is normally thought of as a solution to a problem and getting it accepted and implemented are usually treated separately rather than as complementary aspects of the problem. For example, President Clinton's recent proposed solution of the national health care problem was rejected by Congress, whose approval was required before it could be enacted. Furthermore, many laws are simply not obeyed or enforced and therefore solve nothing, and many solutions are modified when implemented in order to serve the purposes of those who are supposed to implement them. This is often the case in less developed countries when alleged solutions are bent to facilitate corruption.

Mexican peasants (*campesinos*) are generally very poor. They can hardly grow enough food to live on, let alone sell to others. In the 1970s what they could sell to others, they could only sell to the local political boss (the chief, or *casique*), who was the only one accessible to them with enough money to buy their products and with the ability to transport them to markets. He bought the products at a very low price, but he charged those to whom he sold them a much higher price. They, in turn, did the same until the products reached an ultimate consumer, who often had to pay five to ten times what the peasant had received for them.

The Mexican government, through its basic commodity agency, Conasupo, developed a program intended to help peasants. It guaranteed the peasant a higher price for their products than they normally received for them from the *casique*. The government built buying stations in rural areas to which peasants could bring their products to get the supported price for them. All that was required of them was that the products meet some minimal quality standards.

The government had to put someone in charge of each buying station. Local political bosses, almost always *casiques*, were asked to suggest who should run the stations in their areas. Those they suggested were almost always selected for the job.

Subsequently, the peasants eagerly brought their small harvests to these buying stations. The attendant generally rejected them, claiming they were of too low a quality. The peasants had no alternative but to take their products to the *casique*, who was notified by the attendant (they had selected) of the rejection. The *casique* pretended to be reluctant to buy inferior products but offered to do so at lower prices than he had paid for them before installation of the government program.

When the peasants withdrew, poorer and penitent, the *casique* took the products he had bought to the government's buying station at which they had been rejected earlier and received the much higher price the government offered. For this the attendant was suitably rewarded. The *casique* and the attendant prospered for many years until the scheme was disclosed publicly and corrective action was taken by the government.

Ecological Systems

Ecological systems, of which nature itself is an example, contain interacting mechanistic, organismic, and social systems but, unlike social systems, have no purpose of their own. However, they serve the purposes of the organisms and social systems that are their parts and provide necessary inputs to the survival of the inanimate biological systems, such as plants, that they contain. Such service and support is their function.

An ecological system is affected by some of the behavior of its component organismic and social systems, but their effects are determined, as are the behavior and properties of a mechanistic system. For example, the purposeful use of fluorocarbons as a propellant affects the ozone layer in a way that is determined and is not a matter of choice. Like animated and social systems, ecological systems are alive because they too display autopoiesis.

Although the function of an ecological system is to serve its parts, many people assume the existence of a deity whose purposes the universal ecological system is believed to serve. The deity is also assumed to have created this system and, therefore, to own it.

It should be kept in mind that deterministic, animate, social systemic, and ecological models are *classes* of models, within which there are many variations. However, most of these variations derive from different treatments of nonessential variables.

The Mismatching of Models and Social Systems

One can treat (hence model) a part or an aspect of a social system—for example, a corporation's production facility—as a mechanism and by so doing improve that part's performance. However, this can reduce the performance of the system as a whole. Recall that every essential part of a system can affect the performance of the whole but cannot do so independently of all the other essential parts. Therefore, when changing the performance of any of a system's parts, its effect on the system as a whole should be taken into account. Some (nonessential) properties of even a system's essential parts may have no effect on the system as a whole: the color of an automobile's interior may have no effect on its performance and therefore can be modified without affecting performance of the automobile. Similarly, workers may be essential in a corporation, but the color or type of clothing they wear may not be.

The effectiveness of any model used to describe and understand behavior of a particular system ultimately depends on the degree to which that model accurately represents that system. Nevertheless, there have been and are situations in which application of deterministic or animate models to social systems have produced useful results, but these situations are often short lived. In the long run, such mismatches produce less than desirable results because critical aspects of the social system are omitted in the less complex models that are used. This was the case, for example, in the Mexican agricultural product price-support system.

Deterministic Models of Organizations

In the early stages of industrialization, an enterprise was conceptualized much as the universe was by Newton, as a machine created by its god, the owner, to serve his purposes. The owner's principal purpose, of course, was to make a profit. Therefore, the firm's social function and only responsibility was taken to be to provide the owner with a return on his investment. This position is still maintained by Milton Friedman (1970).

Owners had virtually unlimited control over the system they had created. They were unregulated and unconstrained by laws and unions. The human parts of an enterprise were treated as replaceable machine parts. This does not mean that owners were unaware of their employees' humanity, but that the employment agreement implicitly absolved employers of any responsibility for serving their employees' purposes. The only obligation of employers to employees was to pay them for the labor received. The worker was thought of much as a slot machine: one coin in, one unit out; two coins in, two units out; and so on.

This way of thinking about and modeling an enterprise was possible for the following reasons:

1. Workers were poorly educated and relatively unskilled, but were adequate for the simple repetitive tasks assigned to them. These tasks required behavior that was more machine-like than human.
2. Since there was virtually no social security available, unem-

ployment implied financial destitution for many. This resulted in workers who were willing to tolerate working conditions suitable for machines but not people.
3. There was a large pool of people looking for work, hence
workers could easily be replaced, like machine parts, and the
workers knew this.

When societies industrialized, machines replaced thousands of agricultural workers, which resulted in a very large number of unem-
ployed, unskilled agricultural workers. This, in turn, had a
destabilizing effect on society. Disaster was averted because a new
concept of manufacturing "came to the rescue." Production processes
were designed much as a complicated tractor is, consisting of an
assembly of parts each of which involves a very simple and repetitive
task. Unskilled workers could be assigned to these elementary tasks. In
time, this mechanical model of production and the application of
mandatory public education replaced the army of unskilled agricultural workers with semiskilled industrial workers. The impact on productivity of this mechanistic model of organizations was so great that
in one generation it provided an amount of goods and services that
surpassed all expectations.

Although Henry Ford had phenomenal success in the creation of a
mechanistic mass-production system, this system already contained
the seeds of its decline. He showed how he failed to appreciate the
potential of producing a variety of outputs when he said [customers]
can have any color [of automobile] they want as long as it's black. This
misreading gave Alfred Sloan of General Motors the opportunity to
gain domination of the automotive market. Sloan took mass production for granted and focused on the question of how to sell; the marketing era emerged. It gave rise to a new set of challenging questions, the
most important of which was how to organize and manage production,
distribution, and marketing so as to satisfy demand.

As the size and complexity of organizations increased, it became less
effective to manage them as though they were machines. Decentraliz-
ing control became necessary, and this was incompatible with a mechanistic conception of organization. A machine requires centralized control and invariance of output. No driver in his right mind would drive a
car with decentralized (self-determining) front wheels.

However, in an organization that requires invariant functioning of
its parts (as bureaucracies do), decentralization leads to disorganiza-
tion, if not chaos. This occurs because improving the performance of

some parts of an organization taken separately, as happens in decentralization, often reduces the effectiveness of other parts and the whole. The best solution to a production problem taken in isolation (e.g., reducing the number of different products that have to be made) may well be in conflict with the best solution to a marketing problem (e.g., offering a wide variety of products, a complete product line). When it becomes apparent that improvement of the performance of the parts does not improve the performance of the whole, centralization takes place. When it subsequently becomes apparent that a number of parts are not functioning well under centralization, decentralization takes place. It is for this reason that organizations frequently oscillate between centralization and decentralization.

Problems that arose in the production function lent themselves particularly well to mechanistic treatment. A number of mathematical techniques were developed (in operations research and the management sciences) to handle such production-inventory problems in this way: economic lot sizes, production scheduling, sequencing multiple production runs, allocation of production to different facilities or equipment, scheduling of maintenance, repair, and replacement of production equipment and facilities. Although these techniques usually yielded improvements in production, they either did not improve the performance of the system of which production was a part or did not improve production as much as possible. Problems viewed as production problems could usually be treated better by viewing them as social-systemic problems.

> An example of a social-systemic treatment of an production-inventory problem was provided by an abrasive-manufacturing company that offered discounts on purchases that were proportional to the amount of lead time given by the customer for delivery of the goods ordered. This solution converted "demand" into a partially controllable variable by taking into account the purposefulness of the customers. It reduced inventory several times as much as had previously been obtained by use of (mechanistic) economic lot sizes, and it had a very positive effect on customer attitudes toward the company.

Recall the elevator problem described in the preceding chapter. The elevator engineers consulted viewed it mechanistically. All three of their proposed solutions, none of which worked, were derived from a mechanistic model of elevator operations. The young psychologist, however, saw elevators as providing a service within a social system. He looked at the problem from the point of view of animate systems, people, in that social system. As a result, he saw boredom as the problem, not elevator operations, and found an effective way of dealing with it.

Summarizing, deterministic models may work well when applied to parts or aspects of a social system when these parts or aspects are considered in isolation. However, it is possible to simultaneously improve the performance of each part or aspect of a system taken separately and reduce the performance of the whole. This follows from the fact that no part or aspect of a system has an independent effect on the performance of the system. *A system's performance is the product of the interactions of its parts.* Moreover, even the performance of the part of a social system can be improved by looking at it more social systemically.

Animate Models of Organizations

There were a number of developments between the two world wars that made deterministic modeling of social systems, particularly businesses, less and less appropriate. Business and governmental organizations took growth to be necessary in order to respond effectively to demand for an increasing amount and diversity of products and services. Technological developments required workers with increasingly greater skills; as the educational level of workers increased, union and government interventions did also. The threat of financial destitution associated with unemployment decreased as social security emerged. Finally, as businesses went public in order to raise the capital required to fuel growth and technological improvements, management and ownership were separated. The publicly owned company became a *corporation* (derived from "*corpus,*" meaning "body"), with stockholders as owners, and the chief executive became the "head," or management, of the firm. Because of these developments, animate models were increasingly used when dealing with such social systems as corporations.

Sloan's concept of an organization was essentially animate, that of a single-minded biological entity. This provided a relatively effective way to manage an organization's growth and increase the diversity of its outputs. In his implicit model, corporations, like the human bodies, were divided into two distinct parts: (1) management, the *brain*; and (2) the operating unit, the *body.*

The operating unit, the body, was considered to have no choice, no consciousness. It was restricted to reacting deterministically to instructions coming from management, the brain, or events in its environment. Ideally, an operating unit would be a robot programmed to carry out without deviation a set of procedures defined by management. Military organizations, governmental bureaucracies, and autocratic corporations closely approximated the behavior of robots.

The principal purpose of an enterprise conceptualized as an animate system—as an organism—is, of course, survival. Growth is normally taken as essential for survival because the limit of its opposite, contraction, is death. Profit is seen in this context not as an end, but as a means: as Peter Drucker once observed, as oxygen is to a human being, necessary for its survival, but not the reason for it.

Social-Systemic Models of Organizations

As a result of World War II, a large portion of the workforce in western nations was drawn into the military. Replacements included Rosie the Riveter and Tillie the Toiler, new workers who were motivated at least as much by patriotism as by additional income. Such workers could not be treated as replaceable machine parts or organs of a body that only required consideration of the effects of their work on their health and safety. They had to be treated as human beings with purposes of their own. In addition, unions discovered that corporations working under cost-plus contracts or demands for increased production could easily be induced to make concessions to workers' interests. Work rules favoring the workforce went through a profound transformation. Furthermore, because of the great increase in technological developments, the skills required of the workforce increased dramatically. The more skilled the workers, the harder they were to replace. Technological developments required a significant investment in specialized training of the workforce. Management had to obtain an adequate return on its investment. All this produced a need to treat employees as human beings with purposes of their own.

Children of the post–World War II workforce made up the permissive generation, whose members were not about to be treated as other than purposeful entities. They expected their interests to be taken into account by their employers and where they weren't, these workers were alienated and their productivity decreased (HEW, 1973). The quality-of-work-life movement was an effort to correct this.

Subgroups of the purposeful parts of many social systems began to demand that more attention be given to their interests by the systems of which they were a part. The racial equality movement and the women's liberation movement were examples of this, as was the demand of third-world countries for a larger share of the world's economic development. In addition, protest groups, for example, consumerists and environmentalists, formed outside social systems, insisting that their interests be better served by the systems that affected them. As a result, management's social responsibility and its work-related ethics emerged as major concerns. They were even taken up by business schools.

By the end of the 1960s, it was apparent that the West was experiencing both an accelerating rate of change, largely due to technological developments, and increasing complexity, produced by an explosion of interconnections resulting from continuously improving transportation and communications. The socioeconomic environment became turbulent, one in which predictability of the future diminished significantly and the only equilibrium that could be obtained was dynamic, like that of an airplane flying through a storm. These changes undermined whatever effectiveness had been obtained by applying organismic models to social systems. Centralized control and the treatment of subordinates as mindless parts were no longer good practices.

Increasingly, employees could do their jobs better than their immediate bosses, but only if they were given the freedom to do so. Therefore, the mechanistic and organismic concept of management as "command and control," or even softer supervision, became less and less appropriate. The functions of management became

1. to enable and motivate subordinates to do as well as they know how;
2. to develop them so they can do better in the future than the best they can do now;
3. to manage their interactions, not their actions; and
4. to manage the interactions of the unit they manage with other internal and external organizational units and organizations.

This can only be done by using such social-systemic designs as are provided in Part III.

Furthermore, the unprecedented generation and distribution of both wealth and knowledge after World War II resulted in increasing choice and greater interdependency. This changed the nature of social settings and individual behavior. The greater the interactions and interdependencies, the more vulnerable social systems became to the actions of a few (hence, the rise in sabotage and terrorism). The more knowledge available, the greater the value of communication and information. However, advances in information technology and communication did not yield the quality or quantity of control for which managers hoped. Since it was assumed that members of organismically conceptualized organizations would behave like organs in a human body and react mechanistically to information provided by the brain, it appeared reasonable to conclude that the malfunctioning of organizations was due either to the lack of information or noise in the communication channels. Therefore, more and more information and better and better communication facilities were provided.

Unfortunately, this mode of thinking is ineffective in dealing with the complexities of increasing social interactions and interdependencies. It fails to recognize that members of an organization, unlike the parts of an organism, have a choice and do not react deterministically to the information they receive. Imagine a thermostat that developed a mind of its own. If it received information about the temperature in the room that it did not like, it would not react to it. This would result in a chaotic air-conditioning system. The effectiveness of a servomechanism is based on the fact that it does not have a choice and can only react in a predefined manner to the events in its environment. Our organs, as well, cannot decide on their own not to work or how to work for us. Even when they are defective, we do not conclude that they are out to get us.

Another problem arose from the push to improve communications. Increases in information eventually produces a condition Meier (1963) called "information overload": as the amount of information received increases beyond the amount its receivers can handle effectively, they use less and less of it. Not only do receivers become saturated with information—and therefore cannot receive any more—but they can and do become supersaturated and discard some of the information they already have.

Moreover, information can intensify conflict. Organizations with purposeful parts almost inevitably generate internal conflicts. Wherever there is choice, conflict is likely to occur; without choice, there can be no conflict. In conflict situations, organismic thinking is ineffective because it usually tries to resolve conflict by increasing the flow of information between the conflicting parties. Unfortunately, when conflict is based on differing values or scarcity of resources, an increased flow of information, contrary to conventional wisdom, does not improve but aggravates the conflict. For example, the more information enemies at war have about each other, the more harm each can inflict on the other.

However, the biological mode of organization can be successful in the short term in the particular context of paternalistic cultures— where loyalty, conformity, and commitment are considered to be the core virtues. These virtues are reinforced by the security of belonging to a group that protects and provides for its members. For example, Japan, an industrialized society with a relatively strong paternalistic culture, closely approximates an organismic system. Therefore, it has been able to capitalize more effectively on the strength of the biological model of organization. In the context of a strong paternalistic culture, conflict can be resolved by the intervention of a strong father figure, whose command, "Give the apple to your sister," would be respected without much hard feelings. To appreciate the power of this type of leader, recall that such American corporate giants as Ford, DuPont, General Motors, IBM, and Kodak owe much to their paternalistic founding fathers.

The nature of highly developed social systems is fundamentally different from that of a paternalistic culture. Members of societies that have matured past the secure and unifying umbrella of a paternalistic culture insist on the right to make choices, to decide for themselves. But there is a price to be paid for this right; it can induce insecurity and conflict. Purposeful actors, individually or in groups, who pursue incompatible ends or employ incompatible means, generate conflict. Consequently, because of its organismic orientation, corporate America is ill-equipped to deal effectively with internal and external conflict. Furthermore, it finds it almost impossible to make the changes required to flourish in its rapidly changing and increasingly complex environment. A significant part of its energy is wasted on futile efforts to deal with conflict. The frustration that results reinforces its inability to change. This in turn creates a feeling of impotency and hopelessness that immobilizes western governments, institutions, and organizations.

A conflict-free organization can be created by reducing choice, by reducing members to robots. Fascist societies and autocratic organizations have attempted to approximate such a state. But such systems are dehumanizing. Over time they result in reduced productivity of the workforce and reduced quality of its outputs. This produces a precipitous decline of an economy, such as is occurring in many western nations. On the other hand, relying exclusively—as organismic modelers of organizations do—on an increasing flow of information and compromise to reduce conflict does not produce encouraging results. Witness the situation in the UN, which has dramatically increased the flow of information between nations and compromise among them.

Therefore, the challenge before us is to create a type of organization that is capable of continuously dissolving conflict while increasing choice. This requires an organizational concept that is not compatible with either a deterministic or animate model of organization. It requires application of social-systemic models to social systems.

A social-systemically conceptualized enterprise has *development* as its principal objective: its own development, that of its parts, and of the larger systems of which it is a part. Development, contrary to prevailing current usage, is *not* the same as growth and may occur without growth, and growth may occur without development. The nature of development will be explored in detail in Chapter 13.

The Social-Systemic Organization

In Chapters 9, 10, and 11, I propose organizational designs that are based on a social-systemic model. They have the following features, none of which are compatible with any other type of model:

1. The social-systemic model is a *democratic organization*, one in which every individual affected by what that organization does has a voice in deciding what it does, and one in which anyone who has authority over other individuals is subject to their collective authority, hence there is no ultimate authority (Chapter 9).
2. It has an *internal market economy*, one in which every part of the organization can purchase the goods or services it requires from any internal or external source it chooses and can sell its output to any buyer it wants. Both of these types of decision, buying and selling, are subject to overrides by higher authorities, who must, nevertheless, compensate the affected part of the organization for its loss of income or increased costs due to the higher-level intervention (Chapter 10).
3. It has a *multidimensional organizational structure*, one in which units of three different types are located at each level of the organization and are defined by (a) their function (units whose output is primarily consumed internally), (b) their output (product or services primarily consumed externally), and (c) their users (markets, defined by type or location of customers). This type of organization eliminates the need for continual restructuring. Restructuring is replaced by reallocation of resources (Chapter 11).

4. It uses *interactive planning* which involves idealized redesign of the organization and determination of the closest approximation to that design that can be realized. Such planning then involves selection of the means by which the approximation is to be pursued; provision of the resources required by the pursuit; specifying the implementation steps to be taken, when, and by whom; and finally, design of monitoring and controls of both the implementation and the effects of the plan (Chapters 4 to 8).

5. It contains a *decision-support system* that facilitates learning and adaptation by (a) recording the expectations associated with each decision of significance, (b) the assumptions and information on which they are based, and (c) the process by which the decision was reached and by whom it was reached. It then monitors the implementation, assumptions, and effects of every decision; corrects them where assumptions turn out to be wrong or expectations are not met; and retains in an easily accessible memory what has been learned. Finally, it carries out continuous surveillance of the environment to detect changes that have occurred or are about to occur that require adaptation by the organization (Chapter 8).

Any one or subset of these changes can significantly improve organizational performance. However, when all are made together, there is a powerful multiplicative effect, one that is much greater than the sum of its parts.

The Social Functions of a Social System

Recall that the function of organizations viewed deterministically is to provide their gods (owners/creators) with a return on their investments, profit. When organizations are considered as animate organisms, profit is viewed as a means, not an end: it is taken to be like oxygen is to a human being—necessary for its survival but not the reason for it. Profit itself has no value; it is what it can be used for that has value. Therefore, as Ambrose Bierce (1967) observed, it has no value until we get rid of it. The principal objective of any animate organism is survival. Like profit, growth is seen as necessary for survival because the opposite of growth, contraction, ultimately results in death.

Every social system has a function in the larger system(s) of which it is part. In the case of a firm, the function it has is primarily economic. The nature of its economic function is best understood by adopting a *stakeholder view of the firm.* After describing this view and its implications, I consider how this economic function fits into the principal purpose of a social system: to contribute to the development of its parts, itself, and the larger system of which it is part.

A stakeholder is anyone who is *directly* affected by what a firm does. This excludes competitors because they are affected indirectly, through the direct effects of a firm on customers, suppliers, and other stakeholders. The stakeholder view of the firm derives from looking at it as a set of transactions with stakeholders in which an exchange of resources takes place. Using a very simple classification of stakeholders, we get the view shown in Figure 2.1.

Those employed by a firm put their labor in and take money out in the form of compensation. Suppliers put goods and services into the firm and take money out. Customers do exactly the opposite: they take goods and services out and put money in. The goods and services received by customers are usually of greater value to them than those that are put into the firm by suppliers. Therefore, firms usually add value to the goods and services they receive if by no other way than by making them more accessible to customers (as is the case for retail stores).

Investors and lenders put money into the firm, either in the form of investments or as loans, and later take money out, they hope more than they put in. Debtors do the opposite. They first take money out and later put it in. For example, the banks in which a firm's operating capital is held owes that money to the firm and often has to pay for its use. A firm's pension funds are usually invested in other firms, making them debtors to the firm.

Finally there is the government, which also is a supplier of goods (e.g., water) and services (e.g., police and fire protection) in return for money paid either as fees or as taxes. Government is usually differentiated from other suppliers because it can exercise some control over the firm, and the goods and services its provides do not become the property of the firm, although it gets use of them.

This stakeholder view (Fig. 2.1), involving only six stakeholder groups, is about as simple as one can make it. It can be expanded considerably. For example, a distinction can be made between local, state, and federal governments; between wholesale, retail, ultimate customers, and consumers. (Customers and consumers may be different, as in the purchase of children's food and clothing; institutional and individual investors can also be treated separately.) However, no matter how many stakeholder groups are used in developing such a view, each

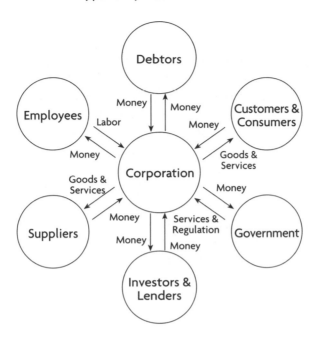

Figure 2.1   A stakeholder view of the firm

is involved in a transaction with the firm that involves an exchange of resources.

The flows of resources in and out of a firm are only of two types; they either involve *consumption by the firm* or *consumption made possible* by the firm. If a firm's consumption is subtracted from the consumption it makes possible and the difference is positive, the firm has created wealth. That firms have the function of creating wealth in society is not a discovery; it has been well-known for a long time. But that the firm also has the function of distributing wealth is a discovery for many, particularly those who manage firms. They distribute wealth by providing the financial resources that can be used to obtain the goods and services that they provide or that are provided by others. This function of firms, the distribution of wealth, is often overlooked or underemphasized.

Productive employment by firms is one of the most important, if not the most important, way by which firms distribute wealth. It is the only way currently available for simultaneously producing and distributing wealth. Therefore, *a major societal function of firms conceptualized as social systems is to create and provide productive employment.*

If in a capitalistic society the amount and quality of productive employment created by nongovernmentally owned firms does not produce an equitable and satisfactory level of wealth, the tenure of their containing societies' governments are usually seriously threatened. In such situations, governments often nationalize firms in order to maintain employment, even when profit has to be sacrificed. Insufficient employment is often more threatening to a government than insufficient profit. Governments are usually very bad in managing enterprises so as to produce wealth, however well they may distribute whatever wealth there is available for distribution. The problem that governments reacting this way have had is that however well they distribute wealth, they are not efficient in producing it. This is what has happened in most communist countries: they wind up distributing poverty because an insufficient amount of wealth is produced. On the other hand, most capitalist countries that have nationalized a large number of industries, like the United Kingdom and Mexico, to preserve employment, have subsequently had to privatize them in order to produce more wealth.

Therefore, from society's point of view the production and maintenance of productive employment is a primary responsibility of private enterprises. In light of this, the currently widespread use of *downsizing* raises fundamental questions about the social responsibility of firms and governments' reactions to their irresponsible behavior. I consider these questions in Chapter 12.

Conclusion

I have argued that it is useful to classify systems and their models as either deterministic, animate, social, or ecological. The differentiating criterion is choice of ends and means in the same and different environments, their purposefulness. Deterministic systems and their parts display no choice; hence, they have no purposes of their own but serve the purpose(s) of external entities, and this is their function(s). Animate systems can display choice; hence, they have a purpose of their own, but their parts don't. Social systems and their parts display choice; hence, they have purposes of their own and are parts of larger systems that have purposes of their own and contain other systems that do so as well. Finally, ecological systems like nature display no choice, hence have no purposes of their own; but some of their parts (animate and social systems) display choice and have purposes of their own.

My point has been that when models of one type are applied to systems of a different type, the possibility of effective choices is significantly reduced. This follows from the fact that the number and types of available choices perceived are significantly reduced when the system and the model applied to it do not match. The amount by which effectiveness is reduced is a function of the level of maturity of the system involved. Our society and the principal private and public organizations and institutions that it contains have reached a level of maturity that eliminates whatever effectiveness applying deterministic and animalistic models to social systems may once have had.

In the chapters that follow, I will discuss the five things I believe corporations must do to function as effectively as currently is possible: plan effectively, learn and adapt rapidly and effectively, democratize, introduce internal market economies, and employ a structure that maximizes their flexibility but minimizes the need for frequent restructuring.

3

Types of Management

Introduction

So much of what we call management consists in making it difficult for people to work.

—Peter Drucker

No two managements are either exactly the same or completely different. The variations, however, are limitless. The only way they can be dealt with effectively is through classification. Fortunately, the traditional forms of management fall into a small number of categories, much as colors do. Although there is a limitless number of colors, all derive from three primary colors. The varieties of traditional management derive out of three primary forms. Like the primary colors, we seldom see the primary forms of management, but even in mixtures we can usually identify the dominant primary type. Although one type usually dominates, all three types appear to some extent in most organizations. Furthermore, individual managers often exhibit different types under different circumstances.

The three primary traditional forms of management derive from their *attitude toward time and change*. Now time is a very obliging variable because it breaks up into three very familiar categories: the past, the present, and the future. Attitudes are even simpler because they are

Table 3.1 The Primary Forms of Traditional Management

| | *Attitudes Toward* | | | |
	Past	*Present*	*Future*	*Change*
Reactive	+	—	—	Undo
Inactive	—	+	—	Prevent
Preactive	—	—	+	Accelerate

either positive (plus) or negative (minus). Attitudes toward time determine attitudes toward change. This, along with the three types and their characteristics, is shown in Table 3.1.

Reactive Management

As can be seen from Table 3.1, reactive management is dissatisfied with the way things are and the way they are going. What they like is the way things once were. Therefore, they select a previous state as their objective and deal with problems and plans in an effort to return to that state (Fig. 3.1).

The reactive approach to a problem is first to identify its cause or source, then to try to remove or suppress it. If successful, this undoes the change that produced the problem and returns the system managed to the state that existed before the problem arose. This process is *problem resolution*. The process is essentially clinical in character, depending primarily on previous problems that are similar to the one now confronted. The thinking directed at them is essentially experiential, qualitative, and common sensical.

For example, when the United States developed an alcohol abuse problem in the early part of this century, the country's government identified alcohol as the cause of the problem and made its production and sale illegal. It did not work. Prohibition did not make alcohol inaccessible because bootlegging became commonplace, which provided easy access to alcoholic beverages, and gave rise to organized crime, which was a much worse social problem than alcohol abuse. Nevertheless, in many cases this way of attacking problems works satisfactorily as, for example, in the treatment of diseases or ailments. Here medical diagnosis tries to find the cause of an illness or disability and remove it. When it succeeds, it usually restores the person involved to health. But it is not unusual for the treatment to cause a worse ailment or disability than the one it was intended to cure.

Organizations in which reactive management is dominant tend to

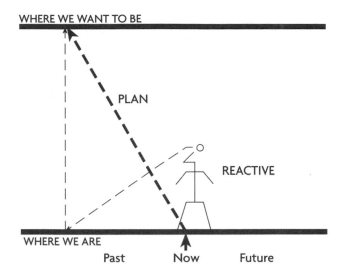

Figure 3.1   Reactive planning

use as their model the oldest and most stable form of organization known, the family. They aspire to make their organization a "great big happy family." The chief executive, like father, is assumed to know best and is, with justification in most cases, referred to as "the old man." The older an executive is, the more experience he (almost never a "she") has had and hence the better able to resolve problems. "Experience is the best teacher" and "The school of hard knocks is the best school" are reactive aphorisms.

Like most families, most reactive organizations function as autocratic hierarchies. Nothing takes place without the explicit or implicit approval of the old man, including planning. His decision to initiate planning is often stimulated by his learning that a reactively managed organization that he admires has done so. If and when he decides he wants a corporate plan, he usually calls in his "oldest sons," those who report to him directly, and addresses them as follows: "Boys, by the end of this year I'd like a corporate plan covering the next five years. This means I will need a divisional plan from each of you in eleven months, leaving me some time to evaluate them and put them together into a comprehensive corporate plan. Is that clear?"

They say yes, click their heels, salute, and take off to call in the younger sons, the next layer down. They are usually addressed as follows: "Boys, the old man wants a five-year corporate plan by the end of the year. This means I have to give him a divisional plan in eleven months, and therefore, you will have to give me your departmental plans in ten months so I can evaluate them and put them together into a divisional plan. Is that clear?"

They, too, say yes, click their heels, salute, leave, and call in their subordinates until they reach Joe, the lowest authority on the totem pole, often a foreman or supervisor. He is the organizational atom, the indivisible particle that matters. He is told by his immediate superior that a plan for his crew will be needed in time for his boss to assemble his plan. If the organization has more than twelve layers of management, Joe may be asked to have his plan ready six months or more ago. Fortunately, he is accustomed to such requests.

It should be noted that although reactive planning is authorized from the top down, the actual planning is carried out from the bottom up.

Now what does Joe do? Since it is a reactive organization, he begins by listing all the things that require reacting to, the things that are wrong with the current situation. For each deficiency, he designs an effort to identify its cause and remove it. Such efforts are called "projects." The costs and benefits associated with each project are estimated, and these are combined one way or another into a measure of performance. The projects are then prioritized based on their estimated performance.

Joe generally has a pretty good idea as to how much money he will get for projects. If the last year was a good one, he is likely to receive 10 to 20 percent more. If it was bad, 10 to 20 percent less. If so-so, no change. But he also knows he must ask for more than he expects to get in order to get any money. He estimates that amount. Then he selects the project with highest priority and subtracts its cost from the total amount he intends to request. He does the same with the second project on his priority list and continues until all the requested funds are allocated. Last, he prepares a document in which he "packages" those that have been selected for financing and submits it as his plan to his immediate superior.

His superior, who has received such a plan from each of his immediate subordinates, does three things. First, he corrects the grammar and the spelling in the plans he receives. He may or may not modify some of their content. Following this, he adds to the plans he has received projects that he has generated, ones that address problems confronting him. Finally, he "repackages" these with those that were passed up to him. This process is then continued up the hierarchy until it reaches the old man.

After discussion of the content of the submissions and some modifications of it, the old man assembles the surviving projects into what is then called the corporate plan. It consists of a large number of projects generated at different levels of the organization, all addressed to improving performance by removing deficiencies.

About 25 percent of the corporate plans and more than 50 percent of the government plans that I have seen are of this type. Very few of these have been fully implemented, fortunately so, because many of them would have destroyed the organization that implemented them. This could happen because there are two serious deficiencies in such planning.

First, they are directed at getting rid of what is not wanted. Unfortunately, when one gets rid of what one does not want, often one does not get what one wants but gets what one wants even less. (Recall Prohibition and organized crime.) This should be obvious. If we turn on a television set during the day, most of us are very unlikely to get a program we want on the channel that comes up. The program, a deficiency, is very easy to get rid of by changing the channel. Unfortunately, when we do so we are more likely to get another program we do not want than one we do, and we are even likely to get one we want even less than the one we are getting rid of. Therefore, a fundamental principle of effective management emerges: *Effective management must be directed at getting what one wants, not getting rid of what one does not want.*

Second, each deficiency is a part of a system of interacting deficiencies, that is, a mess. Therefore, even if each deficiency is removed and replaced with something that is individually better, the system of replacements may be much worse than the system that it replaced. Recall that improving the parts of a system taken separately is not likely to improve the performance of the system as a whole.

The reactive pattern of thought was exemplified by the Luddites in the early part of the nineteenth century. These English handcraftsmen tried to destroy the textile factories and machines that were putting them out of work. In the preceding century, the French philosopher Jean Jacques Rousseau argued that the "natural man" from which his contemporaries had emerged was superior to them. At the end of the last century, William Morris and John Ruskin, also in England, urged artists to return to medieval principles and practices. In the 1960s and 1970s, groups of hippies migrated to places such as western Canada and formed agriculturally based communes that sought a better quality of life by shedding contemporary technology and culture.

Reactive organizations, past and present, are like trains driven from the caboose: their management has a good view of where they have been but none of where they are going. They walk into the future facing the past, backward.

The remnants of those basic industries that have survived the reduction of their roles in the U.S. economy—for example, railroads, steel, and mining—tend to be managed reactively. I was once told by a railroad executive that railroads were confronted with no problems that could not be solved by eliminating trucks and the Interstate Commerce Commission.

Inactive Management

Unlike reactive managers, inactive managers are satisfied with the way things are; they may not be perfect, but they are "good enough." Therefore, "Let well enough alone," "Let nature take its course," and "Don't fix it if it ain't broke" are typical inactive aphorisms. Their objective is to prevent change (Fig. 3.2).

The godfather of inactivity was the German philosopher Liebnitz, who argued that since God was by definition perfect, the world he created could be nothing but perfect. Voltaire expressed his disdain for this belief in his famous novel *Candide*. Few if any would argue today that the world is perfect, but many think it is good enough and therefore should be left alone.

Inactivists believe that if nothing were done, nothing would happen, and that this would be fine; unfortunately many keep trying to make things better, and they almost always make things worse. However, inactivists do not usually respond to such efforts at improvement until they threaten the stability or survival of their organizations, that is, until there is a crisis. Then they react by doing as little as possible to remove the crisis. Unlike the reactivist, who tries to eliminate the cause

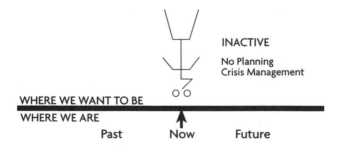

Figure 3.2   Inactive management

of a problem, the inactivist settles for suppressing the symptoms. He practices *crisis management* and, therefore, is an antiplanner. John Foster Dulles, the secretary of state under Eisenhower, introduced crisis management to his department as the official doctrine. However, he renamed it "brinksmanship": wait until you are at the edge of a precipice before you jump and then jump back. The literate British call this doctrine "muddling through." Academics who fear that their students may understand these terms refer to the inactivist's doctrine as "disjointed incrementalism." It suggests doing as little as possible and doing so only when required by external events, not by a plan.

In a world experiencing an accelerating rate of change, as noted by Toffler (1971), and increasing complexity, the number and intensity of crises also keeps increasing. This keeps the inactivist very active trying to prevent change. But he would be very busy even if there were no crises or efforts to change things because people generally, and employees in particular, do not relish sitting around doing nothing. Therefore inactivists must find ways to keep people busy doing nothing. Fortunately for them there is an organizational form that facilitates this, *bureaucracy*. Bureaucracy consists of people organized to engage in "make-work," work with no useful output. Unfortunately, people so organized often create unproductive work for others who have productive work to do, such as red tape.

It often takes a great deal of ingenuity to create make-work, for example, operators of automatic elevators. In one country I visited there was a uniformed young man in the elevator lobby who asked whether you wanted to go up or down and then pushed the appropriate button. The use of lengthy questionnaires, the answers to which may be tabulated but with which nothing further is done, is a productive way of occupying time unproductively. Quality-of-work-life questionnaires distributed to employees are frequently of this type. In the 1970s, by analyzing employment in Mexico's oil industry, I found that Pemex, the national oil monopoly employed seven times as many people as it needed! No wonder it was unprofitable. When I pointed this out to the minister of national patrimony to whom Pemex reported, he informed me that the function of Pemex was not to create profit, but to make work, to create jobs. He argued that making the company profitable by reducing the number of employees might well threaten the stability of the government.

What kind of an organization can survive inactive management? One whose survival is independent of its performance—independent of how well it serves or supplies those it serves or supplies. Subsidized organizations have such independence; they depend on a higher authority for operating funds, not on the users of their products or services. Therefore, they tend to provide poor service and products and, in general, to be unresponsive to their users.

Government agencies, of course, provide many examples of such organizations, but so do many functional service units within firms. These units provide a service such as accounting, data processing, education and training, and personnel and are the only permissible source of a service required by other parts of the organization. Therefore, they are monopolies. Their users usually do not pay for each service they receive, but pay an overhead charge (such as taxes) levied by a higher authority, who then allocates resources to the serving units.

Regulated public utilities whose profits are protected by public utility commissions are, in effect, subsidized and therefore tend to be predominantly inactive. They tend to make only those changes imposed on them. When a public utility—for example, the old AT&T—is deregulated and forced to compete, its style of management and its activity goes through a profound change.

Preactive Management

However good preactivists think the past was or the present is, they think the future will be better (Fig. 3.3). They are anxious to reach that future and therefore devote their efforts to accelerating its approach.

The difference between preactivism, inactivism, and reactivism is perhaps best reflected in a metaphor. Picture a person who goes swimming in the ocean and is carried away from the shore by a strong undertow. If he were reactive, he would turn around and try to swim against the tide, back to shore. If he were inactive, he would like his location and try to throw out an anchor and hold a fixed position, despite the tide. If he were preactive, he would like where the tide is going and would try to get on its leading edge and get to its destination before anyone else does. Then he would climb on shore, turn around, and collect a toll from those who arrive later. For preactive managers, change is opportunity to be exploited.

Preactive managers *predict and prepare*, that is, they attempt to predict the future, then establish the objectives they want to attain (usually in the form of a "vision statement"), and finally create a plan to get from where they are to where they want to be. Their plan is directed at minimizing forecasted threats and maximizing forecasted opportunities. Prediction is taken to be more critical than preparation because if

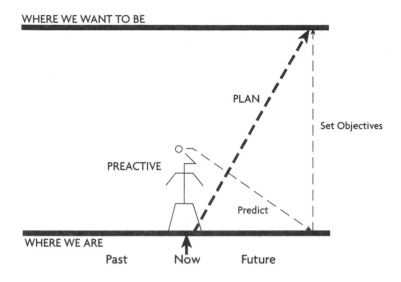

WHERE WE WANT TO BE

PLAN

Set Objectives

PREACTIVE

Predict

WHERE WE ARE

Past		Now		Future

Figure 3.3   Preactive planning

the forecast is wrong, no matter how well it is prepared for, the error is generally more serious than poor preparation for the correct future. For this reason, forecasting is a major preoccupation of preactive managers and their staffs.

Preactive managers are very sensitive to the accelerating rate of change and for this reason do not regard experience as a good teacher or the school of hard knocks as a good school. Change makes experience obsolete; for example, the fact that one has driven an automobile for many years does not equip him or her to pilot a plane or a space vehicle. Therefore, what is required in place of experience is a readiness, willingness, and ability to learn and adapt to change. Two things are implied by this. First, since young people are more flexible and open to learning than older people, the executive function in preactive organizations tends to fall into hands of younger managers. Second, the family does not exemplify an ability to change rapidly and effectively, but winning sports teams do. Therefore, they become the metaphor for successful management, and management tends to be practiced by teams and managers who tend to think of themselves as coaches rather than commanders.

Preactive managers organize for rapid response to change and therefore decentralize, putting decision-making responsibility where internal or external changes requiring organizational changes can first be detected and reacted to quickly. Whereas managers in reactive organizations tend to behave much like administrators carrying out the will of the old man, managers in preactive organizations tend to act more autonomously, but within plans and policies established by and for the organization as a whole.

In *The Two Cultures: a Second Look* (1964), eminent British novelist C. P. Snow contrasted two cultures, the technocratic and humanistic. These are exemplified by preactive and reactive management. The preactive believes there are few problems that hard science and technology cannot solve; the reactive tends to think they can only be solved by a softer humanistic approach. Therefore, it is not surprising that preactive management prevails in technologically oriented firms and business schools.

Unfortunately for preactive managers, as the rate of change in the environment accelerates and the environment becomes more complex, their ability to forecast accurately deteriorates. But this does not deter most preactive managers and planners. They argue that we do not forecast and prepare for the weather perfectly, but we are clearly better off because we do both. And they are right, but this argument is irrelevant for a reason that is important. Preparations for forecast weather have no effect on the weather even though some people believe carrying an umbrella will prevent rain or washing a car will cause it. On the other hand, a firm's preparations for a forecast future are made precisely to change that future. It is the purpose of a plan to modify forecasted customer, supplier, government, and other stakeholder behavior so that they become more favorable to the planning organization. Therefore, the purpose of planning, unlike preparation for forecast weather, is to change the forecast on which it is based.

This means that a successful plan changes the forecast on which it is based and, therefore, that the forecast should be modified. So the plan itself should be modified to take the changed characteristics of the future into account. But this will, in turn, change the forecast, and the process, if not stopped arbitrarily, would go on indefinitely. Preactive planning never goes this far. It is usually stopped. Many, if not most, preactive plans are never completely implemented because errors in the forecasts on which they are based become apparent, nullifying the plan.

However, there is a very much stronger reason for not predicting and preparing. It is revealed by the following example. Suppose you were offered the choice of receiving a perfect weather forecast every day and all the clothing you might want but would have to work out-of-doors. On the other hand you could choose to work in a building. Few, other than those whose work must take place out-of-doors, would choose to work out-of-doors. Yet, for obvious reasons, they do not ask for weather forecasts in the buildings in which they work because a building is an artifact created by man to control the weather, thereby eliminating the need to forecast it. It becomes apparent that the objective of planning should not be to prepare for a future that is largely out of our control, but to control that future as much as possible by "building buildings" to harness those variables that have the most effects on our futures.

Interactive Management

Returning to the undertow-in-the-ocean example, interactive management wants to bring the tide under control. This is not a pipe dream: man has reversed the flow of rivers, moved rivers, put the ocean where it wasn't (the Suez and Panama Canals), and taken it away from where it was (the coast of Holland).

On reflection, it becomes apparent that most of what happens to a firm is a consequence of what it does, not of what is done to it. Therefore, the objective of management and planning should be to *create as much of the future as is possible.* This is the objective of a new type of management, the interactive, which falls off Table 3.1. It falls off because it does not think of good and bad as functions of time and it does not think of what time does to us as good or bad, but of what we do to time as good or bad. Our lot is due more to what we do than what is done to us.

The Interactive Planning Process

Interactive planning (Figs. 3.4 and 3.5) consists of the design of a desired present and the invention or selection of the means for approximating it as closely as possible. Because such planning consists mostly of design and invention—that is, acts of creation—its objective is to create the future. It does so by specifying behavior that constantly closes the gap between where an organization is and where it wants to be now. Why "now"? If we do not know where we would be right now if we could be wherever we wanted, how can we possibly know where we will want to be five or ten years from now? In fact, we can be reasonably sure that five or ten years from now we will not want to be where we say now we will want to be.

Interactive planning has six interactive phases, all or any number of which may and usually do go on simultaneously, but they are usually

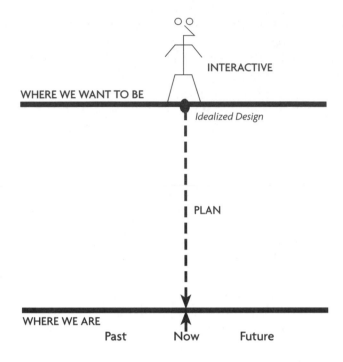

Figure 3.4   Interactive planning

initiated in the order listed below. Therefore, any linear description of these phases is bound to give a false impression of the need to carry them out in a specified order. The order in which I present them implies nothing about the order in which they should be carried out. Since, as we will see, interactive planning is necessarily continuous, it has no last step, and it can begin with any of the six phases.

Formulating the mess: Analysis of the situation. In this phase of the planning process, a description and understanding of the current state of the relevant organization and its environment is developed. Its purpose is to reveal what the organization is and is not capable of and what changes are required to increase its capabilities. In addition, it reveals the seeds of self-destruction that are inherent in the organization and suggests ways such a fate can be avoided. In this way, it reveals the most important choices an organization can make.

Ends planning. This involves specifying the ideals, objectives, and goals to be pursued by the organization: what it wants, not what it does not want. These ends are specified by means of an *idealized redesign* of the organization involved, that is, the design of the system the designers would have if they could have any system they wanted. The design

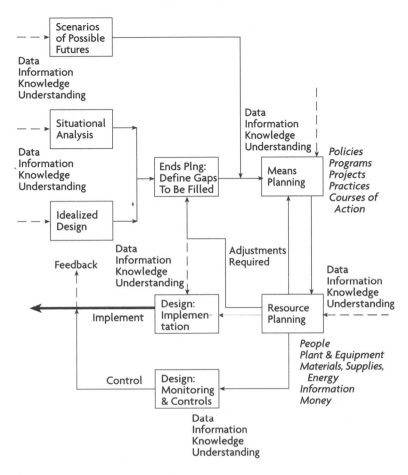

Figure 3.5 The planning process

is subject to only the few minor constraints described below. The differences between this most desired current state of the organization and the future for which the organization is shown to be headed should be formulated and faced. These differences are the gaps to be addressed in the remainder of the planning process.

Means planning. Here, ways of closing the gaps are selected. They may require either invention or discovery. Creativity plays a very large role in inventing or discovering the means to be employed. The means range from very general policies through programs, projects, and practices to very specific courses of action.

Resource planning. This phase of interactive planning is concerned with determining for each type of resource (1) how much will be required, where, and when; (2) how much will be available at the designated time and place; and (3) what is to be done about surpluses or shortages. The following types of resources should be considered: (1) people; (2) plant and equipment (capital expenditures); (3) materials, supplies, and energy (consumables); (4) money; and (5) information.

Implementation and control. In designing the implementation, a determination is made of who is to do what, where, and when and by when it is to be completed. In designing the controls, procedures are specified for identifying and monitoring the assumptions on which the plan is based, the effects it is expected to have, and finally, the method by which errors in expectations and assumptions are to be detected and corrected. It is feedback provided by these three control procedures that makes organizational learning and adaptation possible.

Operating Characteristics of Interactive Planning

Interactive planning differs from all types of conventional planning in three very important ways. First, it plans backward from where the organization wants to be now to where it is now. Second, the planning process is continuous, not an off-again, on-again activity. Third, it provides an opportunity for all an organization's stakeholders, or representatives they select, to participate in the planning process.

Planning backward. Reactive and preactive planners work out from where they are to where they want to be. Interactive planners do the opposite: they plan backward from where they want to be to where they are. This simplifies the planning process considerably by reducing the number of alternatives that have to be considered. As many children have discovered in trying to solve a maze, problems involved in finding a path from a known origin to a known destination are best solved by working from the destination to the origin. Mazes are more easily solved by working from the exit to the entrance.

I was once asked how tennis matches would have to be played in a tournament in which there were 64 players entered. I figured it out as follows. There would be $1/2(64) = 32$ first-round matches; then 16, 8, 4, 2, and 1. I added these up and got 63. The person who gave me the problem asked how many losers there would have to be in such a tournament—sixty-three, of course. No addition or division. How much easier to start at the end rather than the beginning!

A second reason for planning backward from our destination is the effect it has on our concept of feasibility: it makes what otherwise seems infeasible, feasible. I will illustrate this point in Chapter 5.

Continuous planning. Reactive and preactive planning are "sometimes" activities. There is a planning period that ends and is followed by implementation. Implementation may end, followed by a period of no planning-related activity. Then planning starts again. This cycle is repeated periodically. In contrast, interactive planning and its implementation is a continuous process. It frequently does not take time out to prepare a document called "the plan." A plan is considered to be like a still photograph extracted from a motion picture; it is not an adequate basis for evaluating the film. The most important product of interactive planning is the planning process, not plans. It is in the planning process that knowledge, understanding, and wisdom are generated. It is in these acquisitions that the value of planning resides.

Interactive planning is continuous for two reasons. First, it virtually never turns out that the amount of resources required by the means plan is what will be available. A surplus or a shortage of at least some of the types of resource is expected. Therefore, either something in the plan must be changed (upgraded or downgraded) or something must be done to the supply of resources (increased or decreased).

> In a corporate plan prepared for Anheuser-Busch, it was determined that an additional brewery should be built, one that was significantly larger than any that had yet been con-structed. Because of its cost, this required board approval. The board gave approval conditional on the ability of the company to generate internally the additional cash required. The planners went back to the drawing board. Fortunately, they found a way of generating not only the additional cash flow required, but an excess as well. When this solution was presented to the board, it approved the brewery but wanted to know what was planned for the additional cash flow. The planners said they thought it should be used for diversification. The board agreed and instructed the planners to come up with a diversification plan. Again returning to the drawing board, the planners developed three independent diversification plans, each requiring the excess of cash flow that had been produced. The board was asked to select one plan but decided to pursue all three. Since there was not enough cash flow for all three, the planners were instructed to find a way of generating the additional cash required. This was the beginning of a cycle that has never ended.

Second, no planning ever works exactly as expected because either one or more of the assumptions turns out to be wrong or the expectations were in error. The last aspect of planning, control, is designed to reveal such a discrepancy at the earliest possible date so as to make it possible to adjust the plan appropriately. The way this can be done is discussed in Chapter 8.

Participative planning. It should be apparent in light of the preceding discussion that the most important product in planning is process. Engaging in the process develops the knowledge, understanding, and wisdom that make it possible for the organization to work better. The learning that can occur through planning is greater than can be obtained in any other way within the organization. Therefore, the more members of the organization given an opportunity to participate in planning, the greater the individual as well as organizational learning taking place. This considerably increases the chances of successful implementation of plans because those who participate in preparing them have a vested interest in seeing to it that they are implemented as intended.

Moreover, every unit in the organization should engage in interactive planning of that unit and should coordinate and integrate its planning with all units affected by its plans. This enables a comprehensive, coordinated, and integrated plan to emerge. In Chapter 9, I describe a way of organizing and carrying out such a planning effort.

Conclusion

Because the principal product of interactive planning is engagement in the planning process, and because it advocates involving as many employees and other stakeholders in the process as possible, it requires a significant change in the role of professional planners within the company or those employed from without. Their function no longer is to prepare plans for modification, approval, and adoption by others. Rather it is to encourage and facilitate planning by as many of the relevant others as possible. Therefore, their role is much more educational than advisory. In addition to educating those involved relative to the planning process, it is their responsibility to inform them of alternatives of which they may be unaware. For this reason, it is important for the professional planners to keep up with developments in all aspects of management and organization.

Each of the phases of interactive planning is treated in detail in a separate chapter in Part II. The principal characteristics of interactive management other than its planning are discussed in Parts III and IV. An application of the planning process is described in some detail in Appendix B.

Part II

PROCESS

Planning, Design, Implementation, and Learning

4

Formulating the Mess: Sensing and Making Sense of the Situation

It's not the tragedies that kill us, it's the messes.

—Dorothy Parker

Introduction

In order to close the gaps between where an organization is and where it wants to be, one must, of course, know where it is, where it is heading if it does not change its behavior, and what are the internal and external obstructions to its changing. This requires relatively complete knowledge and understanding of the current state of the organization and its environment. Such knowledge and understanding are usually divided among different members of the organization. Therefore, preparation of what might be called the *state of the organization* or a *situational analysis* requires identifying sources, seeking them out, soliciting and collecting their knowledge and understanding, and compiling it into a comprehensible form.

Such a formulation almost always turns out to be of value to the management of the organization involved, independent of its use in the planning process. In many cases, it provides them with their first comprehensive and comprehensible view of the system they manage.

In addition to determining what the state of the organization is, formulation of its mess requires determining its "projected future," where it would be (1) if it were to continue to do what it is doing now and (2) if its environment changed, but only in ways the organization expects.

Note that *both these assumptions are false;* the organization would not be engaged in planning unless it expected to change at least some of its behavior, and every organization expects the unexpected to occur. Therefore, the projection is a "contrary-to-fact-conditional." Nevertheless, it is such a projection that identifies the mess an organization is in; that is, it reveals how the organization will destroy itself unless it changes and what kind of changes are necessary.

There are no special tools or techniques involved in developing a description of the state of the organization. Therefore, what is discussed here is not so much the process, but the content of such a description. On the other hand, determining the projected future of the organization does require discussion of the method of preparing reference projections.

The State of the Organization

Clearly, a description of an organization's state should include a description of what it does. This is usually best provided by use of flow charts: (1) one that describes the flow of orders from their receipt to delivery of final products or services, (2) one that shows the flow of information and instruction that is required by the processes shown in (1), and (3) the flow of financial resources. These descriptions can be prepared separately, but it is usually helpful to combine them into a single chart or to put them on transparent overlays so that their interactions can easily be seen.

In preparing flow charts, I have found the following guidelines very helpful.

1. Show activities in boxes that are clearly labeled.
2. Show flows of material, information, and instructions as directional lines connecting boxes. Each line should be clearly labeled. If the information or instruction is transmitted by means of a document, the number of copies prepared should also be indicated. The ultimate disposition of each copy should be shown on the flow chart. (I have almost always found that this step reveals a number of unused copies, and sometimes an unused original, that can be eliminated without effect. It frequently leads to a significant reduction of the amount of paper floating around the organization.)
3. Where a single instruction or piece of information affects several activities, these activities should be combined. (This simplifies

the diagram and makes it considerably more comprehensible.)
4. A significant effort should be made to avoid diagrams with crossing lines. (It has been my experience that almost every flow chart can be organized so that no lines cross. When this is accomplished, the nature of the flow is much more apparent. An example, prepared for a firm that manufactures sheet aluminum, is shown in Figure 4.1.)

Next, the description of the state of the organization should include "the rules of the game," the behavior and practices that facilitate survival, if not "thrival," of individuals in the organization. These constitute the organization's culture. There is usually a significant difference between the rules and customs practiced and those that are preached. Both should be collected so that the differences between them and their effects can be revealed.

One organization I have worked in claims an "open-door policy." But to get to the open door one must go through two security checks and up to the top floor, where few but the executives and their immedi-

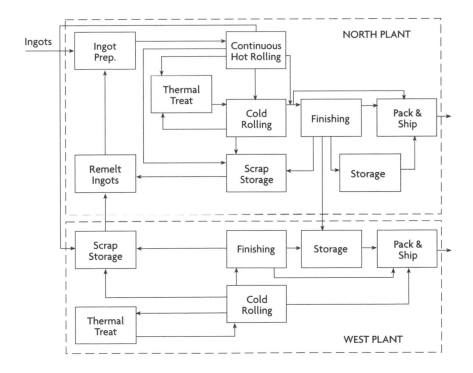

Figure 4.1   A flow of material in two adjacent sheet-aluminum production plants

ate staff members are ever seen. It takes courage and insensitivity to the staring of others to go up there. In addition, the company preaches open communication, but most of the occupants of the top floor never go to any of the lower floors except the one containing the executive dining room, where food is provided at no cost. Not so in the other employees' cafeteria on the ground floor.

In most organizations that have an "open communication" policy, it is dangerous under any condition to criticize, or point out a mistake made by, a superior, especially in public. It is necessary to be aware of such discrepancies if one is to understand an organization's culture. I am reminded of the quotation attributed to Samuel Goldwyn, "I want you to tell me what you think even if you get fired for it." In the course of planning, it is very important for an organization to learn and face the truth about itself.

The practices and procedures that are preached are usually available in documents such as policy manuals and speeches by senior executives. In contrast, the rules that are practiced are best uncovered by interviewing a variety of employees of different status and locations in the organization. If those interviewed are not assured of anonymity, it is difficult to get them to open up, particularly if the interviewer is a member of the organization.

The third component of the description of the state of the organization is a disclosure of the conflicts within the organization that obstruct or otherwise affect performance of either the organization as a whole, its parts, or individuals within it. Consideration should also be given to conflicts with external organizations or individuals. For example, in one organization the purchasing agent refused to deal with the lowest-cost supplier of a material his company used in large quantities because he had once had an argument with that supplier's sales representative.

Finally, the organization's description should identify trends that could affect the organization's performance (for better or worse) if they were to continue. Relevant external trends might include such things as rising costs of raw materials, increasing interest rates on loans, and changing foreign exchange rates. Relevant internal trends could include such things as increases of attrition rates, salaries of new hires, alcohol or drug abuse, and quality-reject rates.

Who Should Prepare It?

Even if an external consultant is used to facilitate preparation of the state of the organization, the bulk of the work should be done by internal personnel. I have found that three to five young professionals who have been with the company no more than five years, preferably less than three, working on this preparation about half time, are able to do the best job. They are less inhibited than old timers and most sensitive to differences between practice and preaching. Furthermore, it provides them with good organization education.

Presenting It

Descriptions of states of the organization are generally much too long to reproduce here. But it may be helpful to include a few selections drawn from several different kinds of organizations.

The first is from the description of the 1987 state of ALAD, the Armco Latin American Division. This division included operations in eight countries: Uruguay, Argentina, Chile, Peru, Brazil, Colombia, Venezuela, and Ecuador. These previously relatively autonomous units had been combined into a division only a few years earlier. Its product line consisted of a wide range of fabricated and forged steel products.

The state of the division was described as follows:

As presently organized ALAD does not constitute a system. It is an aggregation of several operating units pulled together by a central governing body. . . .

Traditionally Armco has relied on its overseas managers as operational managers. They were not expected to be general managers of a business. The technology, products, markets, management practices, and human resource policies were predefined for them. Their role was to manage the operations as efficiently as possible and to meet RONA [return on net assets] and dividend goals established by the Corporation.

This conception has changed drastically in recent years. Now the managers are expected not only to manage an efficient operation and produce acceptable RONAs but also to define the business they *ought to be in* and devise a strategy for the development of these businesses. This clearly involves, among other functions, definition of markets to be served, development of products that meet the needs of that market, establishment of appropriate human resource policies which can attract, retain, and develop the necessary talent for managing these businesses, and financial planning for survival and "thrival" of these businesses.

Conceptually this change has been welcomed and adopted at

the Country Manager's level. In practice they are hindered in their attempts to perform in the new role principally by three factors: training and education, support from levels below, and management systems and processes imposed from above.

1. The group of managers responsible for Armco's businesses are exceptionally young. They are very talented, aggressive, and enthusiastic. For the most part, however, they have not been trained as general managers nor do they have any relevant experience.

They need training in areas of management with which they are unfamiliar, most notably marketing. They also need guidance in standardization of their approach to preparation of business plans, evaluation of diversification opportunities, and development and evaluation of business strategies. Most importantly, they need coaching from the more experienced managers of the Division. Establishment of this coaching relationship is a key element in their development.

2. The functional managers in the business units face a similar problem with training but in their case the most important factor is their refusal to accept a new role. By and large, the managers at this level are waiting to be told what to do and are content with being efficient administrators. This is especially troublesome in the critical areas of Product Management, Finance, and Human Resources.

3. The existing management processes at ALAD correspond to the mode of management for which they were designed: that is, low authority and low responsibility for the business unit managers and strong central controls. In the new approach the managers are given a lot more responsibilities but the level of authority remains practically the same as before. A country manager, for example, cannot purchase a personal computer without approval from the Division. This can only lead to frustration and ineffectiveness.

ALAD was subsequently redesigned and formed into a homogeneous organization with considerable synergy between its parts. Its profitability increased to the point at which its parent company, in critical need of cash, disassembled it and sold its parts.

The next example consists of a small section drawn from a description of the state of the Tennessee Operations of ALCOA (A-T). It was prepared in the early 1980s. Alcoa Tennessee has been completely changed since then, technologically, managerially, and in labor-man-agement relations. It is now an efficient and productive plant, whose products are of very high quality.

A-T management is now discouraged. It has been put in a posi-tion where the future looks so bleak, that it could take steps which might turn these somber forecasts into a self-fulfilling prophesy. It cannot see how the A-T works, with their cost structure unbal-anced by large fixed costs, could ever function at the low produc-tion levels which are imposed on A-T by the corporation. The burden and GASE [General, Administrative, and Selling Expenses] costs have been rising very fast. Only direct labor costs are constant compared to inflation. Together with the fact that their magnitude is only a quarter of the variable burden which is now rising rapidly, this indicates that contracting the A-T opera-tion will put it in the red. In other words, a substantial contracting . . . of the production level at A-T which would reduce revenue by a third would result in a non-proportional, much smaller reduc-tion in total cost (one has to also consider the layoff compensation payments and pensions which would have to be paid).

Moreover, labor is not going to sit still and cooperate in its own demise. The contraction of the work force in 1975–76 has left scars on people's minds as well as a certain number of displaced individuals to act as a reminder, to those eager to cooperate with management, of the "capricious" policy of the company. In this context, job security becomes a real concern. Safety is an issue intertwined with it. The number of injuries is on a slowly declin-ing trend, but there still are nearly 300 per million employee hours. Workers resent the company's "lack of planning" which causes it to push for production in one period, and lay people off in the next. Against the background of such labor relations, it is not clear how management could contract the operations signifi-cantly and still command enough commitment from the remain-ing employees, given their job insecurity. As a result, it is to be expected that labor's negative cooperation to any significant con-traction scheme will aggravate the structural non-proportionality in cost. . . . Together, these effects will render any cost saving largely illusory; the revenue will decrease, but not the cost.

The content of this situational analysis was incorporated into the formulation of Alcoa Tennessee's mess, which is reproduced below.

Reference Projections

A reference projection consists of a projection of the future of the organization based on two false assumptions: that there will be no change in corporate behavior and that the relevant future currently predicted by the organization is complete and correct. Since an infinite number of corporate properties could be projected, those that are most relevant to the future state of the organization should be explored first—the critical success factors. But these are not always apparent. The relevant aspects of the organization are those that will lead to its destruction in its projected (not predicted) future. It may take some detective work to find the relevant factors. It is much like a detective looking for clues to a crime that has not yet been identified but that is known to have been committed.

The projection should extend far enough to allow the relevant variables to do their damage. (A typical example is shown in Fig. 4.2.) Selection of a horizon may also require some trial and error. This, however, is not nearly as difficult as selecting the right variables.

What's the point? No matter how successful an organization may be now, there is a reference projection of that future in which it will cease to exist if it were to continue to behave as it does now. This follows from the fact that the projection assumes no change in the organization's behavior in a changing environment. A failure to adapt to envi-

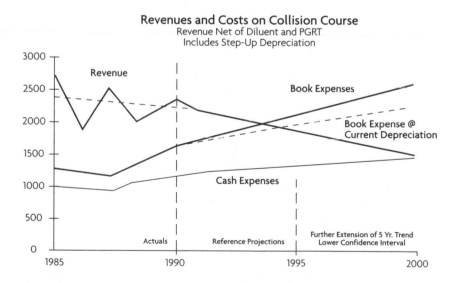

Figure 4.2   A typical projection used in preparing a reference projection

ronmental changes will destroy any organization in time, but this much is known before the projection is made. Then why make it? Because it will reveal *how and why* the organization will destroy itself, the organization's Achilles heel.

The Automotive Industry

The following reference projection was prepared in 1960 for the Ford Motor Company. The company had its internal planners prepare a very long range plan to the year 2000 that assumed no fundamental change in the nature of automobiles. Such a long-range projection allows us to see what actually happened as we near the end of the century.

> Some of us (external personnel working for Ford) doubted the validity of the no-fundamental-change assumption and believed that environmental changes might force fundamental changes of the nature or use of automobiles. The argument that followed could not be settled unless one could reveal the types of change that could be imposed on the automobile and why. This led to a formulation of the mess of the U.S. automotive industry, one based on the following reference projection.
>
> The first step consisted of obtaining an estimate of the population of the United States in the year 2000 assuming no change in the dynamics of population growth. We consulted the U.S. Bureau of the Census and obtained its best (conservative) estimate. Then we requested and received from that Bureau an estimate of the number of people in the year 2000 who would be old enough to drive, assuming no change in the existing driving laws. Using this estimate and information on the number old enough to drive who actually did, we estimated the number who would be driving.
>
> Next, we projected the number of automobiles per driver. This turned out to be 1.54, a number that struck us as very large. We were aware of an argument in the literature to the effect that the upper limit on the number of cars per driver was 1.0. Therefore, we reduced our estimate in order to proceed as conservatively as possible. Then we projected the number of miles per car per year by using data obtained from the petroleum industry. It increased from about 11,800 to 13,200 miles. This mileage was divided into urban and

interurban usage using data obtained from the Highway
Research Board of the Federal Government. It turned out
that by the year 2000 expected urban mileage would be 62
percent of the total.

Now 62 percent of the number of miles per year per car
times the number of cars gave us an estimate of the total
number of automotive miles that would be driven in cities in
the year 2000 if everything went as expected and no changes
were made. This number of miles could not be accommo-
dated on then current streets and expressways in cities; the
resulting congestion would be intolerable. Therefore, we
estimated how many additional lane miles of streets and
expressways would be required to accommodate the additional mileage while maintaining the 1960 level of congestion. It was about 58,000 lane miles. We did not (and did not
need to) take into account the additional parking space that
would be required.

Next, using data again obtained from the Highway
Research Board, an estimate was made of the annual cost of
providing the additional urban lane miles required. This was
more than twelve times as much per year as had ever been
spent for this purpose in the past. Therefore, to assume it
would be spent each year for the next forty years was unreasonable. But this was not the mess. The mess was revealed
by assuming the government would spend the required
money and build the required urban lane miles. *Then, by the
year 2000, 117% percent of the cities' surfaces would be covered
with streets and expressways.*

This was the automotive industry's mess. Now, clearly, this could
not happen. Therefore, expected continuation of the current automobile and its usage was not possible. What would happen to prevent it?
This was an open question that remained to be determined, one that
could be significantly influenced by what the Ford and other automobile manufacturers did. The obvious (nonexclusive) possibilities were:

1.   Greatly increased congestion.

This has, of course, been realized in most large American and foreign cities.

2.   Restrictions imposed on the use of automobiles.

In many cities in the United States and abroad, streets have been closed to automotive traffic for at least part of some days. In some cases (e.g., Rome), large areas have been permanently closed to automotive traffic. In other cities, truck-trailers are not permitted to use the streets during specified hours. In Mexico City, automobiles with license plates ending with specified numbers cannot be used on designated days. It has been necessary on occasion to extend the prohibition to two days per week. (This measure has not had the desired effect because many bought a second car with different last-two numbers on its license plates.)

3. Public transportation can be expanded and made more attractive.

Unfortunately, there has been little success in reducing congestion by increasing public transportation. Those who have a choice prefer the convenience, privacy, and independence offered by a privately owned vehicle.

4. The city can be redesigned so as to minimize the requirement for mechanically aided transportation, and its growth and development can be gradually directed toward realization of that design.

Such a city was subsequently designed and its characteristics largely incorporated into the design of a new city built in Mexico, Cuatitlan Izcalli. Traffic and congestion were significantly lower here than in other cities of the same size. Subsequent changes in the city eradicated this advantage.

5. The automobile can be redesigned to reduce the amount of space required to transport a person.

Ford placed no faith in the projections and, therefore, had no interest in pursuing any of the possibilities at that time. Design of a more appropriate automobile was pursued with other sources of support. This led to a concept of a two-passenger urban automobile (Fig. 4.3). A number of other conceptions have since been developed and brought to the market. Renault has made a two-passenger urban automobile in Europe. Other European manufacturers and Honda are promising or have already made available similar automobiles (Fig. 4.4). Ford has reacted by introducing its four passenger Ka in Europe in October 1997, but indicated it did not plan to bring it to the United States for at least two years ("Cute as a Bug, but You Can't Get It Here," *USA Today*, August 20, 1997).

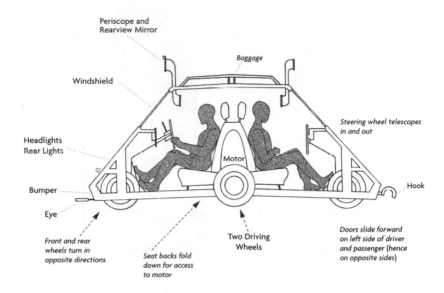

Figure 4.3 A concept of an urban automobile

The point is that the reference projection of the industry revealed the types of change, at least one of which would have to occur. It revealed the need for a smaller car when less than 1 percent of the cars sold in the United States were small cars. Ford did not react to the growing need until the 1970s, when small foreign cars had gained 18 percent of the market, and then Ford got it all wrong with the Pinto. It was not until much later when it produced the Escort that it got it partly right. This is still a long way from the two-passenger urban automobile that ultimately will be required. In the meantime, if designed to be inexpensive, a small urban automobile could find a very large market in less developed countries with temperate climates.

The same study suggested the development of very small coin-operated, drive-it-yourself taxis. Several European cities (Montpelier, France, and Amsterdam, Holland) made a limited number of such vehicles available. This stimulated the design of a large system of this type for Paris (called Tulip) by PSA Peugeot Citroen (Fig. 4.5).

The Federal Reserve Bank

A reference projection for the fourth district of the Federal Reserve Bank was initiated in 1973.

Figure 4.4   A French urban automobile currently available
Source: *Time* magazine, November 5, 1990.

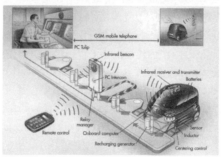

Figure 4.5   A proposed French transportation system. The "tulip" system
consists of two-seater electric vehicles located at a variety of points around a
city. Subscribers of the Tulip network would be free to drive around town,
following their own paths and time schedules, without having to own
and maintain their own cars. The name Tulip is an acronym for Transport
Urbain Libre Individuel et Public (self-service, public, and private
urban transport).
Source: PSA Peugeot Citroën, Communications Director, 75 avenue de la Grande-Armée,
75116 Paris, France.

A time study was conducted to find out how employees of the bank spent their time. It was learned that the largest block of employees' time was spent clearing checks.

A projection was then made of the number of checks that had to be cleared by the bank per unit time. This number was steadily increasing. Then a study was conducted of the number of checks a check clearer could clear per unit time. It was found to be relatively constant. This made it possible to project the number of check clearers that would be required. This was followed by finding the amount of office space required by a check clearer. This amount was then multiplied by the number of check clearers to obtain the total amount of office space that would be required. It exceeded the amount that would be available in the United States.

Therefore, something had to be done about either the rate of increase in the number of checks or the rate at which checks could be cleared. As a result, a coalition of district banks was formed that eventually developed the present system of electronic funds transfer, which in turn stimulated the development of credit and debit cards. Initially, it reduced the rate of increase of checks and has recently reduced their absolute number.

An Insurance Company

In 1982 the National Life Insurance Company (of Montpelier, Vermont) was and had been a very successful writer of large life-insurance policies. It did not anticipate a crisis when it decided to formulate its mess; it did so largely out of curiosity.

The effort to formulate the mess of National Life stalled because all the initial projections indicated continuing success. By a stroke of luck, a young woman in the accounting department turned attention to cash flow. Increases of cash flow, which had been continuous over years, had begun to slow down. It was still positive, but clearly something had changed. A search for the cause was initiated. It turned out that most of the insurance policies were quite old and had been written at a time when the insured were given the right to borrow on their policies at what subsequently turned out to be a very low interest rate. By the 1980s, National Life could not borrow money for as little as those it insured could borrow from it. Its financially sophisticated policyholders found that if they borrowed on their policies they could invest what they had borrowed at a higher rate of interest than they paid for it. An increasing number of those insured were discovering this. Q.E.D., a decreasing cash flow. Continuation of this trend would eventually have produced serious financial difficulties for the company.

Clearly, the policies had to renegotiated so as to replace the fixed borrowing rate with one that was variable and tied to the current prime rate. This was done.

Presentation of the Mess

The state of the organization and its reference projections should be combined into a scenario of the possible future of the organization, a future it would face if it were to make no changes in its current practices, policies, tactics, and strategies, and the environment changed only in expected ways.

It is well known that many organizations will not change their course unless they are in a state of crisis. Reference projections can reveal the crisis the organization will be in unless it changes its behavior. Therefore, it is critical that the mess be presented in as realistic, as believable, and as shocking a way as possible. A drab report of the mess won't do it. A number of ways have been found to make it provocative.

At Alcoa Tennessee, the mess was written as if it were five years in the future, cast in the form of a history of the closing of the facility, portrayed as a natural consequence of what had happened from the real time at which it was written (1980) up to the fictional time at which it was pretended to have been written (1984). Then that account was printed in an imitation of the local newspaper, the *Maryville Times*, with the help of that newspaper. That article is reproduced here.

Blount County To Lose Alcoa Plant and 2,300 Jobs

Economic disaster hit the Maryville town area yesterday.

The largest population center of Blount County lost 3,000 jobs and a substantial portion of its tax base when ALCOA announced it would close its fabricating plant operations in October of 1984.

The full extent of the closing will not be felt for months, but the severity was apparent yesterday.

The $1,300,000 that ALCOA paid in property tax is 60% of the township's taxes. ALCOA spends $400,000,000 a year in Tennessee.

Now most of it is going. "It's certainly a shock," said Mayor Peter S. Smith. Local officials of both ALCOA and Maryville had become concerned by recent layoffs and job reduction at the plant that have reduced the workforce from 4,600 in 1982 to 3,600 (approximately 1,250 jobs are in the smelting plant, which will remain open) in March 1984. The officials had jointly requested, but had not been granted, a meeting with ALCOA to discuss ways the company could be helped.

Peter S. Smith, mayor of Maryville, a community of 16,000 on whose border the plant is located, called the news a "disaster." Smith said ALCOA was the largest employer in the area and it had paid its workers nearly twice as much as other employers. Smith, while not being specific, predicted "major cutbacks" in government services in Maryville and the "possible consolidation and closing" of several schools.

ALCOA's Tennessee plant is the first of two major closings in ALCOA's U. S. operation.

A spokesman for the company denied that the closings are related to the current strike that has closed the Tennessee Operations down for the past six weeks.

The closings are attributed to the banning of aluminum beverage containers (about 50% of A-T's business according to a spokesman).

The spokesman also said that energy costs and a metal shortage contributed to the decision to close. "The cost of energy to smelt aluminum has risen 200% in the past four years, and consequently, most of the metal ingots are used for manufacturing high profit items by other divisions of ALCOA ."

Most of ALCOA's smelting and manufacturing takes place outside the U.S. where energy and labor costs are significantly lower.

United Steel Workers Sub-District Manager Billy Joe Drums said, "I don't believe they are serious about this closing. In 1967 they threatened to do the same thing and didn't." He went on to say, "If those [deleted] in Pittsburgh think they're gonna close this plant for six months to break the strike and then sell it to another operation without the Union, then they'd better think again."

Upon receiving word of the apparently irrevocable plans to close yesterday, about 1,000 strikers stormed the plants in ALCOA and vowed to stay until the company met their demands and rescinded the closing order.

A prepared corporate statement issued at the plant said the closing was due to "the decline in the rolled-container sheet market and increased U.S. energy costs." As recently as January, ALCOA plant officials told the *Times* that they did not foresee additional layoffs beyond the 400 that had occurred from September to

December 1983. "We are looking for increases in employment when conditions get better," a spokesman had said.

ALCOA's Operations Manager, John Olstead, would not elaborate on the terse statement's expression of regret on its employees and the community. That statement said ALCOA would help dismissed workers try to find other jobs.

Olstead said that an aluminum powder facility that employs 50 employees would not be affected by the closing of the manufacturing plants.

The closing will throw 600 management and 1,700 production workers out of jobs, in addition to those already laid off, Olstead said. Olstead, when asked whether the company had considered what it would do eventually with the factory, had no comment.

He did indicate that the company had sought an injunction in Federal court to remove occupying strikers from plant property yesterday.

ALCOA-Tennessee reported a loss of $10 million in the first quarter of its fiscal year. This was mostly attributed to the current protracted strike.

An anonymous source close to ALCOA said that the Tennessee Operation has been in trouble for a long time. Management and the Union were unable to work together on problems of productivity and competitiveness because of a high level of distrust, the source indicated. As a result the Corporate Headquarters have invested few capital funds in Tennessee.

In the past three years ALCOA has invested the majority of its capital funds in international operations. Unfortunately, two South American countries have nationalized ALCOA's operations and projected profits for the next few years are substantially down—this has severely limited the ability of the Corporate Headquarters to sustain operations like Tennessee, the source indicated.

This fictitious account was dated four years in the future, but few who saw the paper caught this inconspicuous fact unless it was pointed out to them. Unfortunately, copies of this "issue" of the newspaper, which were supposed to be tightly controlled, got out. Workers and their union local, overlooking the fictitious date, panicked at the announced closing of the plant and threatened to demonstrate against it. Though unintentional, this response to the story demonstrated to management and the union the realistic nature of the projected crisis.

The mess we formulated for Imperial Oil of Canada was presented in the form of an article published in *Business Week*. Again, it was made to look authentic. Although it caused no panic, its realism and believability caught the attention of even the most skeptical managers. This led to a series of changes that were less than we had hoped, but more than we had expected.

At Metropolitan Life, a group of young professionals produced a video tape of a simulated television network news broadcast in which they recounted the demise of their company, giving the "history" leading up to it. This, too, caught and held management's attention, leading to some significant changes in the company's businesses and organizational structure.

Conclusion

An organization's mess is the future implied by its current plans, policies, and practices, together with the changes it expects in its environment. This future implies the destruction or deterioration of every organization, no matter how successful it may be now, because under these assumptions it would fail to adapt to even expected internal or external changes. The projected future reveals not only what cannot happen, but also suggests what might be done to avoid coming close to it. This provides the organization with an opportunity to control or influence a significant part of its future. If it fails to plan to bring about its future, it will be subject to interventions by others. Therefore, its future will be a product not of what it does, but of what is done to it.

5

Ends Planning: Where to Go

Vision—What management truly wishes your organization would become, namely an engine for churning out acceptable returns to the stockholders and whopping compensation plans for management without the need to subsidize the health insurance of a single full-time employee.

—Jack Gordon

Introduction

In the discussion of reactive management (Chapter 2), I argued that effective management must be directed at getting what is wanted, not at getting rid of what isn't. Ends planning is directed at making explicit exactly what is wanted.

What an organization wants, its ends, is of three types: *ideals*, *objectives*, and *goals*. An ideal is an end that can never be attained, but that can be approached endlessly; the gap between an ideal and where we are can always be reduced. Therefore, an ideal is a limit. Similarly, if we begin the process of dividing 1 by half, we get the series 1, $1/2$, $1/4$, $1/8$, $1/16$, and so on, always getting closer to 0 but never reaching it.

An objective is an end that is attainable only in the long run. A goal, on the other hand, is an end that is attainable in the short run. These terms are frequently used in reverse. I use them this way because in such games as football, soccer, and hockey, goals are intermediate ends, winning is the objective, a longer-run end. But reversal of this usage creates no difficulty if it is applied consistently.

Ends and means are relative concepts. For example, building a bookcase is a means to the end of storing books. But storing books is a means to facilitate our reading them, the end. Reading books, in turn, is a means to acquiring some needed knowledge. And so on and on, until we reach the ultimate end of everyone who has or will ever want anything, that is, the ability to obtain whatever they want. I call this ability "omnicompetence." This is necessarily everyone's ideal because one cannot want anything—including the ultimate nothing, Nirvana—without wanting the ability, the competence, required to obtain it. Although omnicompetence is clearly approachable, it is equally clearly unattainable. (This concept will be dealt with in more detail in Chapter 13.)

The Steps Involved

Ends planning should involve the following steps:

1. A mission statement should be prepared, one that states the organization's reason for being, its ultimate ends, its ideals.

Together with the formulation of the mess, this statement gives direction to the subsequent idealized-design process.

2. The properties that the planners desire the organization and its behavior to have ideally should be specified.
3. An idealized design of the organization should be prepared.
4. The closest approximation to this design that is believed to be attainable should be formulated.

This should be done in such a way as to leave open the possibility of getting still closer to the idealized design in the future, as a result of learning and adaptation to changes in the environment. Furthermore, an organization's ideals, like an individual's ideals, may change over time with increasing age and experience. Once the ideals and the closest feasible approximation to them have been formulated, the final step can be taken.

5. The gaps between that approximation and the current state of the organization should be identified.

The remainder of the planning process is directed at closing these gaps. It is for this reason that I think of formulating the mess and ends planning as the *idealization* phases of planning and the remaining aspects—means, resource, implementation, and control planning—as the *realization* phases of planning.

For reasons discussed in Chapter 3, when the idealized design is completed the designers work back from it to where the organization is now, from destination to origin. Most planning proceeds in the opposite direction. Recall that the reason for working backward, counterintuitively, is that it is simpler, often very much simpler.

The Mission Statement

A mission statement should *not* contain "motherhood statements," tautologies, or pious platitudes. These are statements the negative of which no one would ever make or defend: "to provide the best value for the money" or, as one company put it, to make "intelligent and disciplined application of proven principles of organization and management." No one would argue that an organization should provide the worst value for the money or make an unintelligent or undisciplined application of unproved principles of organization and management.

An organization's mission statement (1) should contain its reasons for existence and its most general aspirations, its ideals. (2) It should identify in very general terms the way(s) by which the organization will pursue its ideals, that is, the business it wants to be in. (3) It should formulate the ways by which it will attempt to serve each of its stakeholder groups. (4) It should meet the preceding requirements in a way that is exciting and challenging to all its stakeholders. Finally, (5) it should establish the uniqueness of the organization.

Once formulated, the mission statement should make a significant difference in what the organization does. If it doesn't, it is useless, as most mission statements are because they fail to meet some or all of the preceding requirements. Consider each in more detail.

1. A mission statement should contain a formulation of the organization's ideals and do so in a way that makes possible evaluation of progress toward them.

If a mission statement cannot be used to evaluate progress, it is hollow, at best propagandistic, not programmatic. It should *not* state what the organization must do to survive; it should state what it *chooses to do to thrive*. For example, to say that a corporation seeks "to make an adequate profit" or "meet shareholder expectations" is like a person saying that his or her mission is to breathe enough air.

2. A mission statement should define the business that the organization wants to be in, not necessarily what it is in.

The business so defined identifies the general means by which the organization intends to pursue its ideals. This formulation should expand the organization's concept of itself. For example, when a company that produces alcoholic beverages consumed primarily by young and middle-aged adults said its business was to "provide products and services that enables people of all ages to spend their discretionary time in more satisfying ways," it opened a vista to products and services that could be provided to senior citizens and children. They have the largest amounts of discretionary time. When a company that produced audio and visual tapes said it was in the "sticking business, putting any two things together," all sorts of exciting possibilities emerged. When a hospital said its business consisted of "producing and preserving health," concluding that "the treatment of sickness and disabilities is a cost, not an output," it generated an entirely new way of paying for health care.

3. An organization's mission should be unique, not suitable for any other organization.

It should establish the uniqueness of the organization. If an organization is not unique, there is not a good reason for its existence. Also, it is very difficult for its stakeholders to identify strongly with and make strong commitments to an organization that is not unique.

4. A mission statement should be relevant to all of the organization's stakeholders by stating its function relative to each type.

It should state how it intends to serve the interests of each class of its stakeholders, not just those of management, stockholders, or both. It should induce a commitment from each group of stakeholders. If it fails to appeal to educated nonmanagerial employees, in particular, pursuit of its mission will never be effective.

5. A mission statement should be exciting, challenging, and inspiring.

If it fails in this regard, it will fail to produce change no matter what its other properties. Even the unattainable can be inspiring if it is approachable, and what appears to be unattainable may not be. José Ortega y Gasset (1966) put it succinctly:

man has been able to grow enthusiastic over his vision of . . . unconvincing enterprises. He has put himself to work for the sake of an idea, seeking by magnificent exertions to arrive at the incredible. And in the end, he has arrived there. Beyond all doubt it is one of the vital sources of man's power, to be thus able to kindle enthusiasm from the mere glimmer of something improbable, difficult, remote. (1)

The mission statement formulated by ALAD, Armco's Latin American Division, tried to satisfy these conditions:

To contribute significantly to the development of Latin America and to the viability of Armco Inc. by:

Producing and/or marketing products and services that provide the most cost-effective solutions to current and emergent needs of Latin-American industries.

Providing conditions of work and a quality of work life for all its employees that will help them realize their personal aspirations.

Developing technologies that are particularly suited to the social, economic, and cultural conditions of the countries in Latin America, and enable them to compete world wide.

Demonstrating that a multi-national company with roots in many Latin American countries can contribute significantly more to the development of each of them than an organization centered in one country only.

A division of a Mexican company, Alfa, formulated its mission as follows:

Through land development and tourism to demonstrate the ability of the private sector of the Mexican economy to contribute significantly to national development while efficiently and effectively pursuing corporate objectives.

To create a wholesome, varied, pluralistic, multi-class recreational area incorporating tourist facilities and permanent residences and to produce locally as much of the goods and services required by the area as possible, so as to improve the standard of living and quality of work life of its inhabitants.

Specifications

Before an architect can design a house for a family, he must find out what properties they would like the house to have: the number of rooms of each type, the style, the approximate cost, and so on. His design is an effort to operationalize these properties by imbedding them in a structure that can be built. Idealized design of an organization or any other type of system is much the same thing. It begins with a listing of the properties that its stakeholders would like it to have.

For example, preparatory to an idealized design of the U.S. telephone system prepared in the early 1950s, such desired properties of the system as these were specified: no wrong numbers, push button phones in place of the dial, phones that could be used with no hands, phones that tell the receiver who is calling before he or she must answer a call, a phone that comes to the receiver wherever he or she is rather than he or she going to the phone, automatic redialing of the last number called. All these properties and many others were incorporated in the design that followed. Almost every change in the telephone system made since 1953 was part of that design. A number have yet to be realized because they are not yet economically feasible.

Prior to preparing its idealized design, the Clark Equipment Corporation prepared extensive specifications of the properties it desired. They were organized under the following general headings. The first item under each heading is also reproduced here to give a flavor of the list. The numbers in parentheses after the heading and "etc." indicate the number of items that followed.

1. General (7)
   1.1. The organization should provide for learning and adaptation through an on-going planning process together with flexibility in functions, workforce training, products, and markets.
2. Organization (3)
   2.1. The organizational design should be flat and as decentralized as possible, recognizing that solutions are best generated at the lowest possible level: where the knowledge exists.
3. Management Style (1)
   3.1. Management style should be interactive and should value and encourage minimum rules and policies; strategic vs. tactical orientation; employee involvement, trust, creativity, and win-win solutions; constructive feedback; etc. (10)
4. People (7)
   4.1. Opportunities should be provided for employee development and experience to enhance self-worth and self-actualization while accomplishing the objectives of the organization.
5. Products (5)

5.1. The products and services should incorporate state-of-the-art technology.
6. Marketing (4)
   6.1. Clark should strive for market leadership.
7. Facilities (2)
   7.1. Design, development, selection, and investment in facilities should be based on the following criteria: least number of facilities compatible with projected capacity needs; location predicated on least cost in relation to markets to be served; etc. (7)
8. Environment (2)
   8.1. Clark management should have excellent working relationships with the following stakeholders: employees, Board members, stockholders, retirees, vendors, suppliers, etc. (11)

Idealized Design

An organization's *vision* should be a verbal picture of what its stakeholders most want it to be. Corporate visions are seldom formulated by a cross section of stakeholders. They are usually formulated by the upper level(s) of management alone. Unless the vision is shared by the various stakeholders, it is unlikely to be pursued effectively.

By a vision, most managements mean a description of what they would like their organization to be at a specified time in the future, usually five or ten years ahead. This ignores the fact that individual and collective aspirations change continually, especially in response to unanticipated changes in their environments. Even if this were not the case, *how can those who formulate a corporate vision know what they will want it to be in the future if they do not know what they want it to be right now?* If they knew what they wanted the organization to be right now—assuming that it could be whatever they wanted—and if they knew how this differed from what it is right now, why would they need to know what they wanted it to be in the future? Whatever we want an organization to be right now necessarily includes what we expect of it in the future. When we build a house now, we do so using assumptions about the use we will put it to in the future. The same is true of organizations.

Corporate visions are usually expressed in very general and abstract terms. They often consist of a list of desired properties and nothing more; they do not consist of a *design* of an organization that has these properties. A design incorporating an organization's current ideals can take the future into account without forecasting that future. Forecasts are uncertain at best. A design can do this by making *assumptions* about the future rather than forecasting it. Some argue that assumptions about the future are nothing but forecasts in disguise, but they are wrong. For example, we carry a spare tire in our automobile not because we forecast we will have a flat tire on our next trip, but because we assume one is *possible*. If we forecast this at all, it would be that we would not have a flat tire. Forecasts are about probabilities; assumptions are about possibilities. Planning that takes possibilities into account is *contingency planning*.

An organization cannot and need not take every possibility into account. It need not do so if it is designed to be ready, willing, and able to change in response to a wide variety of internal and external changes that can affect it. Like a good driver of an automobile, management of such an organization is capable of responding rapidly and effectively to almost any contingency that can arise.

What an organization most wants to be now is best learned and captured in an *idealized design* of that organization. This is a design of what an organization's stakeholders want the organization to be *right now*, assuming that it could be whatever they wanted, subject to only a few relatively unrestrictive constraints that are identified below. There is no more effective way for an organization to create its desired future than by continuously making its present more nearly approximate its current ideals.

The benefits derived from idealized design come from not only implementing the plans that derive from it, but also in the learning and creativity that result from engaging in the design process. In idealized design, as in interactive planning as a whole, process is *the* most important product.

There are two types of idealized design: *bounded* and *unbounded*. Consider each in turn.

Bounded Idealized Design

A bounded idealized design of an organization (or any system) begins with the assumption that the organization (or system) involved was destroyed last night. It no longer exists, but its environment is assumed to remain as it was, untouched. If the organization to be designed is a part of a larger existing organization—for example, a division or a department of a corporation—the rest of the containing organization is initially assumed to remain unchanged. Only the unit to be redesigned is assumed to have been destroyed. Therefore, its replacement to be designed must fit into the containing organization as it is currently.

An idealized design is subject to three constraints:

1. The organization designed must be *technologically feasible*; it must not incorporate any technology that is not currently available.

This requirement does not preclude invention or innovation, but it does prevent the design process from being a work of science fiction. For example, the designers should not employ mental telepathy as a way of communicating between managers and organizational units, but could use a corporately controlled communication satellite or optical fiber network, although they don't have one now, because they know one is possible.

The feasibility of the design, economically or politically (from an internal point of view), is not relevant.

2. Although the design need not be capable of being implemented, it must be *operationally viable,* that is, capable of surviving in what would be its environment if it came into existence now.

Therefore, it must obey current laws and regulations, pay taxes, and, if publicly owned, produce annual reports, and so on. This requirement assures the conceptual feasibility of the design, not its practicality. Obviously, practicality is not required of an idealized design.

3. The organization designed must be *capable of being improved continuously* from within and without.

This requires the organization to be capable of rapid and effective learning and adaptation, and to be subject to change by its stakeholders.

Because idealized designs are capable of being improved, they are neither ideal nor utopian. An ideal or utopian system is one its designers claim to be perfect and, therefore, not subject to improvement. Then why is the process called "idealized" design? Because the product of such a design is the best *ideal-seeking* system that its designers can conceive of now.

An idealized design should cover all aspects of an organization. These vary among organizations. The following is a typical list that was used in one corporation.

Products and services to be offered
Markets to be served
Distribution system
Organizational structure
Internal financial structure
Management style
Internal functions, such as:
    Purchasing
    Manufacturing
    Maintenance
    Engineering
    Marketing and sales
    Research and development
    Finance
    Accounting
    Human resources
    Building and grounds
    Communications internal and external
    Legal
    Planning
    Human resources
    Organizational development
    Computing and data processing
Administrative services (e.g., mail and duplicating)
Facilities
Industry, government, and community affairs

Unbounded Idealized Designs

The bounded idealized design of a system is always limited by the nature of the system(s) that contains it. It is apparent, for example, that an autonomous corporation is constrained by the governments of the countries in which it does business and that a subsidiary or division is constrained by its parent organization.

Because of these constraints, it is desirable to prepare two separate versions of an idealized design, one bounded by its containing system(s) and the other not. The bounded design assumes no changes in any of the relevant containing systems. Even under this assumption, however, most organizations or organizational units can be radically redesigned. In unbounded idealized design, the designers are permitted to design changes of any of the containing systems, but only ones that would improve the performance of the organization being designed.

The constrained design should be prepared first. Surprisingly, the unconstrained design is usually less different from the one that is constrained than the designers expect. This reveals that most of the obstructions between an organization and where its designers would most like it to be lie *inside*—not outside—the minds of the designers and the organization being redesigned.

For example, a government agency in Mexico wanted to incorporate in its idealized design the continuous use of a foreign research group, a practice precluded by the government. The agency was about to exclude this feature from its design when an outsider revealed to it that Mexican universities—even those federally funded—were allowed to employ foreign consultants, and government agencies could employ these universities. Therefore, the agency was able to include the use of a foreign research group in its idealized redesign and subsequently actually used one through an arrangement with a local university.

The ability to "beat a containing system"—that is, to act counter to its intentions—is one of the most important properties an idealized system designer can have. Fortunately, idealized design cultivates such an ability. It does so because it stimulates creativity, which involves the removal of constraints apparently imposed from without by discovering a way around them. (More on hurdling obstructions and creativity in the design process below.)

Most organizations can be significantly improved without changing any of their containing systems. Nevertheless, some additional improvements are almost always possible with changes in one or more of their containing systems. Sometimes these improvements can be dramatic. The following case involved the computing and telecommunication functions at Kodak. Although Eastman Kodak as a whole has hardly provided a role model for other corporations, these two parts of it have.

> Kodak had a computing center serving its corporate headquarters. It also had two larger computing centers that served its line units. The manager of these units, Henry Pfendt (now retired), involved his subordinates and several of his internal customers in an idealized redesign of the headquarter's center. Much of that design was subsequently implemented, leading to significant improvement of the center's operations.

As the bounded design was being implemented, an unbounded design was being prepared. Not surprisingly, it combined the three computing centers into one. Dissemination of this design led to another idealized design effort that involved all three centers jointly. This effort produced a design of an integrated center that was then proposed to corporate management. The proposal was approved and an integrated center was formed. It yielded further improvements in performance.

Meanwhile, the telecommunications unit that served corporate headquarters and reported to the same manager as Kodak's computing center decided to emulate its effort. Telecommunications initiated its own idealized design. This also led to significant improvements in its operations and to subsequent preparation of an unconstrained design. Like its predecessor, the unconstrained design combined several telecommunications departments into one and led to a joint design effort by the relevant units. This, too, resulted in a proposal to combine their activities. The proposal was presented to and accepted by corporate management.

Next, the centralized computing and telecommunications centers jointly prepared an idealized design that combined these two functions within one organizational unit. Their proposal to this effect was also accepted by corporate management and was implemented.

Finally, the integrated computing-and-telecommunication-services unit conducted studies to determine whether even its improved performance was as good as might be obtained by using the services of external suppliers. The result is now well known. Kodak entered into joint ventures with IBM and Digital to provide the company with computing and telecommunication services. This resulted in further improvements in the services provided, and it did so at reduced costs.

Despite Kodak's generally poor performance since these designs were prepared, the joint ventures produced by them continue to function more than satisfactorily.

Creativity and Idealized Design

A creative act involves three steps:

1. identification of self-imposed constraints;
2. their removal; and
3. exploration of the consequences of having done so.

Self-imposed constraints take the form of assumptions made about what can or cannot be done. Most of them are incorrectly assumed to be imposed by external sources; they are actually self-imposed. This was the case in the example given above in which a government agency in Mexico got access to foreign consultants (precluded by the government) by having them hired by a university and hiring the university. Here is a case that illustrates how internally imposed constraints are incorrectly externalized:

> Several years ago, one of Mexico City's prominent planners showed me six alternative transportation plans for that city. He asked if I could suggest a way of determining which one was best. I told him that such an evaluation would be a waste of time because none of them would significantly reduce the congestion in the city; in fact, each of them would increase it. He was both shocked and offended. After putting himself back together, he asked me to explain what he considered to be an outrageous assertion. I pointed out that his plans were based on transportation ideas that had been tried in many other cities and under more favorable conditions than existed in Mexico City. Nevertheless, they had always failed because increases in the supply of transportation create new demands for it that exceed the old demand that it satisfies. In transportation, supply has a greater effect on demand than demand on supply.
>
> He said that if this were true, his city's transportation problems would be unsolvable. I disagreed and pointed out that he had not considered reducing demand rather than increasing supply. He challenged me to suggest a way of doing so that would be acceptable in a democracy. I suggested that a substantial part of the federal government of Mexico be moved out of Mexico City and be dispersed throughout the country. Since the government directly and indirectly provided most of the employment in the city, even

a move of part of the government could reduce its population considerably and this, in turn, would reduce congestion
more than any of his plans for additional supply. I also pointed out that the dispersion of the federal government could
produce a more equitable distribution of development in the
country. (For example, several times as much was spent on
education per child in Mexico City as was spent in the rest of
Mexico.)

The planner reacted by saying, "That's true, but a nation's
capital can't be moved." I pointed out a number of cases in
which capitals had been moved, including two in our country. He claimed that each of the cases I cited was significantly different from Mexico. I was not convinced. This
exchange of reasons and challenges continued until it was
clear that we were getting nowhere. Finally, he said I would
never understand why my suggestion was infeasible because
I wasn't a Mexican. That was that!

After an awkward pause, he asked if I had any other alternatives in mind. I said that I did and suggested changing the
working hours in Mexico City. Most Mexicans employed in
that city have a two- to three-hour midday break, the *siesta*
(which is seldom used for sleeping these days, although the
bedroom is frequently involved). It is used for the midday
meal, for which many either return home or go somewhere
distant from their places of work. By reducing this interval
to no more than one hour, the demand for transportation
would be considerably reduced.

Once again, the planner said that such a change was not
possible. When I asked why, it led to another argument that
ended with his resorting to the impossibility of changing
Mexican culture and his repeating that I could not understand this because I was not a Mexican.

This cycle was repeated several more times. The meeting
eventually ended with both of us frustrated and unaffected
by the other. However, shortly after this exchange, José
Lopez Portillo became president of Mexico. In his inaugural
address, he said he was going to initiate geographic dispersion of the federal government and reduced the length of the
midday break for government employees. Some government agencies were subsequently moved out of Mexico City,
but not enough to reduce automotive congestion signifi-

cantly; and the midday break was reduced, but not enough. Nevertheless, it became apparent that these changes were possible, but they were precluded from the Mexican planner's consideration because of the incorrect assumptions that he had made about his own culture.

It is difficult to identify self-imposed constraints. This is apparent in the difficulty of solving puzzles. A puzzle is a problem that is difficult to solve precisely because of a self-imposed constraint. This is why we are usually surprised and want to kick ourselves when we are shown a simple solution to a puzzle that we were unable to solve. Unfortunately, knowing that creativity and puzzle solving require identification and removal of self-imposed constraints does not, by itself, make identifying such constraints any easier. For example, consider the following common puzzle.

> Nine dots form a square (Fig. 5.1). Place a pen on one of the dots and without raising the pen from the paper draw four straight lines that cover all nine dots.
>
> The most common solution is shown in Figure 5.2. Note that the formulation of the puzzle did not preclude going outside the square, but most people assume this constraint. It is self-imposed.
>
> The puzzle can also be used by folding the paper through the middle of the bottom three dots and placing the bottom of these dots over the bottom of the top three dots, again by folding the paper (Fig. 5.3). By drawing a felt-tip pen across the fold, a line is simultaneously drawn that covers the top three and bottom three dots. Unfold the paper and the rest is easy. With further folds it can even be done with one line.

Figure 5.1   The nine-dot problem

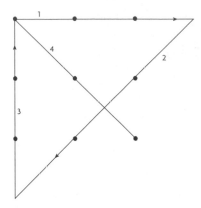

Figure 5.2   A solution to the nine-dot problem

When my youngest daughter was about eight years old, she saw me playing with this problem and asked me to explain it to her. I did and then she asked why I didn't get a great big fat pen and cover all nine dots with one big blob.

Identification of self-imposed constraints is difficult because we are generally unaware of them. However, there are ways of avoiding them or raising them to consciousness. Among such creativity-enhancing procedures are lateral thinking, brainstorming, synectics, TKJ, conceptual block busting, and idealized redesign, which I believe is the most effective. (See Ackoff and Vergara, 1981.)

Idealized redesign of a system releases creativity because it removes many of the constraints that inhibit it. Many, if not most, self-imposed constraints derive from concern with implementability. Implementability, however, is not a requirement imposed on idealized design. Therefore, since it starts with the assumption that the existing system was destroyed last night and imposes a very few and not very restrictive constraints, it tends to liberate the imagination and stimulate the desire to innovate and invent. For example:

In the early 1970s, a group of executives and staff members of a branch of the Federal Reserve Bank were engaged in an unconstrained idealized redesign of their institution and the system that contained it. They were focusing on the problem created by the rapidly increasing number of checks that had to be cleared and the cost of doing so. Therefore, they unanimously agreed that the idealized design should incor-

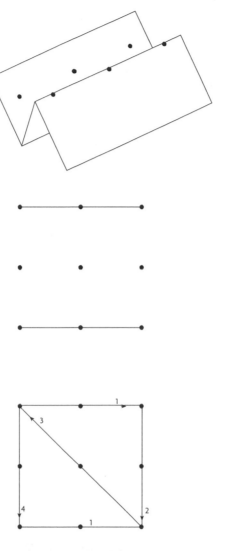

Figure 5.3   Another solution to the nine-dot problem

porate an electronic funds transfer system that would replace checks.

One of the members of the group then suggested that if the banking system required that all payments be made electronically, and each entity was permitted to have only one bank account, banks would have a complete record of everyone's income and revenues. Another pointed out that records of multiple bank accounts could be assembled if every bank account number included a unique identification number assigned to its holder, for example, one's social security number. It was then observed that, if this could be done, banks could prepare income tax returns because they would also have a complete record of expenditures: if all income went into banks, all expenditures would involve withdrawals from them.

"Wait a minute," one of the participants said. "If the system knew how much we spent and what we spent it for, wouldn't it be better for the government to tax consumption rather than income?"

This question released a flood of creative ideas. It began with the observation that if a person were taxed only for consumption, there would be a considerable incentive to leave money in the bank, to save. This would be a larger incentive to save than interest on savings because the tax rate would be higher than the interest rates paid by banks now. Banks would not have to pay any interest on deposits. Because of this, it was argued, banks should not charge interest on loans, but only a service charge for making them. Borrowers, however, would have to pay consumption taxes on what they used.

As details of a possible consumption-based tax system were developed, the designers became convinced that it would be better than the current income-based system.

In conventional system-design processes, the emergence and development of such an innovative idea as a consumption-based tax system would be very unlikely.

Feasibility and Idealized Design

The idealized-design process enlarges the designers' conception of what is feasible. In conventional planning, the implementability of a plan as a whole follows from considering the implementability of each of its parts taken separately. When parts are considered separately, all sorts of obstructions to their change appear, obstructions that disappear when viewed as aspects of the whole. An inspiring vision of the whole sweeps aside apparent obstructions to changing the parts.

An idealized design and the plans based on it are not like chains; they are stronger than their weakest link. They are systems, sets of interacting decisions. This means that the design and plan as wholes have properties that none of their parts have, and their parts acquire properties by being parts of the whole that they do not have when considered separately. Therefore, it is possible to have an implementable plan at least some of whose parts, when considered separately, are not implementable. It is also possible to have an unimplementable plan all of whose parts, when considered separately, are implementable.

The following example illustrates how a firm's concept of what is feasible can be transformed by engaging in an idealized-design process.

In the mid-1980s, the Clark Michigan Company, a wholly owned subsidiary of the Clark Equipment Corporation, was in serious financial trouble. The Japanese company Komatsu had entered Clark's market with better mobile earthmoving equipment that sold at a lower price than Clark's. Clark reduced its price to Komatsu's with the hope of retaining at least some of its market share while studying the possibility of redesigning its products and its production processes in order to compete effectively with Komatsu. In the meantime, it sold products for less than the cost of producing them. This resulted in negative cash flow. Clark's creditors threatened to put the company into bankruptcy and liquidate its assets in order to get their money out. Clark was not given enough time to modify either its subsidiary's products or production processes so as to become profitable. Therefore, it adopted the strategy of dressing up the subsidiary and trying to sell it.

Clark Equipment's board blamed its CEO for this mess and relieved him of his duty. It then had to find a new one very quickly. Because of the rush, it did something unusual: it hired a good one, James Rinehart, then president of General Motors Canada. After joining the company and familiarizing himself with its mess, he called a meeting of its managers. He explained the nature of idealized design to them—a concept with which he was familiar from his earlier experience as head of Packard Electric. He asked the assembled managers to spend several days producing an idealized design of Clark Michigan. They objected, pointing out their studies had indicated that there was nothing they could do to save the company within the amount of time available to them and that he was asking them to imagine they could do whatever they wanted. They wanted to know why. He replied that they would find an answer to that question when engaged in the idealized-design process. They turned to it reluctantly.

A week later, they reported their results to Rinehart, saying that now they understood why they had been asked to prepare such a design. For the first time, they had been able to use all they knew about their industry and, as a result, felt that a company of their design could dominate its industry if it came into existence. But, they added, there was no conceivable way they could get from where they were to that design.

Rinehart told them that was not the right problem to consider. He said he wanted them to work *back* from their design to where they were, not forward from where they were. They did not understand. He explained. He said there were a number of other companies in their industry in states similar to theirs. What combination of these companies with Clark Michigan would give them the closest approximation to their idealized design?

Again they objected, pointing out there was no way they could acquire another company because of their financial condition, and no other company would be willing to acquire them for the same reason. Again Rinehart pressed them.

A week later, after completing this assignment, they expressed surprise over the fact that by combining three companies with Clark Michigan—a German company, a Swedish company, and a Japanese company—they could get a very close approximation to their idealized design. But again they did not see how they could get close to realizing such a union. Rinehart argued that since the companies identified in their design had not seen the design, their reaction to it could not be accurately predicted. Therefore, he organized a visit to the firms to discuss the design they had prepared.

At Daimler-Benz (D-B), they discussed the Euclid Truck company, an American company D-B had acquired a while back. It had never been profitable. D-B, after seeing Clark Michigan's idealized design, decided that survival of the Euclid Truck Company would be considerably enhanced if it become part of the joint venture envisaged in that design;

they offered to sell it to Clark. Rinehart explained that they could not buy it for lack of cash, and a deal was arranged using an exchange of stock. Clark Michigan got Euclid.

At AB Volvo, the discussion focused on Volvo BM, a subsidiary that produced earthmoving equipment. The Volvo executives were impressed by the marketing potential of the joint venture designed, but expressed skepticism about the ability of a cross-cultural management to work effectively. Rinehart admitted to such a possibility but suggested a team of Volvo, Clark, and Euclid managers be formed to design their closest approximation to the four-firm joint venture Clark had prepared. (For legal reasons, the Japanese firm was unable to become involved, although it was greatly interested.)

In April of 1985, such a task force was formed and began work with the help of two professors from the Wharton School as facilitators. By September, a detailed design of a joint venture had been completed with no cross cultural difficulties at all. A proposal to create the joint venture was made to the boards of Clark and Volvo, and they accepted it. After the legal work was completed, in April of 1986, the VME Corporation was created—Volvo, Michigan, Euclid.

After a break-in period of a bit more than a year, VME became profitable and worked well. Then, with the support of Clark Equipment Corporation's senior management, Volvo increasingly sought and gained control over its agenda. It gradually converted Clark Michigan into what was largely a sales organization with only one manufacturing facility. Subsequently, Volvo bought out Clark's share of VME at a price very favorable to Clark.

Clark Michigan had avoided bankruptcy, had survived well for a while, and eventually was sold very profitably by its parent company because it worked backward from where it wanted to be rather than forward from where it was.

Another example that makes a similar point but had a different outcome involved a plan for Paris (see Ozbekhan, 1977). This plan was prepared in the 1970s based on an idealized redesign of the city, including two design features that, had they been proposed independently, would surely have been dismissed as infeasible. The first was that the capital of France be moved out of Paris and the second was that Paris be converted into a self-governing open city, not subject to the government of France. In view of the mission of Paris that was incorporated into its idealized redesign—that it become the informal capital of the world—these two changes not only became feasible, but they were seen as absolutely necessary. For this reason, the then-current government of France committed itself to both changes. However, a subsequent government, seeking to differentiate itself from the one that prepared and adopted the design, broke some of these commitments. Nevertheless, some major aspects of the plan were implemented, including a gradual change in the industries located in Paris and the redistribution of types of industry among the regions of France.

Learning and Idealized Design

Those who design a system can learn how it can be made to work as desired and why existing systems don't work as desired. They can also learn how much control and influence they can exercise over both the systems of which they are a part and other systems of which they are not a part but with which they interact. They can learn this by distinguishing between self-imposed and externally imposed constraints, and by learning how to affect the latter.

Idealized design facilitates *widespread* learning because it encourages and makes possible involvement of all the stakeholders in the design process. (The organizational design of such participation is described in Chapter 9.) In the past, experts were usually considered to be the only ones qualified to design and plan for a system. However, the current focus on Total Quality Management makes it clear that quality improvement requires meeting the expectations of *all* those who hold a stake in the system. (See Flood, 1991, and Ackoff, 1994, chapter 3.) Their expectations cannot effectively be incorporated into a system's redesign and derivative plans without their involvement in the design and planning processes.

The widely accepted requirement for expertise in conventional system design and planning derives from the fact that these processes have been, and still are, preoccupied with determining what is wrong with the existing system and how these deficiencies can be eliminated. The recognition and removal of deficiencies is assumed to require deep (expert) knowledge of the system involved. Experts, however, can seldom think out of the box. Most major innovations in systems come from nonexperts.

It has become increasingly apparent that every stakeholder in a system can recognize and remove some of the system's deficiencies and therefore contribute to continuous improvement. Much more important, however, is the fact (discussed above) that getting rid of what one does not want provides no assurance of getting what one does want. What nonexpert stakeholders in a system want is much more relevant than what experts who are not stakeholders want. Every stakeholder in a system, including those who know little of how it operates but know a great deal about what they expect of it, can make important contributions to its idealized redesign.

Participation in idealized design is usually fun; most creative activities are. Therefore, it is usually easy to obtain and maintain. It provides those who care about a system with an opportunity to think deeply about it, to share their thoughts with others who also care about it, and to affect its future. This encourages the development and exploration of new ideas, and facilitates personal and corporate development.

When preliminary idealized redesigns of Paris (Ozbekhan, 1977), the U.S. Scientific Communication and Technology Transfer [SCATT] System (Ackoff et al., 1976), and the U.S. health care system (Rovin et al., 1994) were prepared, they were disseminated widely with requests for feedback from any who were interested. The feedback in each case was plentiful. Many of the suggestions were incorporated into subsequent versions of the designs. This process was continued in each case until there were few new suggestions received. In some cases, thousands of people have participated.

The idealized redesign of the U.S. health care system was of particular significance because it was a very dramatic example of doing the wrong thing right. It became apparent in the design process that something fundamental was wrong in the current conception of the system. The fundamental flaw in the system derives from the fact that the servers within the system and its serving institutions are compensated for taking care of people when they are sick or disabled. Therefore, the worst thing that could happen to the current system would be the elimination of sickness and disability. Regardless of the good intentions of individual servers, it became apparent that the system is designed and operates so as to preserve sickness and disability, not to promote health.

Within the organization being designed, each unit should ultimately have an opportunity to do an idealized redesign of itself. However, this should be done so as to be compatible with higher-level designs and not be in conflict with designs prepared by other units at the same level. Where such conflicts arise, they should be resolved if at all possible by the units affected. Where this cannot be done, the unresolved issue should go for resolution to the lowest organizational level at which the units involved converge. (Again, details on the organizational aspects of such participation are provided in Chapter 9.)

For example, machine operators who engage in idealized design concern themselves with the operations, layout, and equipment in their shop, not with the behavior of the corporation as a whole. Janitors in the same shop consider different aspects of it, such as the design and location of its lavatories. When the janitors and operators review the design work of others and each other's, they usually find either that critical aspects of the shop's activities have been left out or that both have ignored critical interactions of activities that have been included. This enables them to combine their efforts and produce a more comprehensive and coordinated design than either group can produce separately or others can produce without their participation.

As this process is repeated by different units in a corporation, understanding develops of how the parts interact and how these interactions affect overall corporate performance. This enables those who engage in idealized design to learn how the decisions they make and the activities in which they engage affect the performance of the corporation as a whole. There is an immediate and substantial payoff to the corporation when its parts focus on improving corporate, rather than their own, performance.

Consensus

Idealized design tends to generate a consensus among those who participate in it because it focuses on ultimate values rather than on means for pursuing them. The more ultimate the values, the more agreement they generate. In general, people disagree less about ideals than about shorter-range goals and ways of pursuing them. This is reflected in the fact that the constitutions of the United States and the (now defunct) Soviet Union were surprisingly alike. Most of their many disagreements derived from their differences over choice of means, not ultimate ends. This eluded us at the time because we characterized their differences as ideological. Contrary to what many believe, ideologies have less to do with ideals than with means for pursuing them. For example, the ideological disagreement over who should own the means of production concerned the selection of a way of pursuing a state of *plenty*. Both nations accepted this state as an ideal.

The idealized redesign of Paris was forwarded to the cabinet of

France with the support of every one of its many political parties. These ranged from the extreme right to the extreme left. Nevertheless, they agreed on what Paris ideally ought to be. This may have been the first time these parties agreed on anything.

In an idealized-design exercise conducted in a large American corporation, initial designs were prepared separately by each of the eight members of the corporation's executive committee. These executives, who frequently disagreed on issues considered by their committee as a whole, were amazed at how much their separately prepared designs agreed. This had a major impact on their subsequent behavior. The hostility among them was greatly reduced and their inclination to cooperate was significantly increased.

When agreement is reached on ultimate values, differences over means and short-range goals can often be easily resolved. Furthermore, when such differences cannot be resolved easily, other procedures are available for reaching consensus. These, too, are discussed in Chapter 9.

Commitment

Participation in the preparation of an idealized design and the consensus that emerges from it generate a commitment to the realization of that design. People develop stronger commitments to ideas and ideals that they have had a hand in formulating than to those that they have not. Such commitments considerably reduce the number and difficulty of problems associated with implementation of designs and plans.

Conclusion

An ideal-seeking organization is one that should be able to learn from its own experience and that of others and to adapt rapidly and effectively to changing conditions. This capability does not come to an organization naturally; it has to be designed into it. Such a design is the subject of Chapter 8.

In addition, I will argue that if an organization is to be able to function well in our rapidly changing and increasingly complex environment, it must have three other design features: it must democratize, have an internal market economy, and a multidimensional structure. The design of these and the reasons for them are contained in Part III.

These designs make it clear that if an organization is to be effective, it must *transform* itself—mere reform will not do. In reform, the system involved is not changed in any fundamental way, but its structure and behavior are modified moderately so as to provide improved performance. A transformation involves a radical change in the structure and functioning of an organization. Without such a change, I will argue, the ability of a corporation to survive into the twenty-first century is seriously in doubt. It should be borne in mind that the average life span of a corporation in the United States is about twenty years. This amounts to the length of time they can survive in a radically changing environment without themselves changing in fundamental ways.

6

Means Planning: How to Get There

Make no little plans, they have no magic to stir men's blood.
—David Burnham

Idealized design produces the vision of the organization and its behavior currently most desired. The *gaps* between what the organization is and is now doing and where it wants to be and to be doing, as revealed by its idealized redesign, constitute the problems to be solved independently by means planning. Therefore, the first step in means planning is to identify these gaps.

Means planning determines how the gaps are to be closed or reduced. In architecture, this corresponds to preparation of working drawings once an acceptable design of the building has been prepared. These drawings constitute a set of instructions that enable a contractor to build the building. It makes possible *realization* of the vision or the closest possible approximation to it. Means planning is the preparation of the design's "working drawings," which provide the instructions required to close or reduce the gaps.

Gaps are of three types:

1. *Things to be added* for example, a new factory or products, entry into new markets, or acquisition of a new company.
2. *Things to be eliminated* for example, divestment of an old business, discontinuation of products or services, or closing of a facility.

3. *Things to be changed* for example, restructuring the organization, modifying its distribution system, or reallocation of resources.

Gaps requiring addition or subtraction involve types of means different than those that require change.

Types of Means

The more complex a gap, the more complex the means usually required to treat it. Therefore, since gaps range from ones that can be treated easily and rapidly to ones that require complex sets of actions taken over an extended period of time, the means required vary similarly.

1. *Acts* consist of behavior engaged in once, which ordinarily take relatively little time, for example, buying a book or software, writing a letter, attending a meeting. Acts, however, can be very important, for example, firing an executive or signing a contract.
2. *Courses of action* or *procedures* are actions taken sequentially or simultaneously that are directed at a specific outcome, which actions are separately taken to be necessary and collectively are taken to be sufficient to produce that outcome. Therefore, they are *systems of actions.* For example, looking for and purchasing a building or replacing an executive involves a sequence of steps before the purchase or acquisition is consummated.
3. *Practices* are repeated actions or courses of action, for example, billing customers, credit checks, and performance reviews.
4. *Processes* are courses of action or procedures applied to one thing throughout, for example, manufacturing or distributing a product.
5. *Projects* are systems of simultaneous or sequential courses of action directed at a desired outcome, for example, building a building, developing a new product, or installing a quality assurance program.
6. *Programs* are systems of projects that are directed at producing a set of interacting outcomes, for example, opening new markets abroad or beginning a new business. Programs are usually of longer duration than projects.

7. *Policies* are rules for selecting or excluding means of any type, for example, legislation and regulations.

Plans, of course, usually involve all seven types of means. The importance of the type of means chosen is not necessarily a function of its complexity. A simple act—for example, promoting a manager—may be much more important than a project directed at improving the parking area.

Ways of Controlling and Influencing the Future

The future can be significantly affected by what we do by controlling the causes of uncertainty, controlling their effects, increasing responsiveness to change, using incentives, and inducing cooperation and reducing conflict among stakeholders.

Controlling the Causes of Uncertainty

If mosquitoes bearing yellow fever are coming our way, we can prevent their reaching us by destroying or diverting them. In agriculture, insecticides are used for this purpose. In business, forcing a competitor out of business, out of a market, or out of a retailer's establishment is much the same thing.

Monopolies and oligopolies have more predictable futures than firms in highly competitive businesses precisely because they have few or no competitors. Economic "warfare" is a way of trying to reduce uncertainty. Introducing a product clearly superior to a competitor's or pushing a competitor's product off the market by underpricing are ways of reducing competition. Needless to say, such means of gaining control of an organization's future are not necessarily good for all those affected. Control is a means, not an end, and therefore can be used for either good or evil. Forcing a competitive product off all or part of the market by producing one that is clearly superior is also a way of eliminating an external obstruction to attaining an objective. From the consumers' point of view, it is to be preferred to forcing the competitor out of the market.

Vertical integration is, perhaps, the most common way by which organizations control a major source of uncertainty. It consists of internalizing an external activity that affects the organization significantly. For example, when Ford began to produce its own steel, when Anheuser-Busch began to produce its own cans and grow its own grains, and when IBM acquired Lotus, a software company, all three integrated vertically. When a company's franchises or acquires its distributors or retailers, it also integrates vertically, for example, major oil companies that own some or all of their service stations. The same is true of the Singer Sewing Company and McDonald's. As is apparent, vertical integration can penetrate either the supply (input) side of an organization or the user (output) side.

Vertical integration does not always yield desirable results. In some cases, it involves a company in an activity in which it has no competence and therefore increases its costs of operations considerably. It is for this reason that *outsourcing*, the opposite of vertical integration, often brings costs under control.

Controlling the Effects of Uncertain Causes

The undesirable effect of mosquitoes bearing yellow fever can be eliminated without affecting the mosquitoes by immunizing those potentially affected against yellow fever. Immunization against a disease is an example of *horizontal integration*; it involves incorporating something into a system that precludes a potentially negative effect of an uncontrolled cause.

Adding a product to one's product line that has a demand that is countercyclical to the products already in it may make it possible to smooth production. For example, a company that makes nipples for baby bottles and condoms is less sensitive to changes in the birthrate than a company that makes only one of them. The same is true for a company that makes both summer and winter clothing. It was also true for the Warner-Swasey company, which added mobile road-building equipment to its product line of machine tools. Because both types of product could be made in the same manufacturing facilities with the same equipment, it significantly reduced fluctuations of demand on its production facilities. Moreover, both types of product were sold through the same channels.

Hedging on the commodity exchange is a common example of horizontal integration. It eliminates the effect of uncontrolled price fluctuations on a buyer. A trading company can be used to hedge against changes in foreign exchange rates. When a foreign country devaluates its currency relative to ours, income from that country in our currency is reduced. But if our profits are taken out in the form of goods, now cheaper in our currency, we can maintain or increase our profit by selling those products in other countries at their old prices.

Incentives

Managers, of course, are aware of the ability of incentives to influence the behavior of stakeholders. But they are often unaware of incentives that have been created unconsciously, many of which are dysfunctional, as in this example.

> Repair and maintenance men employed by one of the Bell companies carried a very large number of replacement parts in their vans although they used less than two dozen on most days. This resulted in a huge in-transit inventory carried at a considerable cost. The company wanted to reduce this inventory. An investigation revealed that the company paid the repairmen for each job successfully completed. Therefore, if a repairman could not complete a job for lack of an essential part, he had to return to a warehouse to get it, at a considerable cost because of loss of time. The cause of the excessive inventory was the well-intentioned but ill-conceived incentive to maximize the number of calls a serviceman completed per day.

The following is a case in which incentives produced counterproductive conflict among employees.

> A major city in Europe used double-decker buses for public transportation. Each bus had a driver and a conductor. The driver was seated in a compartment separated by glass from the passengers. The closer the driver kept to schedule, the more he was paid. The conductor collected zoned fares from boarding passengers and was supposed to signal the driver when there were no passengers desiring to get off at the next stop. If the driver did not receive this signal he was supposed to stop. The conductor was also supposed to signal the driver to move on when the bus had finished discharging and loading passengers.
> Undercover inspectors rode the buses periodically to determine whether conductors collected fares from all the boarding passengers. The fewer errors the inspectors observed, the more the conductors were paid.
> To avoid delays during rush hours, conductors usually let passengers board the buses without collecting their fares,

which they tried to collect while the bus was moving between stops. At peak hours, because of crowded conditions on the buses, conductors could not always return to the entrance to signal the driver when not to stop or when to continue after a stop. This required the driver to stop at the next stop even if no passengers wished to disembark, using his rear-view mirror to determine when no one else was embarking or disembarking. These delays were costly to the driver, but supportive of the conductors' functions. Since conductors were not evaluated on the basis of their starting and stopping functions, they sacrificed these for collection of fares. As a result, hostility developed between drivers and conductors. The hostility was exacerbated by the fact that they were members of different unions and that conductors were usually immigrants of a minority race, while the drivers were "true blue." A number of violent confrontations followed.

At first, management did nothing, absolution, hoping that the problem would go away or solve itself. It didn't; it got worse. Therefore, management decided to do something. It tried to resolve the problem by going back to a previous more desirable state, by discontinuing the incentive payments to drivers and conductors. The unions representing drivers and conductors rejected this because it would reduce their members' income, but drivers and conductors were willing to accept the highest salary they had earned under the incentive system as their fixed wage. Management said it was unwilling to do this unless it was guaranteed the same productivity as when they paid the highest wage. The unions turned this down because the productivity of the bus depended on weather, traffic, and other conditions that drivers and conductors did not control. The unions also rejected a subsequently proposed solution that the drivers and conductors share equally their combined incentive payments. Each refused an increased dependency on the other; they did not trust one another.

The problem was then handed over to a consultant. He brought together representatives of the opposing sides for discussions, which he hoped would produce a resolution, if not a solution, to the problem. Unfortunately, each discussion group ended in a fight.

Out of desperation the consultant turned to a friend, who asked: "How many buses operate in the system at peak hours?" The consultant said he did not know, but that the answer was irrelevant since the problem arose on each bus independently of the number involved. However, pressed by his friend, he found the answer: approximately 1250 buses operated at peak hours. The friend then asked: "How many stops there are in the system?" This question also seemed irrelevant to the consultant, but once again he reluctantly returned to the files to find the answer: about 850 stops. This meant that during rush hours there were more buses operating than there were stops.

These system characteristics led the consultant's friend to suggest that *conductors be taken off the buses at peak hours and be placed at the stops.* There they could collect fares from people who were waiting for buses, check the receipts of all those disembarking, and were always in a position to signal the drivers when to move on. (It was then recognized that this is exactly what is done with conductors on British trains.)

The number of conductors required at peak hours was significantly reduced. This made it possible to put most conductors on continuous eight-hour shifts rather than split shifts, shifts that were separated by off-peak hours. At off-peak hours, the conductors were moved back onto the buses.

A very familiar example of counterproductive behavior caused by an incentive involves executives who, although asked to focus on long-run performance, are rewarded financially with bonuses based on the short run. This is particularly true where downsizing occurs. (See Chapter 12 for more discussion of this point.)

If tolls on expressways, bridges, and tunnels were proportional to the number of *empty* seats in an automobile, there would be more effective use of automobiles and less congestion around and on these facilities. A similar effect could be obtained by making the cost of a license for a vehicle a function if its size or weight.

Paying doctors and hospitals for taking care of the sick or disabled (however well intentioned the individual providers are) assures their maintaining (unconsciously, if not consciously) a sufficient number of people in these conditions to keep them occupied and well paid. For example, at an international conference held in Atlanta, Georgia, on March 11, 1998, the Center for Disease Control and Prevention reported that about 2 million people a year pick up infections while in hospitals. Of these, approximately 90,000 die.

If health care providers were paid a flat fee per individual to cover *all* health care services required by those in their care—including fees for specialists, tests, hospital stays, pharmaceuticals, and so on—they would act very differently than they do. This would significantly improve the nation's health and significantly reduce its cost, especially by reducing fraud and unnecessary treatments, tests, and drugs. Steps would have to be taken, of course, to assure sufficient health care. (This has been done in the design described by Rovin et al., 1994.)

Similarly, if teachers were paid for how much their students learned rather than how much they taught, there would be a great deal more learning and much less teaching. In general, compensation should be proportional to the amount of output; never to the amount of input. Even more generally, compensation should be consistent with the objectives of those whose compensation is involved, not only with the objectives of those who pay them. Here is a case in point:

> The productivity of women who inspected ball bearings eight hours per day in a factory that produced them was declining precipitously. Since they worked on a salary basis, the decline had no effect on their income, but did on the company's. The women, most of whom had school-age children, resented management's refusal to change their working hours so they could be home when their children returned from school. A human-resources advisor suggested that management define a fair day's work at the highest level of productivity ever reached and that the women be permitted to leave work whenever they had reached that level. This was done. Both the quantity and quality of inspection soared and most of the women were home to take care of their children as they returned from school.

Responsiveness

To the extent that we can anticipate *possible*—but not necessarily *probable*—futures, we can prepare plans to deal with each should they occur. To do so is contingency planning. Remember forecasts are about probabilities and assumptions about possibilities. Estimates of probabilities are almost always less accurate than identification of possibilities, so planning based on explicit assumptions about the future is almost always better than planning based on forecasts. Assumptions can be monitored continually and, when shown to be wrong, can be corrected.

In addition, the unexpected can always be expected to occur. Therefore, to the extent that an organization can recognize a relevant unexpected event when it occurs and respond to it rapidly and effectively, it can bring its effect under at least partial control. An extreme example was provided by Johnson and Johnson when it responded to the insertion of poison into some packages of Tylenol; the company immediately withdrew all packages from the market.

An organization's responsiveness to change is a function of its ability to learn and adapt quickly and effectively. Organizational learning and adaptation is not equivalent to individual learning and adaptation. Organizational learning takes place when something of relevance to any member of an organization is learned by someone in the organization and made available to other members of that organization, even when the one who acquired it is no longer present. Organizational learning and adaptation does not come naturally to most organizations; it must be designed into them. It requires a support system and a culture that collects, stores, and makes accessible information, knowledge, understanding, and wisdom generated either inside or outside the organization. A description of such a system is provided in Chapter 8.

Inducing Cooperation

It is apparent that there are many things that cannot be controlled without the help of others, but that can be controlled with their help. To the extent that management of an organization can establish cooperative relations with its internal and external stakeholders and competitors, it can gain control over some aspects of its organization's future. Such relations can be obtained by joint ventures, mergers, or strategic alliances. Purchasing cooperatives (e.g., among independently owned hardware stores) and marketing cooperatives (e.g., among Florida's orange growers) remove a great deal of uncertainty. Industry associations and chambers of commerce are other examples of cooperative efforts that bring aspects of the environment under control.

Improving the quality of work life of employees—or better yet, letting employees do this for themselves—can induce their cooperation and reduce uncertainty associated with the quality and quantity of production. (An example of this is described in the discussion of human-resource planning in Chapter 7.)

A very effective way of inducing consumer cooperation is to engage them in design of one's products or marketing and selling operations (Ciccantelli and Magidson, 1993). They tend to be very creative and provide ideas that yield a competitive advantage. For example, a group of men designing their ideal men's store suggested that clothing be arranged in the store by size, not type. This would enable them to do all their shopping in one section rather than having to move from one location to another within the store. They also suggested using sales-women rather than salesmen because, they said, a man's opinion on how a man looks cannot be trusted.

Female customers participating in the redesign of supermarkets pointed out that existing markets differed little relative to packaged products, but these dominated the visual field of the entering cus-tomer. Supermarkets tended to differ more with respect to fresh foods. Therefore, these customers suggested that a new chain be created focusing on fresh foods, locating and displaying them more conspicu-ously and attractively. They also suggested making green the chain's color because it is the symbol of freshness marking the name "Super Fresh." This chain was created by A&P and has been expanding very successfully. It has replaced a number of previously unprofitable A&P stores. Many of its characteristics are now widely imitated.

Reducing Conflict

There is frequently a lack of cooperation within and between organiza-tions; outright conflict or competition is commonplace. A firm seldom benefits from such hostility. Therefore, it is important to be able to reduce or eliminate conflict unless it is part of competition or is used to generate alternative choices of means.

Conflict is usually an obstruction to controlling the future, but when it is imbedded in competition it can yield control. Unfortunately, "con-flict" and "competition" are concepts that are often used interchange-ably. Although related, *they are not the same thing.*

Conflict between entities occurs when one party's gain necessarily involves another party's loss. Therefore, conflict between ends occurs when attainment of one end necessarily means failure to obtain the other. In contrast, cooperation occurs when one party's gain involves another party's gain and the attainment of one end implies the attain-ment of another. *Competition consists of conflict imbedded in cooperation.* For example, in playing tennis with a friend, only one can win, imply-ing that the other will lose, and this means the players are in conflict.

However, there is a more important common objective, *recreation*, which is efficiently served by the conflict. The more intense the conflict, the more fun obtained from playing the game. This means the players are competing.

Competition is conflict according to rules. The rules are intended to assure that the conflict involved serves a more important common objective with respect to which the conflict is cooperative. Competition is of three types, *intensive*, *extensive*, and *mixed.* Intensive competition occurs when the common (cooperative) objective is pursued by the parties who are in conflict, as the friends engaged in a tennis match. Extensive competition occurs when the conflict serves an objective of a third party, for example, a prize fight is a conflict between two opponents imbedded in entertainment of an audience, the cooperative objective. Economic competition between two companies is conflict that is supposed to serve the interests of the consumers. Of course, competition may be both intensive and extensive—that is, mixed—as when friends enjoy playing tennis before an audience while competing for a prize.

Now consider the ways of treating conflict within and between organizations. Rapoport (1960) identified three modes of conflict and ways of treating them—*fights*, *games*, and *debates*: "in a fight the urge is to eliminate the opponent; in a game the problem is to outwit the opponent; in the debate, the goal is to convince the opponent" (p. 215).

Rapoport's classification of intentions may be exhaustive, but his classification of means of intervention is not. It was not intended to be; it was intended to illustrate ways of intensifying conflict (fights), stabilizing them (games), and reducing or eliminating them (debates). A more comprehensive way of classifying treatments of conflict derives from dividing them into those that involve manipulating the environment and those that involve manipulating the individuals involved.

Environmental interventions. Those involved in a conflict can be physically separated in a way that precludes their interacting, as when the location of one or both employees in conflict is changed. (Parents frequently settle conflicts between their children by separating them.) Recall the bus example in which the driver and conductor were separated by taking the conductor off the bus.

Incapacitation of one of the parties is virtual removal of that person from an environment. Killing an opponent or enemy is an extreme way of removing him or her from the environment. (Note: the way conflict is eliminated may not be a good thing.) Alternatively, the environment can be changed so that the ability of one party to affect the behavior of another is eliminated. This involves dividing the environment. For example, erection of a sound barrier may prevent transmission of noise that is the source of a conflict. If two distributors want access to retailers in the same region, the conflict between them can be eliminated by dividing the territory into two areas, each served exclusively by one of the distributors.

An environment in which there is a scarcity of resources tends to generate conflict. For example, two children who want to play with the same toy, or two employees who want the one available office. These conflicts can be eliminated by providing more of what is desired by the parties involved or by changing what at least one of them wants. Wherever there are haves and have nots and scarce resources, there is likely to be conflict between them. Such conflicts usually can only be removed by increasing available resources.

Scarcity of resources is not nearly as important as scarcity of opportunity. Revolutions are less often caused by poverty than by the lack of opportunity to escape it. To discriminate is to limit opportunity. Racial and sexual discrimination in corporations causes many more problems than unequal access to resources. As long as there is discrimination within organizations based on something other than competence, there will be conflict within them.

Behavioral interventions. Conflict can be reduced or eliminated by changing the behavior of one or both parties, the choices they make, the efficiencies of what they do, or the values they place on the outcomes. Such changes can be brought about using incentives, as discussed above, but can also be brought about through communication. The ways of generating consensus in groups discussed in Chapter 9 are examples.

Structural and functional conflicts within organizations. Conflicts often arise within organizations because of conflicting objectives that are imposed on the parties involved. This type of conflict emanates from the structure or functioning of the organization itself. For example, such conflict often arises when one profit center within an organization is required to sell its product to another internal profit center at an established transfer price, and the internal buying unit is not allowed to use any other source of supply. Conflict between these units arises when either the seller can get a higher price outside the organization or the buyer can get a lower price from an external supplier. The only way such conflicts can be resolved is by changing the objectives or constraints explicitly or implicitly imposed on the parts of an organization by its superiors. (A way to dissolve this type of conflict is described in Chapter 10.)

A great deal of small group research has been directed at determining whether cooperative or competitive groups are better at solving problems. In a review of their own work and that of others Raven and Euchus (1963) came to the conclusion that, in situations in which the actions of one group's members do not affect the performance of the others, competition is likely to produce better results than cooperation. However, if the members' actions are interdependent, cooperation is likely to be more effective. This is not surprising. Where actions of organizational units or individual members of the organization are independent of each other, incentive schemes that are based on competition for rewards can be effective. Not so when their actions are interdependent; then each is likely to try to reduce the effectiveness of the other. The organization suffers.

The way to reward interacting members of an organization depends on how their performance should be measured. Performance measures affect both individual and collective behavior. The measures employed for evaluative purposes within an organization can reduce organizational effectiveness even when the members or units involved do their best to meet their objectives. Consider the following example, which is a very much simplified description of a situation found in a large chain of department stores.

> The purchasing department bought products at the beginning of each month in quantities that it determined. When received, these items were placed in stock until withdrawn by the sales department. The sales department set the price at which the products were offered for sale. The lower the price set for an item, the more that could usually be sold, but only if they were in stock; back orders were not common. The amount that would actually be sold at any specified price could not be predicted accurately.
>
> The purchasing department was assigned the objective of minimizing the cost of inventory while providing sufficient stock to meet estimated demand. The sales department was assigned the objective of maximizing gross profit, that is, number of items sold times the difference between the sales and the purchase prices. These were conflicting objectives.
>
> When the sales department set a price for an item for the next period, the purchasing department based its stocking decision on a very conservative estimate of demand because if it bought too much of an item, its costs would increase and

its performance (hence management's compensation) would suffer. On the other hand, the sales department used an optimistic forecast of sales because if too few of the items were available, it would lose sales and thereby experience reduced gross profit. Conflict between the purchasing and sales departments was inevitable. The conflict was resolved when the executive office intervened and prohibited communication between the two managers.

Such conflicts can be dissolved by changing the measures of performance (hence objectives) imposed on the two units. For example, if both parties had the same objective, maximizing net income—which took the cost of the goods sold, the price at which it was sold, and the cost of carrying inventory into account—their cooperation would be induced. Then their joint performance could be used to determine, at least in part, their management's compensation.

Use of Conflicting Ideas to Generate New Alternatives

There are two ways of using deliberately organized conflict of ideas to generate new alternative means: *dialectics* and *countermeasures*. Dialectics are relevant where competition is not a major factor; countermeasures are relevant where competition is.

Dialectics. There are many situations in which a choice of means must be made and in which there is no objective basis for selecting among the perceived alternatives. In such cases, a dialectical procedure either generates a better alternative than those previously considered or provides better reasons for choosing one of the alternatives previously considered. Dialecticians try to combine the good features contained in the opposing positions (the thesis and antithesis) and avoid their deficiencies. Such a search can be conducted by forming two teams, each required to take a different point of view. Each team is directed to develop the strongest possible argument for the position assigned to it. The teams are required to share all data and information; their ultimate differences must be based on different inferences drawn from the shared data and information, not on difference in the data and information used.

The decision makers are then exposed to the arguments developed by the two teams. These arguments are usually presented orally in a debating format. The decision makers then discuss these arguments with the teams and among themselves and either accept the view of one of the teams or derive a position that combines elements of both arguments. (This has sometimes been referred as finding a position in the "muddle.") For example:

> Anheuser-Busch was once offered an opportunity to acquire the Seven-Up Company. There were obvious reasons both for and against such an acquisition. But the balance between them was not clear. Two teams were formed and given the tasks of developing the pro and con positions. Both teams came up with arguments that had not previously been considered. Management listened to the results carefully and decided not to try to acquire the company. It did so with a great deal more confidence than it would have had otherwise. It turned out to be the right decision for Anheuser-Busch.
>
> In another case, Anheuser-Busch was presented with an opportunity to increase its equity position in a foreign brewing company with which it had a strategic alliance. Here, too, two teams were formed and the arguments on both sides were developed—to invest or not. In this case, management was led to formulate an offer that it preferred to the one proposed by its ally. The new offer was accepted with only slight modification.

Countermeasures. There are situations in which the selection of means in the pursuit of an end is certain to provoke a countermove by a competitor. For example, when a market leader reduces the price of one of its products, competitive producers of the same type of product are likely to react. In such cases, decisions usually have to be made sequentially, each one a response to an action taken by the competitor. What sequence of choices should one be prepared to make? Alternatively, if one can identify a competitor's likely reactions to one's actions, it may be possible either to preclude the reactions or assure their ineffectiveness.

Countermeasure groups provide an effective way of dealing with such a situation. I first ran into this idea in the military when the group of which I was a part at Case Institute of Technology obtained a contract from the Air Force to develop an exclusively defensive weapon.

> I was placed in charge of what was called the countermeasure team, a team supposedly representing the enemy. My

team was provided with perfect intelligence about the work being done to develop the weapon. When the design for the first version of the weapon was completed, my team went to work on it and in about a day developed a reaction (a countermeasure) that negated the effectiveness of the weapon. Our reaction was fed back to the design team, which then modified its design to overcome our reaction to the first design. This time it took us a while longer to develop an effective countermeasure, but we did develop one.

We went through four such iterations before a design was developed that required an excessive amount of time for us to develop an effective countermeasure. What was to be considered an excessive amount of time had previously been specified: it was the length of time for which unrestricted use of the weapon would justify its development, even if effective countermeasures were subsequently developed. It was very unlikely, however, that an enemy without as good intelligence as we had would be able to develop a countermeasure faster than we had.

The weapon was developed and it subsequently performed in field tests as intended. Fortunately, its use has never been required.

Recently I was involved in a situation involving a potential purchase of a new factory, but the reaction of a major competitor had to be taken into account.

Shortly before a company went out of business, it had completed construction of a new factory in a part of the country in which the market leader did not have a facility, but its principal competitor did. The leader wanted the factory because it needed additional capacity and because this location would reduce the transportation cost of supplying a large market. However, the leader knew that its principal competitor, who had a factory nearby, would oppose any such acquisition. In all likelihood, the competitor would use antitrust to do so. A team was set up at my institute to represent the competitor. Another team was set up in the company that wanted to buy the factory. The company team generated its first offer. The countermeasure team took action (on paper), which all agreed would make the leader's offer ineffective.

A second and improved offer was prepared. Again, an effective countermeasure was developed, but more time was required to do so. This process continued through several more iterations until my team could find no way of preventing the acquisition of the factory by the leader. At this point the leader made its move. What followed appeared as though the competitor had read our script. Our simulation of reality actually took place.

The leader eventually acquired the factory.

From Efficiency to Effectiveness

Control is a double-edged sword; it involves both doing things right (efficiency) and doing the right thing (effectiveness). It is better to do the right thing wrong than the wrong thing right. Unfortunately, the righter we do the wrong things, the wronger we become. In some cases, increases in efficiency can decrease effectiveness.

The ways of increasing control discussed above can make a system more efficient, but cannot change a system from doing the wrong thing to doing the right thing. They can only increase the efficiency with which a system carries out its functions. To increase its effectiveness, one must understand why it is doing what it is doing and whether what it is doing is the right thing. To transform an organization that is doing the wrong thing or producing the wrong product or service into one that is doing what's right usually requires its comprehensive redesign. Recall (from Chapter 4) the redesign of the automobile to better function in an urban environment.

Design is a synthesizing process. Analysis of a system can reveal how it works and, therefore, how to repair it when it stops working or stops working well. Know-how constitutes *knowledge*. With knowledge alone, we can increase the efficiency of a system, but not its effectiveness. An increase in effectiveness requires *understanding*, but even understanding is not sufficient. To increase the effectiveness of a man-made system, we must be aware of why it does what it does (understanding) and whether it ought to be doing it (wisdom). It takes understanding to be aware of the functions a system serves, but it takes wisdom to know whether these functions are good or bad. Therefore, if a system is doing the wrong thing, *wisdom* is required to identify the error and correct it. Wisdom is holistic, not reductionistic. No amount of analysis will right the wrong thing.

Selection of Means

Recall (from Chapter 1) that when an individual or group is confronted with a gap between where they are and where they most want to be, they can respond in four different ways: absolution, resolution, solution, and dissolution.

Learning and creativity are enhanced more by design (dissolution) than by research (solution), more by research than trial and error (resolution), and more by trial and error than by doing nothing (absolution). It is through design that people have the greatest opportunity to realize their potential. Through design, people contribute to the creation of the world they are going to live in. Therefore, it is through design that people in the West behave as they believe their God did. God is not worshipped for His or Her research or trials-and-errors, but for creation, the products of His or Her design.

When a design is evaluated, it is evaluated as a whole. This means that the interactions of its parts are clearly taken into account. If subsequently there is a desire to change a part, the effect of the change on the whole (as well as on the part) is usually taken onto account.

Evaluating Means

The effectiveness with which means can be selected in the pursuit of an idealized design or an approximation to it depends critically on how well the relevant organization, its environment, and the behavior of both are *understood*. Understanding is based on an ability to explain why things are as they are and why the means chosen produce the outcomes they do. Explanations depend on how well the relevant causal relationships are known. Herein lies the rub! Most evaluations of means are based on an association of the means and one or more outcomes, not on causal connections. There is probably no more prevalent deficiency in management and management education than the lack of understanding of the difference between an *association* (correlation or regression) and a *causal connection* between means and ends.

Two variables are associated if they tend to increase or decrease together (positive correlation) or if when one increases the other tends to decrease (negative correlation). Correlation is a way of measuring these tendencies. However, *variables that are associated are not necessarily connected causally.* For example, weight and height are positively correlated; they tend to increase together. This does not mean that when people put on weight this will cause them to grow taller or that growing taller necessarily involves putting on weight. And one of the earliest studies on the relationship between smoking and cancer issued by the Surgeon General was based on a correlation between tobacco consumption per capita in twenty-one countries and the per capita incidence of lung cancer. The correlation was significantly high, from which it was concluded that smoking causes lung cancer. This may be true, but the analysis did not demonstrate it. I used the same smoking data from the same countries and found its correlation with per capita incidence of cholera. It was even stronger but negative. This, using the same logic, proved that smoking prevented cholera. Unfortunately, the medical journal that published the first study refused to publish mine, claiming it was facetious. I admitted it was but pointed out that the one they published was also. No response was made to this.

Associated variables may be causally related, but the direction of the causality is not revealed by a demonstrated association between them. For example, the volume of a company's sales is usually strongly correlated positively with the amount of advertising it does, that is, they tend to move in the same direction. From this, many infer that advertising produces sales. This may or may not be true, but the data on which it is based provides no relevant evidence to this effect. This can be demonstrated by finding the relationship between sales in one year with advertising in the following year. This turns out to be an even stronger association. Using the same logic, this would prove that sales produce advertising. This also may well be true, and is more likely to be, but again the existence of an association of the variables provides no relevant evidence of causality in either direction.

Managers are seduced by all sorts of panaceas on the basis of alleged demonstrations of the results they bring about, only to learn later that they are often ineffective. Such allegations of effectiveness are almost always based on observed associations, not causal relationships. A large number of studies reported by management gurus—of which Tom Peters is a prime example—and published in the management literature, particularly in the *Harvard Business Review*, are based on the following incorrect methodology. A set of companies are selected that are asserted to be successful and to exemplify the one or more characteristics that the author believes is responsible for their success. Another set of companies is selected that are considered to be unsuccessful and not to have the characteristics hypothesized by the author. Then the success of the successful companies is attributed to the characteristics hypothesized by the author and the failures are attributed to their absence. This is absolute methodological nonsense.

Suppose we select twenty-five very successful businessmen and twenty-five unsuccessful ones. Then we find that the successful ones are all wearing suits that cost over $400 and the unsuccessful ones are wearing suits that cost less. We attribute the success of those designat-
.d as successful to the fact that they wear expensive suits. This is exactly the same logic as fills the management literature, but most managers do not understand causality well enough to detect the scam. The fact that several of the companies Tom Peters originally took to display excellence subsequently did not fare well should have given the show away, but it didn't. He and other like him continue to infer incorrectly from associations of specified characteristics with success.

A little understanding of causality is worth a ton of knowledge of associations. A case in point is provided in detail in Appendix B. Experimentation is required to establish causal relations. Few managers understand the logic of experimentation. They should. An effort to provide them with it is given in Ackoff (1962, chapter 10).

The means plan as a whole should be evaluated by how close it takes the existing organization toward its idealized redesign and how well it prevents the crisis revealed by the mess and takes advantage of the opportunities to create the future that it reveals. This involves a holistic judgment, an evaluation of how well the entire thing, means and ends planning, fulfills the promises formulated in the mission statement.

Conclusion

Ends and means, like the head and tail of a coin, can be viewed and discussed separately, but they cannot be separated. Moreover, they are relative terms, interchangeable, depending on the time frame of the viewer. Within a long enough time frame, every end is converted into a means, and in a short enough time frame, every means is converted into an end.

For example, you ask a salesman who is about to take leave of you where he is going (a means), and he says to buy a desktop computer (an end). You ask why. He answers that it will enable him to keep better records of his sales calls (an end). If you ask why he wants to keep better records (a means), he may say to make his sales calls more effective (an end). This chain of questions and answers (means and ends) can be continued as long as patience permits. Recall that Peter Drucker once said that even profit can be viewed as a means: it is to a corporation what oxygen is to a person, necessary for its existence but not the reason for it. This reflects Ambrose Bierce's insightful definition of "money": "A blessing that is of no advantage to us excepting when we part with it" (in *The Enlarged Devil's Dictionary*, 1967).

Furthermore, as will be discussed in Chapter 13, the ultimate end of everyone who wants anything is necessarily the ability to obtain whatever it is that he or she wants, omnicompetence. Even those who want nothing must want the ability to attain it. But in this ideal, ends and means merge. It is not only the ultimate end, it is also the ultimate means to every other end.

Ends are either positive or negative: things we want and things either we do not want (hence want to avoid) or we already have and want to get rid of. The way to get what we want may involve removing an obstruction, which consists of one or more things we do not want. For example, when we seek consensus from members of a board (an end), even one negative vote is an obstruction. Converting the negative vote into one that is positive, or removing the person casting it, is a means that becomes an end in the short run. On the other hand, we may want one thing because it will enable us to get rid of another thing that we do not want, for example, a court judgment against monopolistic behavior by a competitor. Because pure conflict (conflict not embedded in competition) is often an obstruction to getting what we want, I have discussed its removal here.

Ends and means are relative for another reason. There are many means that we value at least partially for themselves (as an end). This is particularly true where aesthetic values are concerned. For example, red, blue, black, and green ink may all produce equally readable handwriting, but most of us prefer one to the others. Organizations also have color preferences. For example, IBM is associated with blue and McDonald's with red. Every means has some positive or negative aesthetic value, and it may be this kind of value that makes us prefer one means to another.

We enjoy listening to music or seeing a play or film of our choice not for their instrumental value as means, but for the pleasure the event itself brings, as ends in themselves. Preferences for "things in themselves" are aspects of our *styles*. An individual's or organization's style is the collection of all the efficiency-independent (noninstrumental) preferences they have. To be able to understand an organization and be able to plan for it effectively, it is as important to understand its style as it is to understand any other aspect of its culture. One of the principal reasons for an organization rejecting a proposed means to a widely accepted objective is that it is not consistent with the organization's style.

Some corporations collect and display works of graphic art and sculpture in their headquarters; few build a headquarters devoid of aesthetic features. Such activities are not motivated by instrumental considerations, but by aesthetic ones. Of course, a thing or an event may be valued both as a means and an end. For example, an Eames or Eshrick chair may be valued both as a work of art and as a place to sit. Clothing and food are also examples of things valued both instrumentally and aesthetically.

Means also frequently involve ethical as well as aesthetic values. For example, killing someone, however efficient it might be for removing an obstruction, is a no-no for most organizations and individuals. The same is true of price-fixing and stealing a competitor's innovations.

Summarizing, the selection of means in the pursuit of ends is never exclusively a matter of efficiency; aesthetic and ethical values are always involved.

The efficiency and effectiveness of the means selected in means planning are not only matters of selecting one of a set of available means, but are also a matter of *creating* means not previously available. As discussed in Chapter 5, idealized design unleashes creativity in developing a vision to be pursued by an organization. But creativity also has an important role in selecting the means by which to pursue it. (Creativity is required both to formulate a good puzzle and to solve it.) Therefore, the selection of means can also be more a matter of design than of research or commonsensical judgment. Recall the problem created by conflict between bus drivers and conductors. None of the means originally considered handled the problem adequately, but redesigning the system—putting conductors on the stops rather than on the buses at peak hours—did, and did so creatively. Such a creative formulation of a means of solving a problem may very well lead to modifications in the idealized redesign of the organization. For example, moving the conductors off the buses at peak hours may lead to the design and construction of sheltered places for the conductor and those waiting for a bus.

Finally, it should be borne in mind that the gaps treated as problems in means planning are seldom independent of each other. Therefore, their solutions interact systemically. The selection of ways to close the gaps should take into account these interactions, especially their joint effects on the organization's overall performance.

Nevertheless, some problems appear to be susceptible to independent treatment; their solutions do not appear to interact. It is to such problems that operations research and the management sciences have frequently been applied. But the independence of such problems and their solutions often is illusory. For example, consider the problem of determining how many checkout counters should be open for a specified number of customers in a supermarket. The solution to this problem conceptualized as independent of others requires balancing the cost of operating the checkout counters with the cost of losing customers because of long delays. However, the chance of losing a customer, hence the cost associated with it, depends strongly on what else is available in the store. For example, if the store provides banking, pharmaceutical, and take-out food services, customers may feel that the time they save by one-stop shopping makes a longer delay in checking out well worthwhile.

The principal criterion used in evaluating the means plan is whether or not it takes adequate care of the mess, avoiding it and exploiting the opportunities it reveals. This aspect of planning should also be evaluated relative to the mission statement: Does it promise progress in fulfilling the promises made in that statement?

7

Resource Planning: What's Needed to Get There

Human beings aren't resources, they're *assets*.

—Jack Gordon

Introduction

The means selected in means planning require the use of a variety of resources. Five types of resources are usually involved:

1. Money
2. Plant and equipment (Capital Goods)
3. People
4. Consumables (materials, supplies, energy, and services)
5. Data, information, knowledge, understanding, and wisdom

For each of these, the following questions should be asked and answered:

1. How much will be required, where, and when?
2. How much will be available at the required time and place?
3. How should each shortage or excess be treated?

One can be reasonably sure that the required amount and the available amount of each type of resource will not be equal. The differences are often large enough to require modifying the plan to accommodate the differences. If the amount of resources that will be available exceeds the amount required, then either the excess will have to be disposed of or the plan will have to be modified so as to require more of that type of resource. On the other hand, if the amount of resources that will be required exceeds the amount that will be available, the plan will have to be modified either to acquire addional resources or to require fewer. Because the requirements and supply of any resource are seldom, if ever, in perfect balance, resource planning usually creates the requirement for *continuous planning*. Recall the example given in Chapter 3 drawn from Anheuser-Busch involving adding a new brewery, how this started a sequence of plans that involved generation of capital and using the excess capital generated.

This type of cycle is one of the principal reasons that planning should be continuous. A plan is like a still photograph selected from a motion picture; it provides no better a basis for evaluating the dynamic process than a still photograph provides for evaluating a motion picture.

Now consider planning for each type of resource.

Financial Planning

Making a profit was once thought to be the only legitimate objective of an economic enterprise. Some still think so. But times have changed. Profit is now generally considered to be a means, not an end.

Therefore, the financial conditions necessary for survival of a company should be formulated, as well as those required to implement the plan. This usually involves use of a variety of economic measures. For example, unless cash flow is positive, a firm cannot survive in the long run. If it does not produce a return on capital employed that is greater than the cost of capital, the firm will find corporate health and growth almost impossible. Its credit rating is very sensitive to its return on capital employed, but it also depends on other measures of its financial performance.

What is needed is a formulation of the minimal financial conditions required for survival and implementation of the plan. This, in turn, requires a financial model of the organization that can yield estimates of what the relevant financial performance measures will be under a variety of assumed conditions and decisions, that is, a choice of means. An overview of such a model is shown in Figure 7.1 and a flow chart of the model itself is shown in Figures 7.2a, 7.2b, and 7.2c. This model is currently in use by the company that produced it. It is the product of an extended evolution.

Equipped with such a model, estimates can be made of the financial

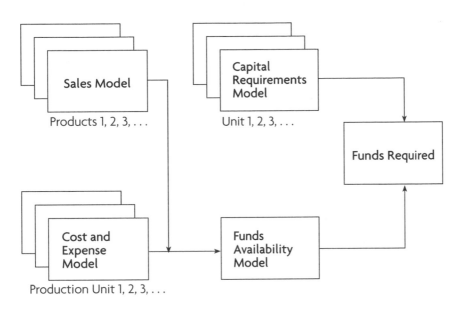

Figure 7.1   A schematic diagram of a typical corporate financial model

consequences of alternative planning decisions and changes in the economies in which the firm operates. This facilitates better choices of financial alternatives than would otherwise be made. A financial model of a corporation with foreign operations is obviously more complicated than that of one operating within one country. Currency exchange rates, inflation rates in the relevant foreign countries, tariffs, and restrictions placed on exportation of capital are factors that usually have to be taken into account.

Construction of a corporate financial model reveals where there is no knowledge of critical relationships. This should direct development of a financial research program designed to improve the ability of the model to estimate critical financial performance characteristics. Improvement of the model, like planning in general, should be a continuous process.

There is a single financial measure that can be used to evaluate the financial performance of a firm or any part of it that can operate as a separate business: the highest price for which it can be sold. By this I do not mean its stock market value, but the price it could obtain if it were put up for sale. When a business is bought, it is bought for its potential—for its future, not its past. The price paid is based in part on an estimate of the value that the acquiring company expects to add to the value of the acquired company. It is this expectation that justifies pay-

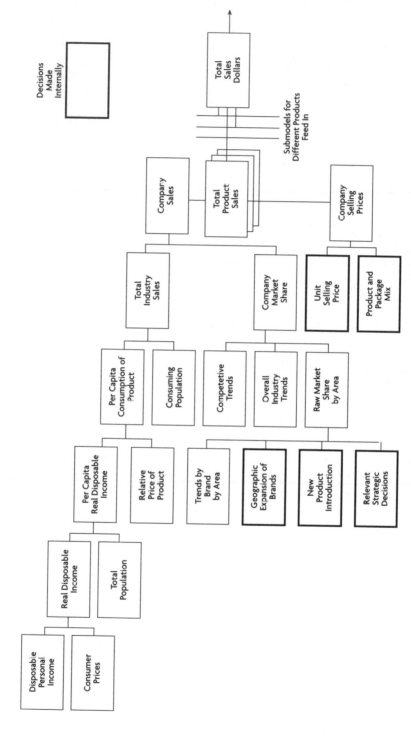

Figure 7.2a A typical sales model for a single product

134

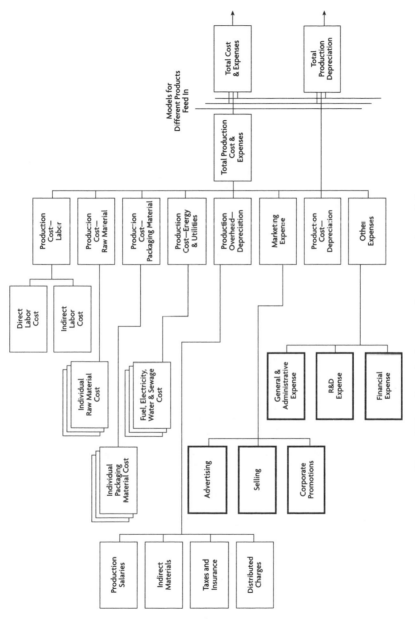

Figure 7.2b A typical cost and expense submodel

135

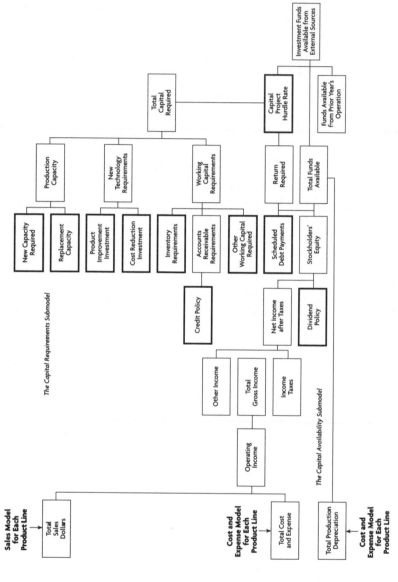

The Capital Requirements Submodel

The Capital Availability Submodel

Figure 7.2c Typical capital-requirements and capital-availability submodels

ing a premium for it. Estimates of a company's value (independent of the acquirer's addition of value) are what other companies pay such specialists as Dillon Reed, Solomon Brothers, and the First National Bank of Boston to prepare for them. However, there is nothing about the estimating procedures used by these consultants that cannot be used by a firm itself.

An effective measure of performance of the financial performance of a business is the *change in its potential selling price* over a specified period of time. It should be noted that this measure is not necessarily positively associated with profitability, at least in the short run. A company can increase its short-run profit while decreasing its potential selling price by reducing maintenance of its facilities and equipment and the quality of its products. On the other hand, a company that invests heavily in upgrading its capabilities may lose money this year but may very well increase its potential selling price. Another example is a company that experiences reduced profits because of opening operations in foreign markets, which may nevertheless increase its value to potential buyers.

The current concern with the breakup values of firms is related to the use of potential selling price as a measure of performance. A firm that is worth more on the market if disassembled than if sold as one unit has negative synergy and should be disassembled. If the parts are worth more together than separately, then there is positive synergy. An individual business that is contained within another larger company and would gain market value if separated should seriously be considered a candidate for separation, such as in the following example.

Clark Equipment Corporation was in serious financial trouble in the early 1980s. Its credit subsidiary, which financed purchases of its heavy and expensive equipment by distributors, suffered as a result. The rate at which it could borrow money was influenced by Clark's poor credit rating. Therefore, it was turned loose and set up as a separate corporation. As such, it acquired a better credit rating than its former parent company. This enabled it to borrow money at a lower rate; hence, it could finance Clark's sales at a lower and more competitive rate. It could also provide credit for other companies. Its profitability increased. Clark benefited from its partial ownership of the company and the reduced cost of the credit it provided to its customers.

Capital Expenditures

Given its planned pursuit of an approximation to its idealized redesign, what new facilities and equipment will a company need? How much of its current plant and equipment should be replaced? How much renewal (modernization) of its current plant and equipment will be required? These are the types of questions to which this aspect of resource planning should be addressed. The needs are usually treated individually and justified by estimated returns on the investment required. So-called hurdle rates are normally established, which are minimally acceptable return rates. Projects whose estimated returns do not meet this minimum are usually rejected. This can be a serious mistake.

Investments that do not meet the hurdle rate when evaluated separately may provide a very good return when considered as a part of a set of interacting investments. For example, investments that improve the quality of work life—like a new cafeteria, improved dressing rooms, a company store offering products at discounted prices—may have no return when considered separately. However, an improvement in the quality of work life may produce increases in the amount and quality of output that more than justify the investment. The interactions of investments are much more important than their effects taken separately. Therefore, even an investment that looks good when considered separately may be poor when considered interactively.

There is a trend, currently in its early stages, that will ultimately have a very significant effect on the kind of resources required to meet consumer demand. It is a trend toward products that are made to unique customer specifications. No two automobiles made in the future may be exactly the same nor two home entertainment centers nor two houses or parts thereof. This implies a growing need for flexibility. Flexible facilities, equipment, and even work forces may cost more initially than those that are less flexible, but flexible facilities may cost a great deal less in the long run.

For example, most university buildings are remodeled every few years at a great cost because they are designed assuming they will not be changed. If they were designed, as many new office buildings are, on the assumption that they will be remodeled frequently, the inevitable changes would be much less costly. Airports provide another case-in-point. Most of them undergo continuous revision, but even the revisions continue to be designed as though they will remain as untouched as the pyramids. In contrast, stages of theaters are designed to be continuously modified; as a result, changing them is simple and relatively inexpensive. The same is true of convention and exhibit halls. Computer-controlled production equipment is gradually making possible virtually continuous production of different products, with minimal time required for setups between products.

Human Resources

People are repeatedly said to be the most valuable resource a company can have. Nevertheless, they are generally used less efficiently than any other type of resource. The waste of employees' time and competence is huge. This is largely due to the fact that the quality and competence of employees has increased significantly during this century, but the way they are managed, organized, and used has not. They are still used primarily as surrogates for machines, where machines are either not available to do the job or are more expensive to use than people. Designs of more productive ways of managing, organizing, and using human resources are the subjects of Chapters 9 to 11. Here I deal with how people are used only insofar as it affects determining how many are required.

A table that facilitates human-resource planning where no increase is assumed in the effectiveness with which people are used is provided in Table 7.1.

Supply of and Demand for People

In estimating the amount of a resource, including people, required, we tend to assume that the supply must increase in proportion to the demand. However, in many cases this is false. For example, in a study conducted for the Lamp Division of the General Electric Company, the frequency of sales calls on customers was doubled. There was an increase in sales, but they were not doubled. When they were doubled again, the percent increase was even smaller. Further increases in sales calls failed to produce any increase in sales, but eventually produced a decline. Customers were not only saturated with GE sales calls, they were *oversaturated* and began to respond negatively. In the research described in Ackoff and Emshoff (1975), it will be seen that continuous increases in the amount of advertising have a similar effect. Imagine how you would respond to a product that was advertised on every commercial shown on television or on every billboard.

Recall also from the discussion of the Mexico City congestion prob-

Table 7.1 A Personnel-Requirements Planning Table

Year _____

Personnel Category		P1	P2	...	Pn	Total
Number available at beginning of year (a)						
Number leaving during year	Fires					
	Quit					
	Retired					
	Total (b)					
Number transferred out to	P1	▓				(j)
	P2		▓			(k)
	...			▓		(l)
	Pn				▓	(m)
	Total (c)					
Number transferred in (d)		(j)	(k)	(l)	(m)	▓
Number available at end of year (e)=(a-b-c+d)						
Number required at end of year (f)						
Number to be acquired (+) or moved out (-) (g)=(f-e)						

lem (Chapter 5) that increases in supply can increase demand, and in some cases, as in traffic, the amount of new demand generated is larger than the old unsatisfied demand that is now satisfied. The relationship between supply and demand in all resource planning is critical, although little is known about it for most types of resource. But opinions are plentiful, and they are contradictory. Planning should include increased research directed at learning about these relationships. Few research activities can provide a greater payoff, particularly where personnel are involved.

In many organizations, there is a tendency to increase the number of people as much as possible, regardless of the output required. The reason is that the importance of organizational units whose performance is not measured objectively tends to be judged by the size of their budgets, hence by the number of people they employ. This, as previously discussed, leads to bureaucracy and the obstructive make-work associated with it.

In a competitive marketplace, organizations tend to learn something about the relationship of supply and demand by trial and error if by no other means. Otherwise, they would not, and do not, survive. This is a major reason for incorporating a market economy within firms as well as within a nation. The design of such an economy is the subject of Chapter 10.

Ignorance of the relationship between the supply of people and their useful output is a major contributor to the currently pervasive downsizing phenomenon. In Chapter 12, I consider the ineffectiveness and irresponsibility of downsizing. I will try to show there that it does not solve the problem of excessive human resources and how such problems can be prevented or dissolved.

Job Descriptions

These tend to restrict an individual's use of their relevant competencies rather than release them. Job descriptions prepared by others should be eliminated. Alternatively, people should be shown where they will be located in the organization. They should be permitted to look around and determine what needs to be done that they can do, then use their observations to prepare a description of what they propose doing. People should be responsible for bringing to the attention of the appropriate persons those needs that they see unsatisfied and that they alone cannot satisfy. They should also design a development program for themselves that will enable them to do the kind of work to which they aspire. These are not so much job descriptions as personal plans. These plans should be discussed with the employees' immediate superiors and the peers with whom they interact and should incorporate any of their modifications. With their agreement, their plans should be used. However, they should be subject to adaptation to reflect changing needs in the workplace and the changing competencies and desires of the persons involved.

> At Alcoa's operations in Tennessee, after the ability of workers to determine the nature of their work was increased, two workers handling sheets of aluminum coming off the end of a rolling mill made a change in their operation that saved the company a large amount of money. I went down to the plant

to congratulate them. In the course of my conversation with them, I asked how long they had known about the improvement they had just made in their operations. With reluctance they eventually told me "Fifteen years." When I expressed surprise and asked why they had waited so long to do something about it, they replied, "The sons of bitches never asked us before."

People tend to fulfill our expectations of them. If these expectations are low, their performance will be. If we expect abusive behavior, we usually get it. But if we expect and facilitate creative and productive behavior, we are just as likely to get that. For example, most professors know that the amount of cheating that takes place on examinations they give is directly proportional to the amount they make it apparent that they expect.

Layering and Spans of Control

I have found that the spans of control of managers and supervisors tend to be quite large at the top and bottom of organizational hierarchies, but very small in the middle. In the companies I have had a chance to study, the average span of control has been slightly more than three. This low average is due to the fact that many managers in the middle had only one or two people reporting to them. Since this is obviously not efficient, I looked for an explanation. I found it: it was usually due to the desire to increase the salaries of persons who were already earning the top salaries permissible in their grades. The only way their salaries could be increased was to promote them into managerial positions. Then somebody had to be assigned to them to justify their title.

This suggests that salary and rank should not be rigorously connected. People's salaries should be based on estimates of their value to the company, not on their rank. Such an evaluation can take place by assuming the person involved has just announced his or her intention to leave the company for a better job elsewhere. How much is the company willing to pay him or her to stay? It is the answer to this question, not rank, that should determine salary.

It is obvious that the smaller the average span of control in an organization, the more layers of management are required. In Japan, the average span of control is more than twice as large as it is in the United States. This suggests that our organizations tend to be overmanaged. Where managers have fewer than five subordinates, their responsibilities should be reconsidered and, where possible, be extended. The fewer the number of levels there are in an organization, the more vertical interacting there can be. With an average span of control of, say, eight, an organization of five levels can have almost 33,000 employees, and with six levels can have 262,000 employees.

The number of people a manager can manage effectively depends on how dissimilar their activities are. If they all have exactly the same function and their activities are independent of each other—for example, clerks processing orders—the number managed by one person can be quite large. On the other hand, if their functions are very different and they interact a great deal, seven, eight, or nine is the right number. Few managers or executives can effectively coordinate the activities of ten or more people who are engaged in different activities. Miller (1956) has shown that seven is the number of distinct activities that a manager can think about simultaneously, hence, interdependently. Nine is the number for exceptional people and five for less-than-average people.

Consumables

Every organization consumes some of the resources it uses, for example, materials, energy, and services. Such resources are supplied by either an internal or external source. In the past, it was generally assumed that it is better for a company to supply itself with any consumable resource that it needed than to obtain it from an external source. Control dominated cost when considering vertical integration. However, it has become increasingly difficult for companies to obtain and retain the competencies required to provide many of these resources economically, and this has hurt their ability to compete. The reason is that people with the competencies required often have no opportunity for advancement in a company devoted to other than their type of activity. Organizations that specialize in providing a particular type of resource can generally do so more efficiently, hence at lower cost and higher quality, than a consuming firm can. As a result, *outsourcing* has become a major issue for many companies.

> Eastman Kodak found that it could not attract or retain those computer-related competencies required to provide the quality and quantity of computer-based services it needed. Movement to the top of Kodak was not open to those with these types of competence. They had to work under a

very transparent but rigid glass ceiling. Confronted with this problem, the director of the internal computing services negotiated a joint venture with IBM that took over responsibility for all of Kodak's computing and all of Kodak's personnel engaged in this activity. People with their skill could move to the top of IBM. The joint venture provided improved services at a lower cost.

There is an alternative to outsourcing. If a company permits its internal source of a consumable resource to sell its product or services externally, that source must compete effectively with external competitors in order to survive. Therefore, its survival provides assurance of the effectiveness with which it can supply what is needed internally. This is precisely what happened when the English branch of the Mars Corporation turned its market research unit loose to compete in the open market for external customers. The quality of the services it provided to internal units improved significantly, while the cost of those services decreased. Several large pharmaceutical companies permit their sales personnel who call on physicians, detail men, to carry noncompetitive products of other companies. This reduces the costs of selling and increases its effectiveness because it reduces the number of detail men a physician would otherwise feel obliged to see.

Contracts for the supply of resources, particularly services, are often written so as to guarantee supplier behavior that is antagonistic to the interests of the customer. For example, when advertising agencies are paid a percentage of a company's expenditures on advertising, it is in their interest to increase advertising, whatever the effect of doing so. The less these effects are known, the better it is for the agencies. Since few companies know the relationship between advertising and sales, the agencies do a real selling job on their customers, better in most cases than on their client's customers. Most contracts with ad agencies are written so as to make them agencies of the media, not their customers. To correct this, the agencies should be compensated for increases in sales obtained without increasing advertising and for decreases in advertising without loss of sales.

In general, all "cost-plus" contracts, in which 'plus' refers to a percentage of cost, operate against the buyers' interests because the profit realized by the suppliers can be increased only by increasing the cost of what they supply. Contracts should be written to do exactly the opposite. For example:

When I built a house for myself and my family, I sent the design and working drawings out to several contractors for competitive bids. When I received the bids, I asked for a meeting with the low bidder. I proposed the following to him. First, that he tell me how much profit he had calculated into his bid. I said I would give him a check then and there to cover it. From then on, I would receive and pay all bills. For every dollar the cost of the house that exceeded his estimate he would receive no additional profit, but he would share equally with me every dollar below his estimated cost for building the house. He was fascinated by these conditions and accepted.

The house actually cost several thousand dollars less than he had estimated, and we divided this amount between us.

It is always desirable to share cost reductions with suppliers so their interests are better served by serving their customer than by increasing their profit at a cost to their customer.

Monopolistic suppliers, unless regulated, can operate much as they want; but the regulators are often more concerned with the welfare of the monopolists than the monopolists' customers. This is frequently the case where public utilities are the suppliers. Also, if a company uses only one supplier and shows reluctance to use any other, a virtual monopoly is created. It is for this reason that it is often a good idea to have at least two different suppliers of any heavily used resource. Where this is not possible, but alternative sources of supply exist, short-term contracts that must be renegotiated frequently are desirable.

Strategic alliances with major suppliers can benefit both suppliers and customers, particularly if the supplier is allowed inside the customer's operation so they can detect possibilities for improvement in what they supply. Conversely, the customer should be permitted inside the supplier's operations for much the same reason. In general, the amount that any supplier can help a customer is proportional to the amount of help a customer can give to the supplier.

Information+

Why the "+"? We tend to use "information" to cover all the content of the human mind. This is a very unfortunate practice because it fails to recognize important differences in the nature and value of different kinds of content of the mind: data, information, knowledge, understanding, and wisdom. In Chapter 8, these are discussed in detail, and ways of gathering, retaining, using, and reusing them are provided in the "Learning and Adaptation Support System" design presented there.

Here I want to discuss a widely held belief that development or operation of a Management Information System (MIS) can provide all the support decision makers require, including implementation of a plan. Because of this belief, conventional planning usually incorporates development of an MIS if one does not already exist and expansion of one that does exist. However, repeated surveys have shown that most MISs miss; they fail to fulfill the promises that were used to justify their development. The reasons for these frequent failures are important, but they are not widely known. Where they are known, they tend to be ignored. In general, managers who are not knowledgeable about computer and telecommunication technology tend to withhold evaluation and criticism of the technologists who design and operate such systems. The managers are embarrassed by their ignorance. They should be.

Incorrect Assumptions About Information

There are five common misassumptions employed in the design of MISs. Any one of them is sufficient to keep the resulting systems from working well, but most such systems that I have observed make most of the incorrect assumptions.

Managers need all the information they can get. It is widely assumed that the most critical information need of decision makers is for more relevant information. This is not true; their most critical need is for *less irrelevant information.* Because of the proliferation of data processing and communication media, information overload is much more common than information underload. Moreover, as the overload increases, the absolute amount of information used (as well as the percentage of it) tends to decrease. For example, in a study done at Case Institute of Technology for the National Science Foundation (Ackoff and Martin, 1963), it was found that if chemists were to allocate all of their reading time to reading abstracts, they would only be able to cover about 2 percent of the chemical literature. When one cannot cover a field in which one is interested, one samples it. When the sample one can obtain is no longer considered to be large enough to represent the whole, the effort to cover the field as a whole is abandoned. Specialization is the result.

It is for this reason that so many have come to know more and more about less and less.

Generalists are a vanishing species. Nevertheless, managers of large complex systems should be generalists. The failure of enterprises in the emerging global economy is due at least in part to the inability of their managers to find the needle (relevant information) in the haystack (which consists largely of irrelevant information). Therefore, *filtration of irrelevant information* and *condensation of relevant information* are badly needed by those who are responsible for our social systems and the organizations they contain. Research in which I have engaged reinforces this point.

> Many years ago, several of my colleagues at Case Institute of Technology and I conducted the following experiment. We listed the more than a hundred articles published within the preceding six months in the five leading English-language journals dealing with operations research. This list was sent to the more than a hundred English-speaking operations researchers around the world whom we knew well enough to address by their first names. They were asked to indicate for each article on the list whether they had read it or not and, if they had, whether they considered its quality to be above average, average, or below average. We received about thirty-five evaluations of each article listed. Only four articles had nothing but above average evaluations. These and four of the six articles exclusively judged to be below average by all of their readers were selected for further use.
>
> Professional science writers were then employed to reduce the length of the eight articles selected but to retain as much of their message as possible. They were limited to removing words, phrases, sentences, and so on; they were not allowed to add anything. They were not told how or why the articles were selected or how they would be used. They reduced these articles by one-third; then reduced these reductions by half, to one-third the original length of the article; and finally produced an abstract of no more than 200 words. At the end of their work, we had eight articles: four originally judged above average, four below, and each one in four different lengths: 100, 67, 33, and about 2 percent of the original length.
>
> While the condensing was taking place, we asked the

authors of the articles, to whom our intentions were not revealed, to prepare examinations that could be graded objectively on a percent scale of zero to one hundred. They were told these examinations would be used to determine how well their intended message had been transmitted to graduate students in operations research. Fortunately, all the authors complied.

Then, in a factorially designed experiment, each member of a large sample of graduate students was asked to read four different articles, none of which he or she had read previously and each of which was in a different percentage of its original length. All students were then given the examinations prepared by the authors of the articles they had read.

The average test scores for the above-average articles were the same for the full-length, 67 percent, and 33 percent versions. However, there was a significant reduction in the average score of those who read only the abstract. This indicated that even scientific writing—which is generally considered to be very compact—could be reduced by at least two-thirds without loss of content.

The average scores for the below-average articles were also essentially the same for all but the abstract. Much to our surprise, the average score obtained by those who read only the abstract was significantly higher. *This suggested that the optimal length of bad writing is zero.*

The implication of all this is that instead of devoting large amounts of resources to generating and distributing more information, as is currently the case, a substantial portion of these resources should be devoted to developing practical ways of filtering out irrelevant and useless information, and condensing useful and relevant information.

There are computer-aided ways of carrying out both these functions. Key-word based filtration systems have become increasingly common. These words are used to characterize each document stored in the system. Users of the system and their requests of it are also characterized by a set of key words. Then, users of the system can be notified of all documents received within a specified period that match, in some predetermined sense, their key-word profiles. The profiles of users can be generated by analyzing the key words of documents they find useful. The validity of their profiles can be checked continually by submitting to users a small percentage of the documents they receive that do not fit their profile but are close to it and by observing how useful the user finds them to be. In addition, feedback from users on the relevance and usefulness of the documents they receive can be employed to update user profiles and the way documents are characterized. (A detailed design of such a system developed by Wladimir Sachs can be found in Ackoff et al., [1976].)

Now that entire texts can be stored within a computer, it is possible to conduct searches for relevant information by using any set of words that users desire. They need not restrict themselves to the words given in a glossary, such as is required for key-word filtration and retrieval systems.

There are several ways of using computers to condense documents. One uses the full text of documents entered into a computer. It conducts a word count, excluding common words such as "and," "but," "is," and "if," then selects those sentences containing the most common word in the document and arranges them in the order in which they appeared. This process can be continued, selecting sentences with the second most commonly appearing word and placing them in the appropriate order. This process is terminated when a desired length is reached. The abstracts produced in this way do not read smoothly, but they do convey a reasonable picture of the documents' content.

An alternative condensing procedure, which can be carried out either by a computer or by hand, involves selecting the first sentence of each paragraph plus numbered equations and printing these in the order in which they appear. The length of the resulting digests cannot be controlled and tend to be longer than what is considered to be a normal abstract, but they are easier to prepare than those based on word counts, and they read better. They have an important additional advantage: the procedure induces authors who are aware of how digests of their works are prepared to paragraph their writing more effectively. It is easy for them to control the digest.

Because of the widespread availability of word-processing equipment, manuscripts are increasingly being prepared on disks, which are submitted to publishers. This reduces publishing costs and makes possible the development of much more effective systems of disseminating information about documents and retrieving them.

For many decision makers, the principal sources of relevant information are friends and colleagues. Here, too, instruments of modern communication and computers make it possible to exchange information and information about information much more efficiently than by mail or phone.

Managers need the information they want. Most designers of MISs determine what information managers need by asking them what they want. Doing so is based on the assumption that managers know what information they need.

For managers to know what information they need (1) they must be aware of each type of decision they should make and (2) they must have an adequate model of each. The second condition, if not the first, is seldom satisfied. The genius of good managers lies in their ability to manage effectively systems that they do not understand well. A system that is completely understood does not require the skills of a manager; those of a scientist who understands it or of a clerk who has been programmed by the scientist are sufficient.

It has long been known in science that the less we understand something, the more variables we require to "explain" it. Therefore, the manager who is asked what information he needs to control something he does not fully understand usually plays it safe by saying he wants as much information as he can get. The MIS designer, who understands the system involved even less than the manager, tries to provide everything. The result is an increase of the overload of information, most of which is irrelevant. The greater this overload, the less likely a manager is to extract and use whatever relevant information it contains.

The moral is simple: one cannot specify what information is needed for decision making, and therefore know what information to want, until a valid explanatory model of the decision situation is available. As shown below, when such a model is available, a manager is not needed to make the decision and should not be burdened with it.

If managers are given the information they need, their decision making will improve. Even if we grant that managers may not know what information they need to make the best possible decision, surely they would do better if they had the information needed. The following example shows that this assumption is not necessarily true. The example deliberately involves about as simple a production problem as one can imagine, one much simpler than any manager has ever had to face.

There are ten products to be made, each requiring time on two machines, M_1 and M_2. Each product must first go to M_1 and then to M_2. The problem consists of finding the order in which to produce the ten products so that the least possible time is required to complete them. Simple enough? All the information required to solve this problem is given in Table 7.2.

Despite the fact that this problem is much simpler than most real

Table 7.2   A Production-Sequencing Problem

Product	Time Required on Machine	
	M_1	M_2
A	7	18
B	3	13
C	12	9
D	14	5
E	20	8
F	4	16
G	2	20
H	9	15
J	19	1
K	6	13

production-management problems and all the data needed to solve it are provided, very few managers can solve it. They cannot do it by trying the alternatives because there are more than 3.5 million of them. Yet the problem can be solved in less than a minute *if one knows how.*

To solve it, take the product with the lowest entry in Table 7.2, product J. Since the entry, 1, appears in the right-hand column, place product J last in the sequence and cross out line J . Next, take the product with the lowest remaining entry, product G with entry 2. Since the 2 appears in the left-hand column, place this product first in the sequence and cross out line G. Then, take the product with the lowest remaining entry, product B with entry 3. Since this entry appears in the left-hand column, place this product second in the sequence and cross out line B. Continue to come in from the left for left-hand column entries and from the right for right-hand column entries until all the products have been placed in order. In case of a tie, either may be selected.

The point of this example is that if we know how to use the information needed to solve a problem, we can either program a computer or instruct a clerk how to solve it. We need not waste a manager's time. If we do not know how to solve a problem, there is no assurance that having the information required to solve it will help.

In most management problems, there are too many possible solutions to expect judgment or intuition to select the best one, even if provided with perfect information. Furthermore, when probabilities are involved, as they usually are, the unguided mind has difficulty in aggregating them in a valid way. There are many simple problems involving probabilities in which untutored intuition usually does very badly; for example, what are the correct odds that at least two out of twenty-five people selected at random will have their birthdays on the same day of the year? They are better than even!

The moral is: if managers do not know how to use the information they need, then giving it to them will only increase their information overload. If they know how to use it, they can instruct someone else to use it for them. This does not mean that managers who do not know how to use the information needed to solve a problem do not need any information. It means that the information that managers need is whatever information enables them to do better with it than without it. To identify such information, experimentation may be required. Therefore, in order to obtain an information system that is capable of improvement, it must be embedded in a management system that can enable a manager to *learn* what he needs. Without such learning, he is bound to ask for and receive more information than he needs.

More communication among parts of an organization produces better performance. One characteristic of most MISs is that they provide managers with more information about what other managers and their units are doing. Better flows of information between parts of an organization is generally thought to be desirable because, it is argued, it enables managers to coordinate their activities better and thus improve overall performance. Not only is this not necessarily so, but it seldom is; one hardly expects two competing companies to become more cooperative if each is provided with more and better information about the other. This analogy is not as far-fetched as one might suppose. Competition between parts of a corporation is often more intense than between corporations and, as has been observed, is often less ethical. A possible consequence of providing corporate parts with more information about each other is revealed by the example, cited in Chapter 6, involving a department store and the parts responsible for its two principal functions, buying and selling. When these departments had access to information about the intention of the other, they adjusted their intended actions appropriately. But these adjustments—reducing the amount to be purchased or increasing the price to be charged—were themselves known by the other and reacted to. Had this process been permitted to go on unabated, nothing would have been purchased and, therefore, nothing sold. Such a state was not reached because the executive office intervened and prohibited communication between the two managers. This did not remove the cause of the problem, faulty measures of performance, but it did alleviate the consequences.

When organizational units have measures of performance that put them in conflict with each other (and this is commonplace), communication between them may hurt overall performance, not help it. The moral is: organizational structure and performance measures should be put right before opening the flood gates and permitting a free flow of information between parts of an organization.

Managers do not have to know how their information systems work. Most designers of MISs try to make their systems innocuous and unobtrusive to managers to avoid frightening them. The designers try to provide managers with easy access to the system and to assure them they need know nothing more about the system than how to use it. The designers usually succeed in keeping managers from knowing any more about the system than this. This leaves managers incapable of evaluating the system as a whole. It often makes them afraid of trying to do so because they do not want to display their computer illiteracy. In failing to evaluate their MISs, managers delegate, in effect, much of their control of the organization to the information system's designers who, whatever else they are, are seldom competent managers. Here is a case in point.

> The chief executive of an equipment manufacturing company asked for help with the following problem. One of his larger divisions had installed a computerized production-inventory control system about a year earlier. About $2 million worth of computing equipment had been purchased for the system. The executive had just received a request from the division for permission to replace the original equipment with new equipment that was considerably more expensive (and advanced). The division had provided an extensive justification for the request. The executive wanted to know whether the request was really justified. He said that he didn't know enough about the system and the relevant equipment to make such an evaluation himself. I agreed to make an evaluation for him, but only if he agreed to increase his knowledge and understanding of computers. He did so and later attended a course put on by IBM for executives.
>
> A meeting was arranged at the division's headquarters, during which I was given an extended and detailed briefing. The system was large but relatively simple. At the heart of it was a computer program for determining a reorder point for each of 26,000 items and its maximum allowable stock level.

The computer kept track of stock, ordered items when required, and generated numerous reports on the status of the inventory.

When the briefing was over, I was asked if I had any questions. I did. I asked whether, when the system had been installed, there had been many parts whose stock level exceeded the maximum allowable under the new system. I was told there had been many. I asked for a list of about thirty and for some graph paper. With the help of the system coordinator and old reports, I began to plot over time the stock level of the first item on the list. When this item came down to the maximum allowable stock level for the first time, much to the surprise of those in attendance, it had been reordered. Continued plotting showed that the item had been reordered every time it reached this maximum allowable level. Clearly, the computer program was confusing the maximum allowable stock level and the reorder point. This turned out to be the case for more than half the items on the list.

Next I asked if they had many paired parts, ones that were used only with each other but were separately numbered, for example, matched nuts and bolts. They had many. A list was produced, and I began to check the withdrawals from stock reported for the previous day. For many of the pairs, the differences in the numbers recorded as withdrawn from stock were very large. No explanation could be provided.

The system was clearly out of control. To determine this I had asked only simple and obvious questions, ones managers would have asked of a hand-operated system. However, they were ashamed to ask the same questions of a computerized system whose workings they did not understand.

The moral is: no MIS should ever be installed unless the managers it serves understand it well enough to evaluate its performance. Managers should control systems that allegedly support them, not be controlled by them.

Conclusion

Resource planning provides an opportunity to organizational personnel to reconsider and upgrade a number of important aspects of their idealized design and means plan. Such planning involves decisions as to how much of each type of resource to spend on each type of activity specified in the means plan. Therefore, these allocations of resources necessarily involve comparisons of the value of the resources to be consumed, inputs, with those to be produced, outputs. These decisions are not often made rationally; most are made irrationally, based on unsubstantiated beliefs. This is true even of those decisions that involve very large sums of money, for example, advertising and promotional expenditures. Ideally such decisions should be based on an understanding of the causal relationships between the resource inputs and the value of the output. The financial model diagrammed in Figures 7.2a, 7.2b, and 7.2c is based on causal models that were developed experimentally and therefore relate monetary inputs, controlled or uncontrolled, to outputs, even those that subsequently become inputs to further outputs.

Financial planning can reveal the need for causal models and good measures of financial performance, especially long-run performance. These measures should not be those used by stock market analysts, but ones that take the interests of all the stakeholders into account, particularly the employees. To paraphrase Charles Handy (1997), to use old concepts to describe new things can hide the emerging future from our eyes. He went on to explain:

> The idea of a corporation as the property of the current holders of its shares is confusing because it does not make clear where power lies. As such, the notion is an affront to natural justice because it gives inadequate recognition to the people who work in the corporation and who are, increasingly, its principal assets. To talk of owning other people, as shareholders implicitly do, might even be considered immoral. Moreover, the language of property and ownership is an insult to democracy. (26)

Planning capital expenditures obviously requires some measure of expected return and some specification of a rate of return that serves as a hurdle. In acquiring another company, it is important not to make the decision based on the return on the acquisitions purchase price that its current operations are likely to yield. No acquisition should be made unless the acquirer can add value to the organization acquired. The value that the acquirer expects to add to the acquired should be taken into account in deciding how much to offer for the prospective acquisition.

People planning involves decisions as to (1) how people can be used by the organization most effectively, and (2) how they can use the organization effectively to facilitate their development and enhance their quality of life.

Operations research and the management sciences have made available mathematical models that assist in making repair-or-replace decisions on facilities and equipment and for selecting maintenance policies. Resource planning of consumables—supplies, energy materials, and services—raises make-or-buy decisions. Should internal or external sourcing be used? This type of decision should be based on more than cost: quality, reliability of delivery, and ability to adapt to abrupt changes in requirements should also be taken into account.

Finally, planning to provide useful inputs to decision making and the ability to identify and learn from mistakes assures improvement of both ends and means planning. A system that (1) supports managers' decision making by providing whatever relevant information, knowledge, understanding, and wisdom are available; and (2) enables them both to learn and adapt rapidly and effectively and to learn how to learn rapidly and effectively is described in the next chapter.

8

Implementation and Control: Doing It and Learning

There is nothing more difficult to carry out, nor more doubtful of success, nor more dangerous to handle, than to initiate a new order of things.

—Niccolo Machiavelli

Introduction

Implementation consists of translating the means selected in means planning into instructions that specify who is to do what, where, and when. Control consists of monitoring all planning decisions, including implementation decisions, to determine the validity of the expectations associated with them and the assumptions on which these expectations are based. If the expectations are not realized, control involves determining why (diagnosis) and trying to correct the decision to take the deviation into account (prescription). Control also involves making relevant corrective changes in the actions taken if the assumptions turn out to be wrong. It is only through the exercise of control that organizational learning can take place as rapidly and effectively as possible.

Even decisions to do nothing require control because they are based on assumptions and expectations that should be monitored. Such decisions are frequently very important and provide the greatest opportunities for learning, as in the decision not to make an acquisition when it is possible, or not to develop and market a product that is proposed. In addition, each implementation decision should be monitored and controlled. Many good decisions go astray because of failure in the implementation phase.

Those who are assigned responsibility for implementing a decision, if different from those who made the decision, should have direct ccess to the decision makers. This may be necessary either to get clarification of the intended effects of the decision to be implemented or to suggest how it might be improved.

Control without learning may improve performance but not eliminate repetition of mistakes. Learning and adaptation, combined with memory, can prevent such repetition. Although learning, in general, and organizational learning, in particular, are widely discussed, these are not generally well understood phenomena. With understanding it becomes apparent that learning, particularly organizational learning, cannot be left to chance. It requires a learning-and-adaptation support system. It is through such a system that control can be exercised.

The extensive literature on learning deals almost exclusively with sociopsychological aspects of learning, that is, how to learn from others. However, all learning ultimately derives from our own or others' experience. Learning from experience is particularly important in organizations because of the continuous flux and turnover of personnel. Therefore, my focus here is on learning from experience in an organizational context. It is meant to redress a shortage of discussion of experiential learning by and control within organizations. This is *not* meant to diminish the important of interpersonal learning within organizations, but people and organizations can learn nothing, even from each other, that does not derive from experience.

I begin with definitions of the different kinds of things that can be learned: data, information, knowledge, understanding, and wisdom. This is intended to rectify the bias in much of the organizational-learning literature toward consideration of information and knowledge to the exclusion of understanding and wisdom. Then I distinguish between "learning" and "adaptation." I have also found confusion in the literature on this distinction (e.g., Haeckel, 1996). In particular, I will deal with the very important role of "mistakes" in learning and adaptation. I will also deal with learning how to learn, what Gregory Bateson (1972) called "deutero-learning."

Finally, in this chapter I present a design of a Management Learning and Adaptation System that meets the varied requirements formulated earlier.

The Types of Learning

The learning literature contains very little about what can be learned. What one learns consists of either *data, information, knowledge, understanding,* or *wisdom.* Unfortunately, we tend to use these terms interchangeably. "Data" and "information" are frequently confused. A distinction between "knowledge" and "understanding" is seldom made. Furthermore, "knowledge" is used in several different senses, for example, as awareness—"I know you are there"—and as ability—"I know how to drive a car." Wisdom is seldom defined and is usually treated as mysterious and indefinable.

Not only are the differences between the contents of learning important, but they form a hierarchy of increasing value, as reflected in the following adage:

> An ounce of information is worth a pound of data;
> an ounce of knowledge is worth a pound of information;
> an ounce of understanding is worth a pound of knowledge; and
> an ounce of wisdom is worth a pound of understanding.

Nevertheless, most of our formal education and most computer-based corporate systems are primarily devoted to the less important types of learning: to the acquisition, processing, and transmission of data and information. There is less effort devoted to the transmission of knowledge and practically none to the transmission of understanding. Even less is devoted to wisdom. This allocation of effort is reflected in the popular and persistent preoccupation with information in the press, on television game shows, and in such popular parlor games as "Trivial Pursuit." How appropriate this name!

Data

Data consist of symbols that represent objects, events, and their properties. They are products of *observation.* Observations are made either by people or instruments, for example, thermometers, ohmmeters, and speedometers. The dashboards of automobiles and airplanes are filled with such devices.

Data that have been processed into a useful form constitute *information.* Therefore, information also consists of symbols that represent objects, events, and their properties, but the difference between data and information is their usefulness. Data are to information what iron ore is to iron. There is very little we can do with iron ore itself, but once it has been processed into iron, its uses are unlimited.

Information

Information is contained in descriptions, in answers to questions that begin with such words as who, what, where, when, *and* how many? It is usable in deciding what to do, not how to do it. For example, a list of the films currently playing in movie houses enables us to select one to see, but it does not tell us how to get there; similarly, the address of a cinema tells us where it is, but still does not tell us how to get there. Answers to how-to questions constitute knowledge.

Knowledge

Knowledge is contained in instructions. It consists of *know-how*, for example, knowing how a system works or how to make it work in a desired way, and it makes maintenance and control of objects, systems, and events possible. To control something is to make it work or behave efficiently for an intended end. The efficiency of a course of action is usually measured either by (1) its probability of producing an intended outcome when a specified amount of resources is used; (2) the amount of resources required to attain a specified probability of success; or (3) a function of resources and probability, such as "expected cost."

Knowledge can be obtained either from experience—for example, by trial and error or by experimentation—or from someone who has obtained it from experience, their own or that of others. When computers are programmed and people are instructed, they are taught how to do something. Training is the transmission of knowledge. *Training and education are not the same thing.* Education is the transmission of understanding and wisdom. Failure to distinguish between training and education is commonplace. It results in a schools and teaching that devote a good deal more time to training than to education.

Computer-based expert systems are systems that have had the knowledge of an expert programmed into them. They store and dispense knowledge. In addition—at least since Shannon developed his electronic maze-solving rat—computers have been programmed to acquire knowledge, and this is a type of learning, but it is only a type, and not the most important type. Programs for acquiring knowledge are still very limited.

Intelligence is the ability to acquire knowledge. Therefore, the proper measure of intelligence is an individual's rate of learning, how rapidly one can acquire knowledge, not how much one knows. Expert systems that do not learn—and most do not—cannot correctly be said to have intelligence, artificial or otherwise. Unintelligent systems, ones with no ability to learn, can possess knowledge, but cannot acquire it on their own.

Management obviously requires knowledge as well as information, but information and knowledge are not enough. It also needs understanding. Management suffers more from lack of knowledge than from lack of information, and more from lack of understanding than from lack of knowledge. As I discussed in Chapter 7, most managers suffer from too much information, information overload, but not from an excess of knowledge or understanding.

Understanding

Understanding is contained in explanations, answers to "why" questions. We do not learn how to do something by doing it correctly because we already know how to do it. The most we can get out of doing something correctly is confirmation of what we already know. However, we can acquire knowledge from doing something incorrectly, but only if we can determine the cause of the error and correct it. Mistakes can be corrected by trial and error, but this is often very time-consuming and costly. There is a significant need for systems that can identify mistakes, determine their causes, and correct for them, that is, learn and adapt. A mistake that can be explained by identifying what produced it is said to be understood. Understanding facilitates and accelerates the acquisition of knowledge.

Understanding is required to determine the relevance of data and information, understanding why the situation is what it is and how its characteristics are causally related to our objectives. On the other hand, explanations can be, and frequently are, suggested by observations. Theories, of course, embody explanations. All explanations are deductions from implicit or explicit theories that are confirmed or disconfirmed by experience.

Objects, events, or their properties may be explained by identifying their cause or producer, for example: "The boy is going to the store because his mother sent him." However, the behavior of an entity that can display choice may also be explained by identifying that entity's intended outcome, for example: "The boy is going to the store to buy an ice cream cone." Only purposeful entities have intentions. (A pur-

poseful entity is one that can pursue the same end (1) in different ways
in the same environment, and (2) the same way in different environments.) Therefore, to say that an apple falls from a tree because it
wants to get to the ground is no explanation at all, but to say that a person climbed a tree to pick an apple is.

It is possible to construct computer-based systems that explain the
failures of some relatively simple mechanical systems. For example,
some automobile manufacturing companies have developed sensing
devices that can be applied to their motors. The data collected are then
processed by a computer to determine whether the engine is defective
and, if so, what is the cause of the defect or its location. The Russians
developed a number of such systems for application to heavy military
vehicles.

Some computerized systems have been developed to diagnose the
malfunctioning of organisms, but are in relative infancy. The types of
malfunctioning that can be explained by computerized diagnostic systems do not involve choice, purposefulness. As yet, we do not have the
ability to program computers to determine the intentions behind or
producers of purposeful behavior. Computers have made inroads into
storing and providing data, information, knowledge, and understanding, but I am not aware of any computerized wisdom-generating or
wisdom-disseminating systems.

Data, information, knowledge, and understanding presuppose each
other. They are acquired and develop interdependently. Although they
form a hierarchy with respect to value, none is more fundamental than
the others.

Wisdom

Recall the distinction made earlier between doing things right and
doing the right thing. This distinction is the same as that between efficiency and effectiveness. Information, knowledge, and understanding
contribute primarily to efficiency, but provide little assurance of effectiveness. For effectiveness, wisdom is required.

*Wisdom is the ability to perceive and evaluate the long-run consequences of
behavior.* It is normally associated with a willingness to make short-run
sacrifices for the sake of long-run gains. It is also normally associated
with age for an obvious reason: the elderly have the most experience
with long-run effects.

What one does is clearly the product of the information, knowledge,
and understanding one has. The value of information, knowledge, and

understanding is instrumental; it lies in their ability to facilitate the pursuit of ends. Although one must be aware of the end that is being pursued in order to determine the efficiency of a means for pursuing it, one need not be aware of the value of that end to do so. Therefore, one can talk about the efficiency of immoral as well as moral acts, for example, the relative efficiency of different ways of breaking the law or harming another.

On the other hand, the effectiveness of behavior necessarily takes the value of its outcomes into account. Effectiveness in the pursuit of an end is the product of the efficiency of that pursuit and the value of that end, the *expected value*. Therefore, the inefficient pursuit of a valuable end may be more effective than the very efficient pursuit of one that has little or negative value.

Wisdom is normative as well as instrumental. The difference between efficiency and effectiveness—which differentiates wisdom from understanding, knowledge, and information—is also reflected in the difference between *growth* and *development* (the subject of Chapter 13). As will be seen, development cannot occur without wisdom; growth can.

One who seeks to increase wisdom must be concerned with the value of outcomes (long run as well as short run), but the value to whom? One person's behavior usually affects others. Then, ideally, all our behavior should serve the legitimate needs and desires of all those it affects, its stakeholders. This means that effective decisions must be value-full, not value-free. Objectivity, which is usually defined as the absence of value considerations in decision making, is antithetical to effectiveness, hence to wisdom. Objectivity is better taken to be value-full, not value-free, that is, as a property of decisions that make them valuable to *all* they affect, whatever their legitimate values.

Evaluation of outcomes is a product of *judgment*. As yet, we do not know how to program the process of making value judgments. In fact, this appears to be unprogrammable. On the other hand, the determination of efficiency can often be programmed because, among other things, the efficiency of an act is independent of the actor. Not so for effectiveness. The value of the outcome of an act is *never* independent of the actor and seldom is the same for two actors, even when they act in the same way in the same environment. It may not even be the same for the same actor in different environments or in the same environment at different times. In contrast, the efficiency of an act in a specified environment is constant regardless of time.

Values are matters of personal or organizational concern. Therefore, wisdom-generating systems are ones that are very likely to continue to require human or organizational participation. It may well be that wisdom, which is essential to the effective pursuit of all ends, is a characteristic of humans and their organizations, a characteristic that ultimately differentiates them from machines and other organisms.

Learning and Adaptation

To *learn* is to acquire information, knowledge, understanding, or wisdom. Systems that facilitate learning, computer based or otherwise, can be called "learning support systems." The varieties of learning—acquisition of information, knowledge, understanding, or wisdom—can, but need not, take place independently of each other.

Individuals acquire information when their range of possible choices increases. To inform someone is to increase his or her probability of making one or more specific choices. For example, to tell someone that it is raining outside is likely to increase the probability of his or her carrying an umbrella.

Learning can increase under constant conditions, as in successive tries at hitting a target with rifle shots. It can also take place when the conditions affecting one's choice change, as when a strong crosswind arises or a distracting noise interferes with target shooting. Under such changing conditions, new learning is required to maintain, let alone increase, efficiency and effectiveness. Such learning is called *adaptation*.

> To adapt is to change oneself or one's environment so as to maintain or increase efficiency or effectiveness when changes of internal or external conditions, if not responded to, result in decreased efficiency or effectiveness. Therefore, adaptation is learning under changing conditions.

Mistakes, the Ultimate Source of Learning

As noted above, one does not learn from doing something right, but one can, although not necessarily, learn from doing something wrong, by making a mistake. In order to learn from mistakes, they must first be detected—this requires information. Then their cause or source must be identified—this requires understanding. Finally, successful corrective action must be taken—this requires knowledge. Therefore, *a complete learning system is one that detects errors, diagnoses them, and prescribes corrective action and these activities require information, knowledge, and understanding.* The values served by such a system are those of the persons served by the system; hence, those values reflect their wisdom, or lack of it.

It should be noted that in most organizations mistakes tend to be concealed even from those who make them. The likelihood of such concealment increases with rank or status. Therefore, the higher the rank, the greater the claim to omniscience. This implies that learning is least likely to occur the higher one goes in an organization.

Types of mistakes. There are two kinds of mistakes, *errors of commission*, doing something that should not have been done; and *errors of omission*, not doing something that should have been done. Those organizations that reveal mistakes generally reveal only errors of commission, not omission. Errors of omission include lost opportunities. Unfortunately, the decline or demise of organizations is generally more likely to derive from errors of omission than from errors of commission. It is much harder to correct errors of omission, which, like Clementine, are usually "lost and gone forever."

Learning how to learn. In order to accelerate learning, decisions must be made and monitored in such a way as to continuously improve the ability to learn. Remember, learning how to learn is called deutero-learning. Such learning occurs when we identify and correct mistakes made in trying to correct mistakes. Because of the accelerating rate of change in our environment and its increasing complexity, much of what we know becomes obsolete in less and less time. Therefore, learning how to learn has become more important than what we learn.

Unlearning. Most learning by adults and organizations involves replacing something thought to be known or understood by something new, that is, much learning presupposes unlearning. Nevertheless, the literature on organizational learning has virtually ignored the unlearning process until recently when Peters (1994) and Hamel and Prahalad (1994, p. 59), among others, have given it a some attention. The system described below not only facilitates learning, including adaptation, but it also facilitates deutero-learning and the unlearning often required.

Requirements for Control, Learning, and Adaptation

Only entities that can display choice, that is, only *purposeful* individuals or systems, can learn and unlearn. Learning and unlearning can only take place in the context of decision making. Therefore, systems that support decision making should facilitate control and rapid and effective learning and unlearning and, of course, the acquisition and development of information, knowledge, and understanding. In addition, a Learning and Adaptation Support System should facilitate the following aspects of decision making:

- Identification and formulation of problems.
- Making decisions, that is, selecting a course of action.
- Implementing the decision made.
- Controlling implementation of the decision, its effects and the assumptions on which it is based.
- Providing the information required to carry out these functions.

Designing a Learning and Adaptation Support System

The design that follows (see Figure 8.1) is meant to be treated as a theme around which each organization should write its own variation, one suited to the uniqueness of its structure, business, and environment. No two of its applications have ever been exactly the same. For example, its application in the North American Organization of General Motors is very different from its application in one of the divisions of DuPont. It should be noted that the apparent complexity of the design derives from the not-so-apparent complexity of the processes of control, learning, and adaptation. All the functions contained in the model can be carried out in the mind of one person, or each can be carried out by different organizational units.

The numbers and letters in parentheses that follow refer to Figure 8.1. The boxes there represent functions, not individuals or groups. As will be seen, they may be performed not only by individuals or groups, but (in some cases) even by use of a computer and related technologies.

Since the support of learning should be continuous, a description of it can begin at any point, but it is easiest to follow if we begin with the generation of *data, information, knowledge,* or *understanding* (1) about the behavior of the **organization** being managed and its **environment**. These inputs are received by the **decision support function**. The inputs may come in a variety of forms, for example, oral or written, published or personal.

Recall that in the preceding chapter I argued that management suffers more from an overabundance of irrelevant information than from a shortage of relevant information. Therefore, I suggested that a management support system should *filter* incoming messages for relevance and *condense* them so as to minimize the times required to acquire their

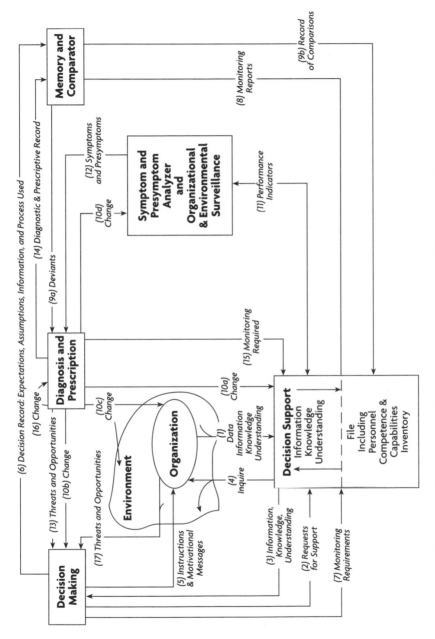

Figure 8.1 Organizational Learning, Adaptation, and Management Support System

167

content. These two functions have received relatively little attention in the learning literature. This, in my opinion, is a serious deficiency. Data should be processed to convert them into information, knowledge, or understanding; therefore, data processing is a necessary part of the **decision support** function. *Information, knowledge* or *understanding* (3) are transmitted to the **decision making** function in response to its *requests for support* (2).

When the decision makers receive the information, knowledge, or understanding with which they are provided, they do not always find it useful, complete, or even correct. They may find it unreadable, incomprehensible, doubt its validity, or question its completeness. Therefore, the receipt of information often leads them to additional *requests for support* (2). Such requests require two additional capabilities of the **decision support** function. This subsystem must be able to generate new data—that is, *inquire* (4) into the **organization** and its **environment** so that the additional *data, information, knowledge, or understanding* (1) required can be obtained. It must also have the ability to reuse data, information, knowledge, or understanding previously received or generated. This means that it must be able to store data in retrievable form. A data-storage facility is a **file** whether it resides in a drawer or a computer. It should be a part of the **decision support** function.

The request-fulfillment cycle—(1), (2), (3), and (4)—may continue until the decision makers either have all the information, knowledge, or understanding they want or have run out of time and must make a decision with whatever they have. In some cases, they may believe that the time and cost of further inquiry is not justified by the improvement or increase of information, knowledge, or understanding they believe is possible.

The output of a decision to do something consists of *instructions and motivational messages* (5) and is addressed to those in the organization whose responsibility it will be to carry out the instructions or whose motivation is the target. An instruction is a message to others or oneself that is intended to increase or maintain the efficiency of the organization. A motivational message is one intended to affect the organization's values, or those of some of its (internal or external) stakeholders', hence the organization's effectiveness. A decision, of course, may be to do nothing as well as to do something. A *decision record* (6) is required for all significant decisions, whether to do something or nothing.

Every decision has only one of two possible purposes: to make something happen that otherwise wouldn't or to keep something from happening that otherwise would. In addition, there is always a time by which the effect of the decision is expected. Therefore, in order to control a decision, its expected effects and the expected times of their realizations should be made explicit and recorded. All this is equally true of decisions involving the implementation of a decision. If, for example, a decision has been made to build a new factory, there are expectations about when it should be completed, what it should cost, and so on. Implementation decisions should be separately recorded and tracked. In addition to the expected effects and when they are expected, a record should be kept of the information and assumptions on which the expectations are based and the process by which the decision was reached, by whom it was reached, and when.

All this should be recorded in the *decision record* (6) that should be placed and stored in an inactive **memory and comparator** (more on the comparator below). An example of a decision record that has been used is shown in Figure 8.2 (see page 170). Because human memories over time are inclined to modify their content, especially forecasts and expectations, it is important that the memory employed be completely inactive. Inactive storage of forecasts and expectations may be the only thing a computer can do that a human can't.

A version of the *decision record* (6), the *monitoring requirements* (7), should be sent to the **decision support** function, which is responsible for checking the validity of the expectations, assumptions, and information used in making the decision and its implementation. When obtained, information about the validity of the expected effects, the relevant assumptions, and the information used should be sent to the **memory and comparator** in the form of *monitoring reports* (8). Then, using the information on the *decision record* (6) stored in the **memory** and the *monitoring reports* (8), a comparison should be made of the actual and expected effects, and of the assumptions and relevant occurrences.

When the **comparator** finds no significant difference between expectations and assumptions, and the performance actually observed and reported in the *monitoring report* (8), nothing need be done other than enter a *record of comparisons* (9b) in the **file** for future reference. This record preserves what is known or believed. Therefore, it should be stored in an easily retrievable form, for example, by the use of key words. However, if a significant difference is found, it is reported as a *deviant* (9a) to the **diagnosis and prescription** function.

Such deviations indicate that something has gone wrong. A diagnosis is required to determine what has and what should be done about it.

DECISION RECORD

Date: _____

Identification Number: _____

Report Prepared by: _____

Report Checked by: _____

KEY WORDS _____

DESCRIPTION OF ISSUE _____
_____
_____

IS ISSUE PRIMARILY AN _____ Opportunity OR A _____ Threat (check One)

OUTCOME (Check One):

_____ No Decision   _____ Decision to Do Nothing

_____ Decision to Do Something (Describe): _____
_____

ARGUMENTS PRO: _____

ARGUMENTS CON: _____

EXPECTED CONSEQUENCES OR EFFECTS AND WHEN THEY ARE EXPECTED:
_____

ASSUMPTIONS ON WHICH EXPECTATIONS ARE BASED: _____

INFORMATION USED: _____
_____

WHO PARTICIPATED IN MAKING THE DECISION? _____

THE DECISION MAKING PROCESS: _____
_____

WHO IS RESPONSIBLE FOR IMPLEMENTATION (f anyone)? _____

IMPLEMENTATION PLAN: _____

OBSERVATIONS AND COMMENTS: _____
_____

Figure 8.2   An example of a Decision Record

The purpose of the diagnosis is to find what is responsible for the deviations and to prescribe corrective action. In other words, the diagnostic function consists of explaining the mistake and, therefore, producing understanding of it.

There are only a few possible sources of error, each of which requires a different type of corrective action.

1. The *information, knowledge,* or *understanding* (3) used in making the original decision was in error; therefore, the **decision support** function requires *change* (10a) so that it will not repeat that type of error. The information used in decision making can also come from the **symptom and presymptom analyzer**, which is described below. Therefore, it, too, may require *change* (10d).
2. The **decision making** may have been faulty. In such a case a *change* (10b) in this subsystem should be made.
3. The decision may have been correct but was not implemented properly. In such a case, *changes* (10c) are required in the behavior of those in the **organization** who were responsible for implementing the communication, the *instructions and motivational messages* (5).
4. The **environment** may have changed in a way that was not anticipated. In such cases, what is needed is a better way of either anticipating such changes, decreasing sensitivity to them, or reducing their likelihood. Such changes involve changes (10a, 10b, or 10c) in either the **decision support** function, the **decision making** function, or the **organization**.

Through these types of corrective actions, the **diagnosis and prescription function** assures both learning and adaptation.

Now consider how threats and opportunities that are not related to previous decisions are identified and formulated. A "symptom" indicates the presence of a threat or an opportunity. It is one of a range of values of a variable that usually occurs when something is exceptionally right or wrong, but seldom when things are normal. For example, a fever is an abnormally high body temperature that is seldom associated with good health but frequently associated with illness.

Variables used as symptoms are properties of the behavior of the **organization** or its **environment**. Such variables can also be used dynamically as presymptoms or omens, as indicators of future opportunities or problems. A presymptom is nonrandom normal behavior: a trend, a (statistical) run, or a cycle. Therefore, a trend of rising body temperature, each of which is separately within the normal range, is a predictor of a coming fever. There are many statistical tests for non-randomness, hence for presymptoms, but the naked eye and common sense can identify many of them.

A complete Learning and Adaptation Support System regularly obtains information on a number of internal and external *performance indicators* (11), some of whose values are revealed as *symptoms and presymptoms* (12) by the **symptom and presymptom analyzer**. When *symptoms and presymptoms* (12) are found, they are sent to the **diagnosis and prescription** function. Once a diagnosis is obtained, the *threats and opportunities* (13) revealed are reported to the **decision making** function.

Whenever the **diagnosis and prescription** function prescribes a change, a *diagnostic and prescriptive record* (14) of it should be prepared. This record is sent to the **memory and comparator**, where its content can be compared with the facts supplied by the **decision support** function in response to the *monitoring required* (15) of its decisions (prescriptions) issued by the **diagnosis and prescription** function. *Deviants* (9a) are then reported to the **diagnosis and prescription** function, where corrective action should be taken. Such corrective action may involve *change* (16) of the **diagnosis and prescription** function or making any of the types of change previously referred to. Such changes are what makes deutero-learning possible.

Finally, information on *threats and opportunities* (17) may be sent directly to the **decision making** function by a source within the **organization** or its **environment**.

Implementing a Learning and Adaptation Support System

As noted above, the functions shown in Figure 8.1 may be carried out by individuals or organizational units. In a small organization, the entire system can be carried out by one person. All the functions except **diagnosis and prescription** can currently be automated to some degree. This ability increases over time with the development of computer and communication technologies. (A computerized template of part of this system was developed by LOTUS.)

Parts of the system can be created separately. Obviously, free standing MISs are commonplace, but I believe it is wrong to start by building such a system. I think it is wrong because the other parts of the Learning and Adaptation Support System are seldom added subsequently when a Management Information Subsystem is created first. The problems of maintaining such a system are so great that little energy and time are left for extending the system to other functions. In general, it is better to create a complete Learning and Adaptation Support System for part of an organization than a subsystem for all of the organization. Complete and coordinated systems are more likely to be developed by other parts of the organization than are other subsystems to serve the entire organization.

If only one part of a system is to be developed separately, then it should be the control subsystem: the monitoring of decisions made, correction of errors, and detection of changes in the organization managed or its environment that require attention. There are several reason for this. First, the payoffs come much sooner than from constructing an information system and are much more visible. Second, a successful control system in one part of the organization invites other parts to follow suit. Third, the successful operation of a control subsystem leads naturally to inclusion of the other functions. Unlike an information system, a control system does not give the impression of being self-sufficient. Finally, without the type of control described here, unlearning is not very likely, and without unlearning, learning is difficult or impossible to achieve.

Acquiring Wisdom

We normally do not refer to the acquisition of wisdom as learning, perhaps because it is not normally associated with schooling or teaching. It tends to be anything but systematic.

Because wisdom involves awareness of the *long-run* consequences of actions and their *evaluation*, it necessarily requires ethical judgments. This is the subject of Chapter 13. It is shown there that ethical judgments require the maintenance, if not the increase, of options for two reasons. First, we cannot forecast with accuracy most long-range consequences of choices made today, so we must allow for possible error; second, we cannot predict with accuracy what choices we and others will value in the future. Both of these deficiencies are exacerbated by the accelerating rate of change occurring in our environments and their increasing complexity.

To assist in the acquisition of wisdom, a record should be made of the expected long-range effects of decisions, if any, and their ethical evaluations. When the actual consequences become apparent, they should be assessed ethically. The assessment process should be treated much like the diagnostic and prescriptive function in the system described above. Where an unethical consequence occurs, it should be noted and recorded in a memory so that future wrongs of this type can be avoided or made less likely.

Individual Learning and Adaptation

With minor additions, the system described here can support the learning and adaptation of individuals. The principal additional requirement is the use of key words to characterize the content of documents and the interests of individuals, which then make it possible to supply individuals with material that will maintain or increase their competence in areas they designate. A particularly sophisticated system of this type was designed by Wladimir Sachs (chapter 3 in Ackoff et al., 1976).

Conclusion

I have tried to show how learning and adaptation—the acquisition and preservation of information, knowledge, and understanding—can be facilitated. A good deal of such a system can be computerized but need not be. The entire system can be installed in either a single mind or multiple units of a large organization. In addition, I suggested how the acquisition and preservation of wisdom might be initiated in a manner similar to the way information, knowledge, and understanding are treated in the Learning and Adaptation Support System described here. The principal difference in the acquisition of wisdom lies in the amount of lapsed time between decision and evaluation of consequences. This increases the importance of acquiring it whenever and wherever it is possible to do so.

Finally, with minor modifications, the system described here can be made to support the learning and adaptation of individuals.

Postscript

As noted in the Preface, I am a designer rather than a scholar. My professional career began in architecture. Architects do not footnote their designs with references to those whose ideas they use or by whom they were stimulated. Therefore, I am not aware of all those whose thinking may have preceded mine and been similar to it. Failure to cite them may be offensive to some. For this, I apologize. Nevertheless, friends whose opinions I respect a great deal have asked, referring to the design presented in this chapter, "How does the work of X, Y, and Z relate to your work?" I try to reply in what follows.

Nonaka and Takeuchi (1995), and later Choo (1998), have built their work on learning organizations on the distinction between tacit and explicit knowledge.

Tacit knowledge is the implicit knowledge used by organizational members to perform their work and make sense of their worlds.... Tacit knowledge is hard to verbalize because it is expressed through action-based skills and cannot be reduced to rules and recipe. (Choo, 111)

Explicit knowledge is knowledge that can be expressed formally using a system of symbols, and can therefore be easily communicated and diffused. (112)

Clearly, explicit knowledge creates no problem for the Learning and Adaptation Support System described in this chapter. Since the way such knowledge is used in decision making can be verbalized, it can be recorded in the decision record. What can be recorded can be stored in the knowledge bank and made accessible as, for example, by use of key words.

Not so for implicit knowledge. The way a decision based on it was reached cannot, by definition, be recorded. Nevertheless, decisions based on it can be controlled; errors they produce can be detected and even diagnosed and corrected (by prescription). This would call to attention of the decision makers the fact that the tacit knowledge used in making a particular decision was in error. They can then engage in trial and error in an effort to find a better decision, or they can find by research the reasons for the mistake and thereby raise the tacit knowledge to consciousness and make it explicit. Nonaka, Takeuchi, and Choo do write that tacit knowledge can be converted to explicit knowledge and that this is desirable because it can be more easily communicated than tacit knowledge.

Where tacit knowledge yields effective decisions, it would be left alone in my system. Although it can't be stored and made accessible to others, those who have it can be identified in a file so that others can get access to them if not what they know.

Neither Nonaka and Takeuchi nor Choo differentiate understanding and wisdom from knowledge. I suspect they meant to include them under the concept "knowledge." If so, that would be a disservice because the acquisition and use of understanding and wisdom are significantly different than the acquisition and use of knowledge. If they did not intend knowledge to be so inclusive, the omission is serious.

Argyris and Schon (1978), and later Argyris (1982), together with Senge (1990), have made among the most widely known contributions to organizational learning theory and practice. Argyris, with and without Schon, is primarily concerned with how knowledge can be brought up to consciousness (i.e., transformed from tacit to implicit), transmitted, and shared. This concern is with knowledge already possessed by someone. But, as I discussed above, all knowledge (and understanding and wisdom) derives from experience. The Learning and Adaptation Support System, therefore, is primarily concerned with learning from experience. However, what is learned is preserved and made available to others.

Argyris and Schon are also concerned with the diagnosis of errors. Their processes could well be used in the diagnostic and prescriptive function in the Learning and Adaptation Support System. Senge is concerned with diagnosis of system errors. He argues that systems thinking is necessary to produce knowledge and understanding, if not wisdom, but he did not create a system, such as the one presented here, that would facilitate the process.

The diagnostic process is by far the most complex and difficult part of the Learning and Adaptation Support System. This process has been discussed and developed by, among others, Churchman (1971), philosophically and provocatively, and Checkland (1981), pragmatically.

Part III

DESIGNS

Democracy, Economy, and Flexibility

9

A Democratic Hierarchy:
The Circular Organization

Democracy is the worst form of government except all others.
—Winston Churchill

Introduction

In the course of applying interactive planning and idealized design, several kinds of problems have occurred repeatedly. Over time, these problems have generated designs that dissolve problems. One of these designs, that of a democratic hierarchy, arises from several different but related issues.

The first problem derives from a systemic requirement that management focus on the *interactions* of parts rather than their actions taken separately. Interactions within organizations can be either horizontal or vertical. If horizontal, *coordination* is required. If vertical, *integration* is required. The question is how to organize so as to facilitate the management of both horizontal and vertical interactions. The organizational phenomenon often referred to as "silos" reflects the inability of the parts of organizations to interact horizontally. The unidirectionality of communication in most organizations, primarily down, reflects the inability to deal effectively with vertical interactions.

The second recurrent problem derives from the increasing level of education attained by the workforce. In the nineteenth century, most employees were barely literate, but today most have at least a high

school education. Because of this and the way managers were selected—they were the best in the ranks from which they rose—most nineteenth century employees could not do their jobs as well as their bosses
could. Today, most employees can do their jobs better than their bosses
can. This means that supervision is no longer the appropriate function
of management. Their principal functions should be (1) to create an
environment in which their subordinates are encouraged and enabled
to do as well as they know how, and (2) to enable their subordinates to
do better tomorrow than the best they can do today. This requires,
among other things, providing subordinates with a quality of work life
that challenges and excites them and education that makes possible
their continuous development. For educated employees, this in turn
requires the ability to control a significant part of what they do, to
exercise freedom of choice. How can all this be done in a way that fur-
thers organizational objectives?

The higher educational level of the workforce has another consequence that hinges on the distinction between "power over" and
"power to." *Power over* is the ability to reward or punish those who do
or do not do one's bidding, that is, the ability to exercise authority.
Power to is the ability to induce others to do voluntarily what one wants
them to do, often by wanting them to do what they want to do. The
more educated one's subordinates are, the less effective power over is as
a way to get them to do what one wants. Put another way, the educational level of subordinates and the effectiveness of power over are
negatively correlated. This is particularly apparent in universities,
which have a very highly educated workforce; little wonder managing a
university has been compared to herding a bunch of cats. The same is
true of high-powered research and development (R and D) organizations. And the shah of Iran, legally one of the most powerful rulers on
earth, was unable to get his subordinates, for whose extensive education abroad he had provided, to execute his policies and programs. He
discovered that there is nothing a superior can do that educated subordinates cannot subvert if they want to.

Third, employees at all levels, but particularly in the lower half of
organizations, are increasingly disturbed by the inconsistency of living
in a society dedicated to the pursuit of democracy, but working in organizations that are as autocratic as fascist dictatorships. Democracy is a
political system that has two essential characteristics: first, everyone—
with the exception of the very young, criminals, and the mentally
handicapped—has the right to participate directly or indirectly

(through representatives they can help select) in making decisions that affect them directly. And second, there is no ultimate authority; anyone who has authority over others individually is subject to the authority of the others collectively (the deposing of President Nixon was a dramatic exemplification of this aspect of democracy). In a democracy, control is circular, not linear. It is for this reason that a democratic hierarchy is called a *circular organization.*

Many of those who advocate democratic organizations argue that the only way to get them is to abolish hierarchy. This has led to concepts such as "heterarchy" (flat or horizontal organizations), and networks. These efforts have failed because divided labor must be coordinated and multiple coordinators must be coordinated; therefore, where complex tasks are involved, hierarchy cannot be avoided. Furthermore, hierarchies, contrary to what many assume, need not be autocratic. Not only are democratic hierarchies possible, a number already exist.

The Design

It should be borne in mind that the design that follows is a theme on which each organization must write its own variation. It is not cast in concrete. It is, however, that version of the design that has most frequently and successfully been used.

The fundamental organizational idea underlying the design is that every manager is provided with a board. It is worth noting that the value of organizational boards has seldom been questioned. To be sure, the value of particular boards has frequently been denied. But even in these cases, the recommendation has not been to eliminate the board, but to select members who will make it function as it should. It is through its board that the interests of an organization's various stakeholders can be brought into consideration in discussions leading up to decisions. The number and variety of stakeholders represented on corporate boards has increased dramatically in the last twenty-five years. Boards have significantly contributed to the humanization and environmentalization of corporations, as well as to increasing the effectiveness with which they can pursue their own objectives and ideals.

Figure 9.1 shows a simple, conventional three-layered organization in which every manager, represented by a small circle, is provided with a board. Three questions must be answered about them: Who should be on the boards, what responsibilities and authority should the boards have, and how should they operate?

Composition of the Boards

Every manager's board should *minimally* consist of:

1. The manager whose board it is, otherwise communication between a manager and his or her board would be very difficult. It is for this reason that corporate CEOs are virtually always members of their corporations' boards, which, more often than not, they chair.
2. The immediate superior of this manager, if any; without such participation, conflict between a manager's board and his or her superior could easily arise.
3. The immediate subordinates of this manager. It is their participation that is necessary, although not sufficient, for democracy. Sufficient conditions are discussed below.

Others from within or outside the organizational unit involved can be invited by a board to participate in a way defined by the board.

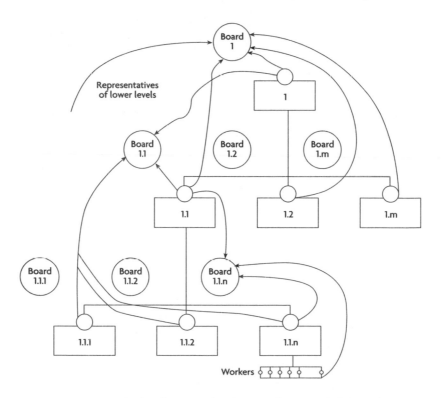

Figure 9.1   A circular organization—a democratic hierarchy

However, the number of others drawn from any one special interest group who are invited to participate should not exceed the number of subordinates on the board. The subordinates of the manager whose board it is should constitute a plurality. Those added to a board by its members may either have full, limited, or no voting privileges. They may be exclusively advisory and ad hoc. The nature of their participation should be specified by the board that invites their participation.

In most applications of this design, the principal external as well as internal stakeholders in the units involved have been asked to participate on the boards of these units, for example, the unit's principal external and internal customers or suppliers. In addition, experts in areas of importance to the unit involved have also frequently been invited to participate, usually as nonvoting advisors. Their expertise may be technical, managerial, organizational, or functional. In some organizations—for example, Alcoa Tennessee—appropriate union representatives have been asked to serve on boards.

Note that every manager except those at the top and bottom participate in three levels of boards, one at the level of their superior, one of their subordinates, and one of their own. Therefore, they interact with *five* levels of management, four others than their own, two above and two below. The highest level they interact with has access to as many as two higher levels; the lowest level they interact with has access to as many as two lower levels. This amount of interaction and access is not to be found in most conventional organizations. It significantly reduces the number and intensity of internally generated problems, as we will see below.

The boards at the top and bottom of an organization require special treatment.

The top board. At the top of most organizations, CEOs report to corporate boards collectively, but these boards differ from the managerial boards referred to here. Corporate boards seldom include all the CEO's subordinates and their functions differ from those of what might be called "managerial boards." Representatives of the corporate board can well be on the CEO's managerial board, particularly members of the corporate board's executive committee. Increasingly, these boards contain representatives of the principal extraorganizational stakeholder groups, particularly customers, consumers, minority, and public-interest groups. In some cases, for example, at Kodak's computing center, rotating representatives of the lowest-level employees were also invited to participate in the board of the center's director.

The lowest-level board. In the lowest level board, numbers can be a problem.

The Harvard psychologist George Miller (1956) has shown that the person of average intelligence can deal with only seven distinct entities and their interactions; with exceptional people able to go as high as nine and those at the lower end able to deal with only five. An effective board must enable each member to deal with the uniqueness and individuality of each other member. Therefore, the manager plus seven to nine others, or eight to ten total, is the most desirable size of a board. This does not mean that larger boards will not function at all, but that they generally do not function as well as those that do not exceed ten members. The larger the board, the less evenly participation is distributed within it.

For example, at the Krey Meat Packing Company (since acquired by another company), the lowest-level manager, a foreman, had as many as thirty-five workers reporting to him. A board of thirty-seven people would be completely dysfunctional. For this reason, we asked those reporting to the foreman to elect six representatives because boards of from seven to ten are optimal.

But the use of six representatives was a complete failure; most of those elected resigned after serving a very short time. We found out why. Because of their interactions with two higher-level managers, the worker-representatives began to understand why managers did some of the things that appeared irrational to the workers. They tried to justify these things to those they represented and, therefore, increasingly came to be seen by the workers as representing—"having sold out to"—management. As a result, the constituents distanced themselves socially from their representatives.

On the other hand, the representatives often defended the point of view of the workers they represented to the managers on their board and, therefore, were perceived and treated by them as workers. As a result, the elected representatives were caught in between two groups, not welcomed by either. Little wonder they elected to return to the group from which they had come.

A solution was found by dividing the work groups of approximately thirty-five into four groups of eight or nine each. Each was asked to select a leader for whatever terms they wanted. For example, they could rotate the leadership or select one for a fixed term. Then this leader, however he was selected, was given a board consisting of the other members of the group that selected him and the manager to whom the group reported. This enabled the company to reduce the number of first-line managers by about half. Then one first-line manager could handle eight groups, or between sixty-five and seventy workers, twice as many as before. This arrangement worked well and has been used ever since. It gave rise to the following important organizational principal: every employee should have the opportunity of serving on his or her immediate superior's board.

Executive Staff Boards

Senior executives frequently have a staff, consisting of deputies and assistants. This staff usually has a chief. That chief should have a board on which the executive served should be a member but only be expected to attend when an issue of direct importance to him or her is on the agenda.

Managers who do not have staffs but do have a secretary or assistant find it helpful to have them participate on their boards. They frequently provide the best input to discussions of even important issues. Moreover, it lends a dignity to their functions and encourages them to enlarge the scope of their jobs and become much more useful to the manager they serve.

Functions of the Boards

The boards are usually given seven functions: planning, policy, coordination, integration, quality of work life, performance improvement, and approval of the boss. Some organizations elect to hold off on the last of these functions until confidence in the use of boards has been established.

Planning

Each board is responsible for planning for the unit whose board it is. Their effort must be coordinated and integrated with the planning being done at other levels. This is done in the ways described below. Each unit is allowed to implement any decision that does not affect any other unit or the organization as a whole. If one of its decisions would affect another unit (or units) and their agreement is obtained, it can be implemented without further approval. If agreement cannot be reached, the issue involved should be taken for resolution to the lowest-level board at which the disagreeing units converge. Any unit can ask the highest-level planning staff—for example, corporate—to determine whether or not a part of anyone else's plan affects their own plan.

Note that this principle eliminates the need to discuss centralization and decentralization. By using it, each decision—imbedded in planning or not—finds its appropriate organizational level.

Conversely, no manager should be permitted to make a decision that has no effect on the organizational unit for which he or she is responsible but does affect others.

> I was once asked by senior managers why the workers in their factory did not use the new cafeteria that had been built for their convenience. We found that the cafeteria was not used by management, who ate in a separate dining room or out. Almost all the workers were Mexican, and they did not like the "American" food served in the cafeteria. As a result many brought their own tortillas, enchiladas, tamales, and so on, from home and ate out on the street, using Mexican street vendors for whatever else they wanted. When control of the cafeteria's menu was turned over to the workers, they began to use it heavily.

Policy

Each board is responsible for making policies that affect the unit whose board it is and all units reporting to that unit, directly or indirectly. A policy is a rule, a regulation, or a law, not a decision. For example, "No one can be paid a higher salary than that of his or her boss" is a rule, a policy, but the setting of an individual's salary is a decision. In a university, "All chair holders must have a doctorate" is a policy; the appointment of someone to a chair is a decision. The Congress of the United States is basically a policy-making body, not a decision-making one; the executive branch is supposed to make decisions, not policy. The point is that the boards in a democratic hierarchy are not management committees, but policy-making bodies—boards, not committees. Committees are only advisory and do not have authority or responsibilities, but boards do.

Managers may ask their boards for advice on decisions the managers must make and even ask for a vote on them, but however boards are involved in decision making, responsibility for the decisions made lies with the managers, not the boards. Policies, on the other hand, are the responsibility of boards, not managers.

Coordination

Each board is responsible for assuring the compatibility of plans and policies made in all boards reporting to it from the next lower level. Since the managers of the units at the next lower level are on the board making these coordinating decisions, coordination is largely self-administered with the participation of two higher-level managers. This makes the formation and preservation of silos virtually impossible. Boards provide a means for managing horizontal interactions.

It has been my experience that when boards are first formed the subordinates on them act as advocates of their unit's interests. With the passage of time, they go through a significant transformation; increasingly they act as comanagers of the unit whose board they serve on. It becomes almost impossible to identify the unit from which they come.

Integration

Each board is responsible for seeing to it that none of its plans or policies conflict with plans or policies made at relevant higher levels of the organization. Hierarchy is preserved, but with a significant difference. In conventional organizations, many of the problems that confront a manager are due to plans, policies, or decisions made at a higher level without awareness of their effects down below. For example:

> The largest division of a Fortune 500 company produced a type of product for which demand was virtually flat. As a result, it was experiencing declining profit. In an effort to maintain its leading market share, it increased advertising and sales promotions and lowered prices. To offset these increased costs and reduced income, corporate headquarters instructed every division to decrease its expenditures on personnel by a specified percentage. In effect, it ordered a downsizing.
>
> One of the smaller, but not insignificant, divisions provided a service that was experiencing increasing demand and profit, selling the time of its professionals. Therefore, the order to cut back on personnel expenditures meant a decrease in this division's sales and profits, exacerbating the corporation's problems and creating one for the division.

The larger a corporation and the more layers it has, the more likely it is that decisions made at the top will reduce performance below and that this will reflect up on corporate performance. Such a conflict is unlikely in the kind of democratic hierarchy described here because each board has members who sit on boards two levels down who can see the effect of a decision at these levels. And they understand the intentions behind policies and plans made at two higher levels because they have participants in boards at those levels on their board. Furthermore, they can easily appeal a higher-level plan or policy through their ranking members.

Quality of Work Life

Each board has responsibility for the quality of work life in the level below it, from which a plurality of board members come. This is the only domain in which a board can make decisions. As with other functions, it can do whatever it wants that does not affect others. If the decision affects others and they agree, the board can go ahead. Otherwise, it must appeal to the lowest-level board at which the disagreeing units converge for a resolution of the difference.

> A vice president of a major corporation who was in charge of one of its two manufacturing divisions had installed a circular organization. Shortly thereafter he called me, greatly upset. He asked rhetorically, "Do you know what those guys working in the main factory did this last weekend?" I said I didn't. He told me that they had called a meeting of the entire hourly workforce and decided to eliminate time cards and time clocks. They had come to him that morning to so inform him but said this was for his information only since they had the right to do this under the new operating rules.
>
> The manager told me that he could not let them go ahead. I asked why. He said there were certain critical machine centers in the factory that if not properly manned, would affect the whole factory negatively. He could not risk this occurring. I asked him if the workers were aware of the importance of these centers. He said they were. Then I asked what he thought they thought he would do if the critical centers were not properly manned. He thought for a while and said he guessed that they thought he would return the time clock and cards. I agreed but asked him, "Then why do you think they have made the change?" He paused again

and replied that he guessed that they did not expect this to happen. Then I suggested he let them go ahead for a period of time long enough to determine its effect on the quantity and quality of production. He agreed.

Several months later he called, and after a very cheerful greeting, he told me that the plant had experienced a dramatic increase in productivity and quality of output. I asked him how it has been brought about. He answered, "I don't know and I'm not going to try to find out."

The vice president had learned the value of the rules governing board behavior. Similar increases in productivity and quality were obtained at the Tennessee Operations of Alcoa when boards were established down on the shop floor. Most of their activities in the first year were directed at quality-of-work-life issues. Then they turned gradually to issues affecting productivity and quality of output, both of which increased significantly.

Performance Improvement

No less frequently than once per year, the subordinates on each board should meet separately to formulate suggestions to the manager to whom they report as to what that manager could do that would enable them to do their jobs better. Note that this is not even indirectly critical of the boss, but a way of asking for their immediate superior's help in improving their performance, from which their boss would also benefit.

In a number of such sessions that I have attended, a subordinate has voiced an opinion about an individual problem that the boss could eliminate, which others in the group have argued the subordinate could solve him or herself, without the superior's intervention. This produces significant learning and self-awareness.

Once the suggestions are formulated, they should be prioritized and a decision made as to who will present them to the manager. The first meeting of this type is often facilitated by an outsider, who is sometimes asked to make the presentation. When I have been asked to do so, I usually agree, but only for the first such meeting. The subordinates must agree to make the presentations in subsequent meetings. In some cases the first and subsequent presentations are made by the subordinates, rotating the presentation, each one taking up an issue in turn.

The presentation is made in a face-to-face meeting with the immediate superior. That manager has three optional responses to each suggestion. First, he or she can say, "Yes, I will do it. It's a good idea." This has been the case in about 75 percent of the suggestions at meetings where I have been present. The manager usually goes on to say that had he or she been aware of the desire expressed in the suggestion, it would have been responded to earlier. The manager then usually asks his or her subordinates to bring such matters to his or her attention when they arise, not to wait for such meetings to present them. Second, as in about 15 percent of the cases, the manager says no and is required to give his or her reasons for saying so. The subordinates do not have to agree with the reasons presented, but they do have to understand them. In my experience the principal reason given usually refers to a higher-level policy or plan. In such cases, where appropriate, the group may decide to request a change in that policy or aspect of the plan. Finally, in a small percentage of the cases, the manager can ask for more time and receive up to one month to return with a decision.

These meetings often transform the relationship between manager and subordinates from adversarial to collaborative because each one begins to appreciate the reasonableness of the other. For example:

> I facilitated a meeting of eleven vice presidents who reported to the CEO of a large corporation. They came up with eighteen suggestions. They asked me to make the presentation because I had been associated with the CEO longer than any of the vice presidents. I agreed, but only for the first time.
>
> We met in the board room. I explained the procedure to the CEO and took the first item on the list. I said, "Vacations." He immediately broke in and asked, "What are you complaining about? We have one of the best vacation policies in the United States." Then he went on to describe it in detail. When he had finished, I told him that he had not let me finish my statement. He asked what more there was to say. I replied by asking him a question, "How many weeks did you take last year?" He thought for a moment and replied that something had come up the preceding summer that had kept him at the office so he had only taken a few days off. Then I asked him about the preceding year. His reply was similar. Then I turned to his subordinates and asked how many had taken the six weeks to which they were

entitled. No hands went up. I followed by asking how many had taken four weeks. No hands went up. I asked how many had taken two weeks. No hands went up. When I asked how many had taken one week, two hands went up. The CEO looked at his subordinates and asked, "Why in the world don't you take your vacations?"

I asked him to answer that question. He paused to think, then blushed and said, "They don't take their vacations because I don't take mine, and they think I'll hold it against them if they do." I said, "You got it!" They all nodded agreement. The CEO said he was sorry and that he had not been aware of this effect on them; he promised that he would take at least four weeks off in that and coming years and asked that they do the same. They all did.

Most of the other suggestions had similar treatment. It is easy to see why all left that meeting feeling better about the other.

As a result of research in which some of my colleagues and I had participated, Imperial Oil of Canada established a business unit to handle liquid gases. Without consulting others, the president of Imperial appointed a young man to head the unit. Most of those subsequently appointed to report to him were older and had more experience with liquid gases. Their resentment of his appointment was considerable.

The young head of the unit instituted the circular organization at the very beginning. His own board did not work well, in fact, not at all. After several months of frustrating efforts to make it effective, he asked me to look at the problem. After doing so, I suggested a meeting of those reporting to him to produce suggestions to him that would enable them to do their jobs better. He agreed.

That meeting was held; I facilitated. It produced forty-two suggestions that the subordinates decided they would present to the head themselves. The met with him almost immediately afterward. About six suggestions were put forth, all of which he agreed to immediately and enthusiastically, saying he wished they had been brought to his attention earlier. At that point, the oldest of those reporting to him, one who had hoped to head the unit and believed himself to be more qualified to do so, broke in and said to the

young head, "Bill, I want to apologize. Sitting here and listening to you I realize that you are a reasonable guy and that
you did not appoint yourself to your job, one I wanted badly.
Now I realize that I have been unjustified in trying to have
you moved out by trying to make you look as bad in the job
as possible. I'm sorry and I want to assure you it's over."

The young head replied, "Jim, I appreciate what you just
said more than you can know. Of course, I've been aware of
your efforts and therefore have been trying to get you reas-
signed to another unit. I'll no longer make that effort. It,
too, is over. I hope we will be able to work together from
here on."

The others at the meeting then began to confess to their
disruptive and uncooperative efforts and promised to
change their behavior and intentions. It sounded like a
"born again" meeting. It went on to handle all the suggestions. At the end, the group that left was a cohesive and dedicated team.

John Purnell, president of Anheuser-Busch International, added a
very good feature to the procedure just described, one I have used ever
since. After his subordinates had gone through their suggestions, each
of which received a positive response, he made a number of suggestions to them as to how they could enable him to do his job better. His
subordinates responded as positively to these as he had to their suggestions. There was a very warm feeling shared by all who attended this
session, including me. It was clear that the relationship been the boss
and his subordinates was collaborative, not adversarial.

Approval of the Boss

In order to meet the important requirement of a democracy that there
be no ultimate authority, each board must be able to remove the manager whose board it is from his position. The board should not be able
to fire a manager, but be able to have him or her relocated. Only a
manager's boss can fire him or her. This means that all managers
require the approval of both their subordinates and their superiors.

I have only experienced one case in which a manager was moved out
of his job by his board. Once the relationship between managers and
their subordinates becomes completely cooperative, there is seldom
reason for moving the managers.

One company has carried shared responsibility for managerial appointments even further. It requires that any managerial appointment be approved first by those who will be the appointee's subordinates, then his or her peers, and finally, his or her boss. As a result, they seldom get a manager who does not appear to perform well because subordinates who are partially responsible for picking their manager, are anxious to make that manager look good. They often succeed in doing so. On the other hand, it is apparent that hostile subordinates can almost always make their immediate superior look bad.

How the Boards Operate

Whenever I have presented this design to an audience of managers, they ask a number of good questions. These are not defensive or negatively oriented questions, but genuine efforts to understand the design, its consequences, and problems associated with its implementation. I consider here the questions most frequently asked.

How Often Do the Boards Meet and How Long Do Their Meetings Last?

More pointedly, I am asked, "How does a manager get his work done when he has ten or even more board meetings to attend?"—both are very good questions, which take I will up in turn.

The frequency and duration of board meetings depends on how dispersed their members are. Where all the members are together in one location, boards generally meet once or twice a month. After a short break-in period, these meetings generally take about four hours per month. Where the members are dispersed, they tend to hold meetings when they get together for other reasons. For example, in one case where each of the board members resides and works in a different country, they meet quarterly by regions. One or part of a day is set aside for a board meeting.

Managers have seldom had to spend more than about forty hours per month in board meetings. Since virtually all managers work more than forty hours per week, board meetings usually take no more than 25 percent of their time. Studies of how managers spend their time reveal that they seldom spend more than 20 percent of their time in activities that require their being a manager. This means that at least half their time is spent in activities that, however important they may be, do not require a manager to engage in them. This in turn suggests that a more appropriate question than the one usually asked, "What do managers do with the half or more of their time they spend in other than board meetings and managing?"

The partial answer to this question is, "They spend it in meetings, most of which accomplish nothing." Boards generally reduce the amount of time required for other meetings by more than the time required for board meetings. Therefore, most managers that have tried to evaluate their time as a result of the boards have found that they have about 25 percent more time than they had before the boards, time in which to do whatever they want Furthermore, they find that the board meetings do not interrupt their work, but are a means by which they can get the most important aspects of their work done effectively and quickly. Managerial boards facilitate management; they do not obstruct or divert it. Most important, they enable managers to manage the interactions of (1) their subordinates, (2) the unit they manage with other units in the organization, and (3) relevant external organizations.

How are Decisions Made in Board Meetings?

Boards should operate by *consensus*, not majority or plurality rule. Tyrannies are frequently the product of majority rule. Even where majorities are not tyrannical, they tend to disenfranchise minorities. The requirement for consensus avoids these possibilities. But if decisions have to be reached by complete agreement, how do they ever get made? The answer to this question requires understanding the type of agreement required by consensus. It is agreement *in practice*, not in principle. I explain by example.

> A CEO of a midsized corporation arranged a week-long retreat of about seventy-five managers. He broke the group up into eight teams and assigned each of them the same task: redesigning the corporation. They were to finish by Friday and report their results back to the entire group at that time.
>
> None of the designs reported on Friday were exactly the same, although many were similar. After all the designs had been presented, the CEO asked the group how many thought the first design presented was the best. About one-eighth of those attending raised their hands—the members of the team that prepared that design. He continued but got the same result when he asked about the next two designs.

Then he stopped, looked at me sitting directly in front of him in the front row, and asked, "What am I supposed to do now? We don't even have a majority on any one design."

I indicated that he was asking the wrong question. He then challenged me to ask the right one. I asked the group to choose between my selecting one of the eight designs at random and their keeping their current organization. The vote approving of my selecting one at random was unanimous. This induced them to return to the drawing board and come up with a design that all considered to be better than what they had and the best to which all could agree.

Boards who cannot agree on what is the *best* thing to do can often agree on what is *better*. This is consensus: agreement in practice but not in principle.

In the relatively rare cases in which consensus is not reached through discussion, there are two other ways that have been used to obtain it: consensus through experimentation or test and consensus through the chairman's intervention.

Consensus through experimentation or test. Very frequently, when consensus does not emerge, discussion reveals that the issue involved is a question of fact. Where this question is revealed, research can often resolve the issue and yield consensus. For example:

> In a company that had twelve factories, all producing the same products but supplying different regions, the question arose as to whether maintenance engineering should report to the plant manager or to the vice president of engineering at corporate headquarters. Agreement could not be reached. The underlying question of fact was: Which arrangement produced the best maintenance services? A test was designed to which all agreed, along with a commitment to abide by its outcome, whatever it was. Half the factories selected at random had their maintenance manager report to the plant manager; the other half to the vice president of engineering. A measure of performance was also agreed to. It turned out that neither arrangement was uniformly the best; different arrangements performed best depending on other plant characteristics. Agreement was reached to make the decision plant by plant and how to do so.

The most dramatic case of this type I have encountered occurred in Mexico in a small Indian village in a very remote part of the Sierra Nevada mountains.

> The Office of the Secretary of the Presidency (similar to the OMB in the United States) provided a university-based research group of which I was a part with funds for an experiment in communal self-development. A small, remote village was selected, and the money was offered to the village for use in its development, provided all the decisions were made democratically. The offer was accepted. We had to spend some time making clear what the nature of development is and how democracy had to be practiced.
>
> The villagers first proposed that the money be divided equally among all the families in the village. We had to explain that this was not an investment in development, that such investment had to increase their ability to obtain what they wanted in the future. (The first project would create an irrigation system and bring water into the village.)
>
> The village had been formed when Cortez had invaded Mexico and a group of Indians had retreated to the mountains and hidden there. For this reason, it did not recognize the federal government of Mexico as legitimate, but as a government of occupation. So the village decided to create a formal government and have it administer the funds. To do this, it required a constitution. The villagers went to work in town meetings to prepare one.
>
> During these meetings, a strong disagreement arose over the issue of capital punishment. Should it be allowed or not? Some argued that it was necessary in order to deter capital crimes. Others argued that these crimes were committed in a passionate moment in which the fear of punishment was not present.
>
> Through discussion, agreement was reached that both sides wanted to minimize the number of capital crimes. The question as to whether or not capital punishment did so was a question of fact. We showed the community how this could be determined for Mexico as a whole by analyzing four types of states: those that had capital punishment five years ago and still did; those that had had it but discontinued

it, those that had not had it and still didn't, and those had not had it but introduced it subsequently.

The analysis was carried out, and it showed that capital punishment did not reduce capital crimes in Mexico. With complete agreement, the community precluded capital punishment in their constitution.

In cases in which those holding opposing points of view cannot agree on what is an underlying factual disagreement, the following procedure—a variation of one developed by Rapoport (1960)—can sometimes uncover the nature of that disagreement:

1. Each party is required to state the opposing party's point of view in a way that is acceptable to the other party.

This may require several iterations. If one of the parties wants to maintain the current state of affairs, that party should be the first required to formulate the other's position correctly. The reason for this is that the party wanting to maintain the current state is less likely to understand the other's position than the converse. As Ambrose Bierce (1967) once wrote, "there is but one way to do nothing and diverse ways to do something."

2. Once the first step is completed, each party should state the conditions under which that party believes the other's position would be valid.

The conditions identified in this way are often ones that are predicted, that is, the disagreement over what to do now may be based on different predictions of what is expected to happen in the future. For example, a recent disagreement in one company's top management board over action that might be taken to improve relations with a partner in a strategic alliance was based on different beliefs as to how the partner would react to a proposed action.

In other cases, the disagreement may be based on beliefs about what happened in the past. For example, in considering a proposed increase in advertising, did a similar increase that was previously made actually produce the increase in sales expected from that action? Or in the capital punishment issue described above, has the use of capital punishment actually deterred the occurrence of capital crimes?

If agreement cannot be reached on the underlying nature of the disagreement, then the board may have to resort to the chairman's inter-

vention in a way described below. This may be the case when the basis
of disagreement is a matter of values rather than fact. This was the case
in one company's board when one party never wanted to hold a minority position in a partnership; the other was willing to do so under certain conditions. The value of the ability to exercise control was the
issue here.

3. Once the factual basis of the disagreement is revealed, each
   party should formulate a test to determine which fact or facts
   actually pertain and, if necessary, modify their formulations until
   they reach agreement. The opposing parties should then agree
   to abide by the outcome of the test, whatever it may be.

For example, in the case of determining to whom the plant-based
maintenance engineers should report, both sides formulated a test in
which some plants were run one way and the remainder run another,
and agreed to abide by the outcome.

Here, too, if agreement cannot be reached, the chairman's intervention in a way described below may have to be resorted to.

4. The test agreed to should actually be carried out and the
   implications of its outcome should be implemented.

If there is neither time nor the inclination to conduct a test, sometimes
finding which of the opposing points of view has the *minimal maximum
regret* associated with it can produce agreement. This requires that a
table like that shown in Table 9.1 be prepared.

5. Then each party estimates the seriousness of error—the
   maximum error if there is more than one—associated with each
   position. If they agree on the relative magnitudes of these errors,
   they select that course of action that has the smallest
   (maximum) error associated with it.

An error is an outcome of a decision that deviates from the one that
would have been made had those making the decision had the benefit

Table 9.1 A Table of Possible Errors on the Issue of Capital Punishment

Positions	*Justifying Conditions*	
	Capital Punishment Deters Capital Crimes	Capital Punishment Does Not Deter Capital Crimes
For capital punishment	x	Error 1
Against capital punishment	Error 2	x

of hindsight. Rank ordering of the magnitudes of the errors can be used or, as is often the case, estimates of the costs associated with them.

Once again, if agreement cannot be reached, the following alternative may have to be resorted to.

Consensus through the chairman's intervention. When it becomes apparent that consensus cannot be generated any other way, the chairman asks each person in attendance to summarize his or her position very briefly. When this is completed, the issue is generally quite clear. The chairman then tells the group what he will do if they do not reach agreement. But if they reach agreement, he will abide by their position whether or not it agrees with his.

Then the chairman goes back around the room asking each person to state his or her position. If two people still disagree with each other, they force adoption of the chairman's position. Although this procedure appears to be a tour de force, most boards agree that it is fair and assures that action will be taken on important issues; they will not be let go by default.

The use of the chairman's intervention, as well as resorting to tests, should be agreed to by consensus when a board is established. They should become standard operating procedures. I have never experienced a case in which consensus could not be reached by one of them.

Where Is the Best Place in an Organization to Start Converting to a Democratic Hierarchy?

The answer to this question is usually very difficult for the one who asks it to accept. The answer is: wherever you are. There is never a better place to start anything than where you are. When everyone looks for a place other than where they are to start, a start is seldom if ever made. For example:

> A number of years ago, I was doing research for an automotive company. One day the vice president in charge of executive development asked me if I would be willing to put on a two-day course for the top 200 executives of the company. Of course, I said. He told me he wanted to have small classes of 20, hence ten classes. He then went on to tell me that the first four classes would be for the most junior vice presidents; the next three for intermediate-level vice presidents; the next two for senior vice presidents; and the final session would be for the executive office, including the CEO.

In the open discussion that came at the end of the first class, one of the attendees told me how excited he was about what he had heard and how anxious he was to use it. But, he said, he was the wrong one to have been exposed to what I had to say; it should have been told to his boss because his approval was required before anything could be done. I explained that his boss would eventually be exposed to the same material. This satisfied him and he said he would wait to "attack" his boss as he came out of his last session with me.

The same issue arose in each of the first four classes. In each of the three sessions at the next higher level, the same question was raised with respect to their bosses, the senior vice presidents. Then, in the two sessions with the seniors, they told me that without the approval of the CEO they could not go ahead.

I could hardly wait to hear what would be said at the last session with the members of the executive office. I found out when the CEO told me how impressed he was with the material I had presented and how anxious he was to use it. However, he said, he could not do so without the support of his subordinates. Then he asked if I would have an opportunity to present it to them.

This was a paralyzed organization where every executive tried to escape responsibility for innovation and play it safe by getting authorization from others. Needless to say, nothing was ever done about my presentation or anyone else's as far as I could tell.

Circular organizations have been initiated at every level of organizations: the top, middle, bottom, and combinations of these. If it succeeds in improving performance, as it usually does, imitation is never far behind. Nothing succeeds like success.

The Director General of the Equipment Division of the Secretariat of Public Works (SOP) in Mexico introduced the circular arrangement in his third-level unit. It was very successful. As a result, when the incumbent president of Mexico left office and the new one took over, he was the only old director general retained in the agency. The new appointees into his peers' positions were naturally curious as why he had been retained. They inquired and learned about the circular organization, and a number of them adopted it.

At Anheuser-Busch, a variant of the board was established at the very top. Some of the vice presidents who were members of this policy committee, as it was called, subsequently adopted the idea at their level, and one moved it further down until it reached bottom. At Alcoa Tennessee, boards were simultaneously created at the top and the bottom, and they moved from these two location up and down until they converged into the middle of the organization. At Eastman Kodak, boards were initiated in a sixth-level organizational unit and spread from there over and up into other units. In the White House Communication Agency, boards were installed all over at once.

Who Should Chair the Boards?

Generally, the manager whose board it is. Rotation among the subordinates has also been used successfully. The one thing not to do is to have the boss of the manager whose board it is chair the board; this reinforces autocratic hierarchy and makes unconstrained discussion difficult.

Who Sets the Agenda?

Any member of a board should be able to place an item on its agenda by giving the item to the secretary of the manager whose board it is or some other designated person. Agenda items should be entered at least three days before a board meeting so the agenda can be circulated beforehand. This provides an opportunity for preparatory thinking about the issues involved.

Is Facilitation of Board Meetings Required?

No, but it is helpful, particularly in the early meetings if no one on the board had has previous experience with them. If a facilitator is used, he or she is seldom required for more than two or three meetings. He or she may be invited to participate past this, but not to chair the meetings, because of the kinds of knowledge he or she can bring to bear on the issues that come before the board.

At Metropolitan Life, the number of boards set up was so large that a large number of internal facilitators had to be trained. The training program was developed internally with some outside help. The heads of the many quality circles operating in the company at the time were selected for such training.

Is It Desirable to Have Some Training in Group Processes
Provided to the Members of Each Board?

Usually, yes. At Alcoa's Tennessee Operations, for example, everyone was put through several days of such a program. (Union officers as well as managers and hourly paid employees attended.) Some organizations have used the National Training Laboratories for this purpose. Others have used in-house human-resource personnel. There are no shortage of sources of such aid.

Have Any Organizations that Adopted the Circular
Organization Later Abandoned It?

Yes, a few, and all for the same reason: a new executive came in who cleared the decks of remnants of his predecessor. This was true both in the Naval Personnel and Training function, and the U.S. Army in Europe. Similar purges have occurred in a few corporations.

What is the Principal Obstruction to Adopting
the Circular Organization?

The satisfaction some managers derive from exercising authority over others and the conviction that without their doing so "things would fall apart." This was the excuse the shah of Iran used for not giving up power when faced with increasing opposition. He was convinced that without his rule the communists would take over. (Talk about looking in the wrong direction!)

For many managers, power-over is an end in itself rather than a means. They are latent dictators. The fact that power-over usually reduces their power-to escapes them. In fascist countries, those with complete power over others could get done whatever they wanted. But not so where subordinates have freedom of choice and free speech.

What Should Be Done with Existing Quality Circles or Other
Groups with Lasting Assignments?

Wherever possible, the quality-promotion function can be added to the responsibilities of the boards. Metropolitan Life did just this with all its quality circles. After very little training, the heads of the circles, as noted above, made very good facilitators of boards.

Does the Presence of a Union Make a Difference?

Yes and no. It depends on the attitudes toward democracy in the work place of both management and the union. At Alcoa Tennessee, Local 309 of the United Steel Workers Union made the process work, but only because they were invited to do so by management. Similarly the union at Westinghouse Furniture Systems in Grand Rapids, Michigan, eventually came completely on board. However, there are cases in which unions fought the introduction of boards, interpreting them as replacing contract negotiations and thereby reducing the power of the union. Not so. When boards have been set up in unionized organizations, contract issues are excluded from discussion by the boards. But the number of issues that arise for contract negotiation tends to be significantly reduced because of board activities, particularly with respect to quality of work life.

Can the Circular Organization Be Superimposed on Any Type of Organization?

Yes. It has been used with matrix organizations, networks, heterarchies, and so on. I have never encountered a structure to which this design could not be fitted.

Isn't the Circular Organization a Communist Concept?

Absolutely not, but it is important to understand why. This question is asked by those who do not know the difference between communism and democracy. Communism has to do with public ownership of the means of production. Its opposite is capitalism, in which the means of production are owned privately. Democracy, as we saw, involves political processes, not management of production. Therefore, there have been undemocratic capitalistic countries—Franco's Spain and Mussolini's Italy—and there have been democratic communistic communities, such as those the hippies formed in British Columbia in the 1960s. Nevertheless, most communist countries have been autocratic, not democratic, and most capitalistic countries have been democratic, not autocratic. However, there is no necessary association of democracy with either capitalism or communism.

Is the Circular Organization Applicable to Organizations in Less Developed Countries?

Yes. I have had the opportunity to install the design in a variety of less developed countries in Latin America and in the near East. The idea was embraced with enthusiasm in every one of these cases. If anything, people who have been living in a less free society than ours welcome freedom when it becomes available, even if only at work.

Conclusion

The democratization of corporations is consistent with an increasing amount of dissatisfaction with the prevailing concept of what a corporation is and who owns it. Such dissatisfaction is increasingly expressed in the management literature. For example, Charles Handy (1997) has said:

> One of the great paradoxes of our time is that it is totalitarian, centrally planned organizations, owned by outsiders, that are providing the material wherewithall of the great democracies. . . .
>
> A public corporation should now be regarded not as a piece of property but as a community—although a community created by common purpose rather than a common place. No one owns a community. Communities, as democracies know them, have constitutions that recognize the rights of their different constituencies, and that lay down the methods of governance. The core members of communities are more properly regarded as citizens rather than as employees or "human resources"—citizens with responsibilities as well as rights. (27–28)

In an article in *Business Week* entitled, "The Battle for Corporate Control" (1987), Andrew C. Sigler, chairman of Champion International Corporation, said: "What right does someone who owns the stock for an hour have to decide a company's fate? That's the law and it's wrong" (103). Another corporate executive, Hicks B. Waldron, chairman of Avon Products, Inc., was also reported as saying: "We have 40,000 employees and 1.3 million representatives around the world. We have a number of suppliers, institutions, customers, communities. None of them have the democratic freedom as shareholders do to buy or sell their shares. They have much deeper and much more important stakes in our company than our shareholders" (103).

The *Business Week* article concluded with the observation: "labor's aggressive use of the tools of ownership is fast eroding the old concept that only management has the right to run the business" (107).

Therefore, the question developing for corporate management appears to be: Do we democratize *now* or have democracy imposed on us *later*? Their answer to this question depends on the answers to two other questions: Does power-to, in contrast to power-over, increase my ability to get what I want done now? and do I value power-over more than I value an increase in my ability to get what I want done, an increase that can result from replacing power-over with power-to?

10

The Internal Market Economy

In all recorded history there has not been one economist
who has had to worry about where his next meal would
come from.

—Peter Drucker

Introduction

Over the years, I have been confronted with many corporate problems involving internal finance, problems that appeared to be
very different but surprisingly turned out to have a common solution.
The solution consisted of replacing a centrally planned and controlled
corporate economy with an internal market. Before describing such an
economy, consider a few of the problems that led me to it.

A major electrical manufacturing company has two strategic
business units (SBUs) that interact a great deal. One is a
major manufacturer of small motors used in household
appliances. Though it had relatively few customers, its volume was large and it was profitable. The other division supplied electrical-equipment distributors with replacement
parts, including small motors. It, too, was profitable. The
corporation required the second SBU to buy its motors
from the first. Since both operated as profit centers, a transfer price had to be imposed on their transactions.
    Herein lies the rub, as it has wherever I have seen transfer
pricing used: it instigates conflict between the units

involved. Other manufacturers of motors operating at considerably less than capacity are willing to price their motors
marginally, hence offer them for less than the transfer price
paid by the second SBU. However, this unit was precluded
from buying externally produced motors by corporate edict.
This affected its profitability, hence its manager's compensation. As a result, he had very negative feelings about the
motor-manufacturing unit. There was no more collaboration between these two units than was required by the need
for motors.

On the other hand, the manufacturing unit could usually
get a higher price for its motors from its customers than
from the second unit. Therefore, when it was operating near
capacity and had to use some of that capacity to supply the
other internal unit, it sacrificed profit. Naturally, it resented
the second unit at least as much as the second resented it.

Transfer pricing can have even more serious consequences, as attest-
ed to by James Rinehart, former president of GM, Canada.

How was it possible in just twenty-two years for GM to have lost
so much ground? It is worth a few minutes to identify the culprits.
The root of the problem was that transfer prices from divisions
like Packard Electric were kept above competitive levels by a
deliberate policy of GM management. The result was enormous
slack that was soon filled by rising costs, leading to the noncompetitive situation . . . in 1975. (Halal, Geranmayeh, and
Pourdehnad, 1993, 146)

Rinehart went on to identify two additional problems associated with
transfer pricing, "keeping internal profitability a secret" and preventing "the end-product divisions from outsourcing any product made by
a supplying division without corporate permission." The result was

not only a loss of overall product competitiveness, but, even
worse, a lack of knowledge of what domestic competitive levels
actually were, and, beyond this, what was going on in Japan. In
1953 the fact was that GM internally supplied 65 percent of the
components as opposed to 50 percent at Ford and 35 percent at
Chrysler, was seen as a competitive advantage because it was considered greater added value. But because the 65 percent "value

added" actually consisted of inflated costs, by 1975 this supposed advantage had been transformed into a millstone around GM's neck. (146–147)

Transfer pricing, which is a surrogate for market pricing in a centrally planned and controlled economy, generally tends to produce intense internal conflict and competition. Peter Drucker once observed that competition within corporations is much more intense than competition between them and, moreover, is a lot less ethical. Corporate units usually have much more cooperative relationships with their external suppliers than with their internal sources of goods and services. As will be seen, an internal market economy can eliminate the conflict between SBUs produced by transfer pricing. It can also solve the two problems identified by Rinehart.

A different but related problem arose in Mobil Oil in the days of large mainframe computers.

> This case involved Mobil's corporate computing center and a new CEO who had just come on the job. He had a financial background and, therefore, during his orientation projected all sorts of future costs. He found that if the company's then-current trends were to continue, in a short time it would be spending more on computers than on people. He was not sure that this was the wrong thing to do, but because no measure of the value of the computing center's output was available, he asked my colleagues and me to develop a way of evaluating its output.
>
> We found that none of the internal users of the center paid directly for the services it provided. It was budgeted and subsidized from above. Since its services appeared to be costless to its users, they overloaded the center and were annoyed by the way priorities were set in the center and by the quality of the service they received. Needless to say, the head of the center reciprocated with little sympathy for the users. Because he thought that their requests were unreasonable, he was not responsive to them.
>
> We identified the major types of work done by the computing center—schedules for the refineries and shipping—but found it impossible to evaluate them. The outputs were never used directly, but were taken as an input to a qualitative judgmental process. Records of the changes made in the

computer-generated schedules and reasons for them were not kept. Therefore, we could not isolate the effects of these schedules no matter how hard we tried.

In desperation, we invoked the principle if you can't solve the problem you're facing, you must be facing the wrong problem. We asked: Why should a third party (us) be trying to evaluate a service provided by a first party to a second? Obviously, the evaluation should be made by the recipients of the services, the second party. But this could only be done if they could choose among alternative sources of the service they wanted.

Therefore, we suggested that the computing center be made a profit center that could charge its customers whatever it wanted and that the internal users be permitted to use external service organizations. In addition, we suggested that the computing center be permitted to sell its services externally.

These suggestions were accepted and implemented. The number of computers required by the internal center was significantly reduced because internal customers stopped asking for unnecessary service now that they had to pay for it. The service provided by the center improved markedly, and it acquired a substantial amount of external business. It became a profitable enterprise.

A very similar problem arose with a marketing-research group in England that was reviled by its internal users, who were allowed no alternative source of the research they needed. Essentially the same changes were made here as were made at Mobil, with similar results. The quality of the research rose significantly once the group had to compete for the opportunity to do it. After a period in which it lost almost all internal business, it was gradually regained as its internal customers saw that its external customers valued highly the sevice they received.

Situations like those described here made me reflect generally on the way internal financial decisions and transactions are usually handled in corporations. They are generally handled much the way they were in the Soviet Union, centrally planned and controlled. Then, not surprisingly, at least some of the financial problems that plague corporations in the West correspond to those encountered at the national level in the Soviet Union.

What's Wrong with a Centrally Planned and Controlled Economy?

Perestroika, the Russian word for "restructuring," was applied to the efforts of the Soviet Union to convert from a centrally planned and controlled economy to a market economy. Not one centrally planned and controlled national economy has ever attained as high a level of economic development as has been attained by national market economies. Of course, not every national market economy has flourished, but every economy that has, has been a market economy. This indicates that a market economy is necessary, but not sufficient, for an effective economy.

Recognizing that their country had developed economically as much as it could with a centrally planned and controlled economy, Gorbachev started, and Yeltsin continues, to try to convert the economy of Russia into one that is market based.

In search of economies of scale, centrally planned and controlled economies in nations and corporations tend to create internal service providers that are bureaucratic and monopolistic. In corporations, departments such as accounting, human resource, and R and D, departments are usually organized and operated as subsidized monopolies. They are subsidized in the sense that the users of their products or services do not pay for them directly. The serving units are supported financially by funds that are provided from above. The pool from which these funds are drawn is covered by an overhead charge (a "tax") imposed on the units served.

Subsidized monopolies are generally insensitive and unresponsive to the users of their services, but they are sensitive and responsive to those who subsidize them. Their subsidizers are even more removed from the users of the services than those who provide them, hence less aware of the services' deficiencies from the users' point of view.

This is only the beginning of the problems that centrally planned and controlled economies create within nations, institutions, and public and private organizations, including corporations. Other problems include bureaucratizing, oversizing, excessive layering of management along with spans of control that are too small, and disinclination to innovate and adopt innovations made by others. Bureaucracies try to ensure their survival by becoming as large as possible; they operate on the (not unreasonable) assumption that the larger they are, the more important they are and the more difficult they are to eliminate. As a result, oversizing is a congenital problem in bureaucratic organizations.

Centralized economic planning and control allows lower-level organizational units to become bloated largely because those who subsidize them get little or no feedback from those these units serve. Subsidizers use the so-called information supplied by the managers of the bureaucratic service units. This information is usually generated by managers to justify whatever their units are doing, however inefficient it may be. The current rash of down- and rightsizing activities in American corporations reflects the growing awareness of the virtually complete lack of size control that a centrally planned and controlled corporate economy exercises. (Downsizing is discussed in detail in Chapter 12.)

Centrally planned and controlled economies stimulate the increases in costs of internally provided products and services because the supplying units do not need to compare their costs and prices with those of external suppliers. Furthermore, the larger their costs, the greater their subsidy. As a result, they seldom know what their internal costs actually are. They have no systematic way of *benchmarking* them. In contrast, units operating in a competitive economy cannot survive without knowing and meeting the prices at which their competitors provide comparable goods and services.

It is almost impossible to determine the economic value of a subsidized internal unit that is a monopolistic provider of a service or product, for example, a corporate computing or telecommunication center, a centralized R and D unit, or a human resources or organizational development department. In a market economy, users, not subsidizers, evaluate suppliers and express their evaluation in a way that counts—by their purchases.

The managers of most so-called business units within corporations do not know what their total costs are. In particular, they seldom know how much capital they employ and what the cost of that capital is. Their cost of capital is usually hidden in costs allocated to them from above. How can managers reasonably be held responsible for the financial performance of their units when they do not know and therefore cannot control a large portion of their costs?

As organizations of any kind become larger and more complex, the ability of centralized controllers to know all they need to know to manage their organizations effectively diminishes. It is just not possible for them to have an adequate mental model of all the parts and their interactions. This is why a market economy works better in large systems: it disperses economic control among many enterprises that must compete with others in order to survive. And survival requires meeting or exceeding the expectations of customers and consumers.

Macro Versus Micro Economies

Why do we have one type of economy at the national level and another at the organizational and institutional level? Some argue that the economic problems of a nation are of a different magnitude and complexity than those of business enterprises, but this is not so. According to the Conference Board in 1991, 47 of the world's 100 largest economies are corporations; General Motors is number twenty. Very few nations have larger economies than GM. Even fewer are as complex.

The macro economy of the United States involves relatively autonomous competitive suppliers of goods and services. Some regulation of these units is required because, among other things, they do not have perfect information about the market or their effects on each other. Further, they do not always behave ethically or in the best interests of their stakeholders, their environments, or the systems that contain them. Centralized control is supposed to provide only enough regulation to enable the market to operate effectively.

Such considerations lead to some questions. What effects would installing market economies within corporations and public institutions have? How could this be done, and if this were done, how would their performance be affected?

Internal Market Economies

The first requirement of a market economy within a corporation is that every unit within it, including the executive office, be either a profit center or a cost center that is part of a profit center that is responsible for the cost center's performance. Units whose output cannot or should not be provided to any external user, and which have only one internal user, must necessarily be cost centers. The corporate secretary, for example, serves the chief executive officer and no one else. The same may be true of the corporate planning department. Therefore, this secretary and the planning department should operate as cost centers attached to the executive office, which—as we will see below—should operate as a profit center. A unit that produces a product whose composition or method of production is secret for competitive reasons would not be expected to operate as a profit center and, therefore, would operate as a cost center that is a part of a profit center. A unit that contains a competence that gives a corporation a unique competitive advantage should not operate as a profit center. This is analagous to a government prohibiting companies from supplying enemies with their knowledge and products during a hot or cold war.

Profit centers are not necessarily expected to be profitable, but their profitability should be taken into account in evaluating their performance. For example, a company may retain an unprofitable unit because of the prestige it brings the parent—for example, Steuben Glass at Corning—or because the unit's product is used as a loss leader. It may also be used to produce a product or provide a service that is required to complete or round out a product or service line; that is, it may facilitate the sale of other products, ones that are profitable. For example, a company may have a unit that makes razors that it sells at a loss because they require blades that are unique, are only made by that company, and are sold at a handsome profit.

Subject to a constraint discussed below, profit centers should have the freedom to buy any service or product they want from whatever source they want, and to sell their outputs to whomever they want at whatever price they want or are willing to accept. Because some corporate units may lack relevant information about other corporate units and their complex interactions, they may not act in the best interests of the corporation as a whole. Therefore, higher-level units must be able to intervene when lower-level units fail to serve these interests.

One way a corporation can add value to its business units is to provide them with internal customers they would otherwise be unlikely to obtain if they operated outside the company. Therefore, it is reasonable to require internal units that intend to purchase goods or services externally to give internal units that can supply the desired goods or services an opportunity to compete for the business. However, even if the internal supplier meets or goes under an externally quoted price, the internal buyer can elect to use the external supplier. The buying unit may choose to do so for reasons other than cost, for example, because of superior quality of products or services provided by the external supplier. Also, external suppliers cannot be expected to provide price quotes that are not even occasionally accepted. If they come to believe that asking for quotes is a hollow ritual, they will deliberately inflate the prices quoted.

The only justification for a corporation's containing a unit that is a profit center and that provides goods or services available from external—hence competitive—sources is that the unit can operate more profitably within the corporation than it can outside it. In this way, the corporation and the unit contribute to each other's value. A corporate unit that reduces the value of the corporation should not be part of it no matter how profitable it is when considered separately. Therefore, the corporation must retain the ability to intervene in a unit's purchases and sales, but should do so only when it benefits the corporation as a whole.

Executive Overrides

At times a corporate executive may believe that a purchase made by a subordinate unit from an external source, even at a lower price than an internal supplier would charge, would be harmful to the corporation. For example, putting the order outside might require the internal supplier to lay off employees, and this would cost more than is saved by buying from the external supplier. Moreover, the company wants to stabilize employment as much as possible in order to maintain a high morale. A high morale pays off in greater productivity and quality of outputs. In such a case, the executive can require that the purchase be made from the internal supplier, but that *executive* must pay for the difference between the internal and external price. This means that the buying unit will *not* have to pay more than it would have had to pay if it had been free to buy from the external source. In addition, since an executive who overrides a subordinate unit will also be a profit center or part of one, he or she will have to consider explicitly the benefits as well as the costs of such interventions.

In a corporation that had just converted to an internal market economy, an executive vice president consistently required one internal unit to buy a major component of its product line from another internal unit. In many cases, the component could have been obtained externally for less money. As a result, at the end of the first year the vice president had paid several million dollars for his overrides. He could not identify what this expenditure had bought for the corporation. Therefore, he reevaluated his policy and decided to free the units to do as they wanted the following year. Not only did each unit improve its financial performance, but these previously antagonistic units became friendly and cooperative, and the executive stopped feeling like a referee of a prize fight, disliked by both parties.

When a corporate executive believes a sale to an external customer that an internal unit wants to make is not in the corporation's best interests, he or she can override the sale, but only by providing the internal unit with the amount of profit it would have made from that sale. This means that a selling unit will never have to sell its output at a price lower than it wants to and can.

When a manager believes that an external purchase or sale should never be made, he or she can act like a government, relative to his or her subordinate units, by establishing appropriate restrictive rules or regulations. The federal government of the United States prevents the sale of certain (e.g., military) products to certain foreign countries because it considers such sales to be against our national interests. Corporate managers may act similarly. For example, they may preclude use of an external source to make a food product sold by the company because the product's formula is considered to be of competitive value. Coca-Cola is not about to allow an external supplier make Coke syrup.

The override provision of the internal market economy to a large extent makes operational the *management of interactions*. A manager does not tell his or her subordinate units what to buy and sell and where to do so unless he perceives some negative effect on other parts of the corporation or the corporation as a whole. His concern is with the interactions of subordinate units and their interactions with the rest of the corporation, not their actions taken separately.

The Executive Unit

As noted earlier, the executive unit operates as a profit center. It incurs costs when it overrides purchasing or selling decisions of subordinate units. It also incurs other types of cost, for example, for externally provided services, for interest on money it has borrowed for taxes, and for dividends.

The executive unit has two major sources of income. First, it charges for the operating and investment capital it supplies to subordinate units. This charge should cover more than its cost of the capital obtained from external sources. Presumably, it obtains capital at a lower price than its subordinate units could. If not, they might be better off outside the corporation. The difference between the actual cost of the capital and what the units would otherwise have to pay might well be divided between the executive office and the units. The way it is divided can reflect the riskiness of the proposed use of the capital by the units involved.

This aspect of the internal market economy makes corporate units aware of the amount of capital they use and how well they use it. They can calculate their return on the capital they employ. Therefore, they are more likely to use it effectively and sparingly than they would in a centrally planned and controlled corporate economy.

The second source of income to the executive unit is a tax it imposes on the profitability of each unit. It operates both as an owner as well as a bank. As such, it has a right to share in the value it adds to its units. The tax on profits that it levies should cover the operating cost of the executive unit, and the taxes it must pay to various governmental agencies. It should charge units directly for any services or facilities it provides to its units, for example, rental for office space, which includes the cost of utilities, janitorial services, telephone services, and so on.

When Imperial Oil of Canada initiated such charges, a number of units moved out of corporate headquarters to less expensive facilities that they also considered to be better located. Eventually, headquarters itself moved to less expensive facilities.

The tax rate established by the executive unit should be specified in advance of the period in which it is applied, with the participation of the taxed units. There should be no taxation without representation. The circular organization facilitates such representation.

Profit Accumulation

Each profit center should be permitted to accumulate profit up to a level set by negotiation with the executive office. This level will vary by unit, reflecting its ability to invest or use capital profitably. Profit accumulated up to that limit should be available to the unit for its discretionary use as long as that use can be shown not to have an adverse effect on any other part of the corporation or the corporation as a whole. If a unit's use of its discretionary capital has any effect on another unit or units, the ones affected must agree to it. If they don't, it goes for resolution to the lowest level of management at which the affected units converge.

Accumulations of capital in excess of the specified amount should be passed up to the corporate level for its use. A unit that provides its excess profit to the corporation should be paid interest on it by the executive office. The rate of interest paid to the unit should be the same as that paid by the unit to the corporation for the capital it employs. This, in effect, reduces the amount of capital it has taken from the corporation by the amount it turns back to it. When the amount turned back to the corporation exceeds the unit's debt to the corporation, it would receive the same rate of interest the corporation pays for capital it borrows from external sources. This would be added to its discretionary funds, which it could use as it sees fit. This arrangement changes the status of cash cows in the organization; they come to be seen as major sources of capital for investment in growth of other parts of the corporation and the corporation itself, and they would be able to use their discretionary funds to provide their members with an enviable quality of work life.

Public Sector Applications

The use of internal market economies is by no means restricted to private for-profit organizations. It can be and has been used effectively in the public sector and in not-for-profit organizations. It should be borne in mind that profit is not at all irrelevant to those not-for-profit organizations that do not depend on charity or subsidies for survival. The principal difference between unsubsidized not-for-profit and for-profit organizations lies in how they can use the profit they make. For both, profit is necessary for survival, but not the reason for it.

A familiar example of the use of a market economy in the public sector is the proposed use of educational vouchers. This idea was originally developed by Christopher Jenks of Harvard University (1970), publicized by Milton Friedman (1973), and expanded by Ackoff (1974). In the latter version, the only income a public school would receive would be obtained from cashing vouchers, supplied by local governments, given to it by parents of children who have applied to and been accepted by the school. Children and their parents would be able to apply to any school they wanted. Applicants would have to be accepted by schools that are responsible for the area in which they live. Schools that could accept vouchers would, when they had more applicants from outside their areas of responsibility than openings, have to select randomly from among them. Every school that could cash in vouchers would have a rated capacity and would not be permitted to go beyond it.

When an applicant is accepted by a public school in an area in which they do not reside, that school receives the voucher and the school in the area in which they live must provide the student with transportation to the accepting school or its cost by other means. Vouchers can also be used to cover all or part of the tuition required by private schools. However, transportation costs to private schools would not be covered by the local public school.

The voucher system not only puts public schools into competition with each other, but it also makes them compete with private schools. Only those schools survive that provide a service sufficiently valued by students and their parents to induce them to turn over their vouchers to them.

It is worth noting that because schools are required to select among applicants from outside their areas of responsibility at random, segregation in schools would become a nonissue. If it occurred, it would be by choice.

To take another example:

> A centralized licensing bureau in Mexico City had a terrible record of inefficiency and poor service. It was broken up into small offices that were placed in each section (*colonia*) of the city. The income of each office was derived exclusively from a fee paid to it by the city government for each license it issued. (The amount varied by type of license.) Those wanting a license could obtain it from any office. Unlike the one centralized bureaucratic monopoly that these offices replaced, the new offices could only survive by attracting and satisfying customers. Service time decreased, service quality increased, and overall costs and corruption within the offices decreased.

The moral here is that it is much better to subsidize users than suppliers because doing so puts the choice of supplier in consumers' hands and thus forces the suppliers to compete for their business. The use of food stamps to subsidize the poor is much more effective than subsidizing food distributors. An internal market economy can be employed by many government service agencies and, to the extent that it is, pressure to privatize these services can be significantly reduced.

Possible Disadvantages

Proposals for the introduction of a market economy in an organization usually give rise to four types of concerns.

First, skeptics argue that the additional amount of accounting required by such a system would be horrendous. Not true. The amount of accounting required is actually reduced because most of the accounting and reporting currently done by organizational units is done to facilitate their control by higher-level units. In an internal market economy, however, all that needs to be provided to higher-level units are the equivalent of a profit-and-loss statement and a balance sheet. Any additional information requested by a higher-level unit should be paid for by that unit. This has a strong tendency to reduce the amount of unnecessary information flowing up within organizations.

Second, some argue that an internal market economy will increase conflict and competition between internal units. Again, not true. Most organizational units have much better relations with their external suppliers than they do with internal units whose services or products they are forced to use or with whom they compete for scarce resources. Internal suppliers who must compete with external suppliers for internal business are much more responsive to internal customers than monopolistic internal suppliers.

Third, those who reject the adoption of an internal market economy argue that it cannot be installed in a part of an organization, only in the whole. It is asserted that a partial installation may be very difficult, if not impossible, to arrange. Difficult, yes, but not impossible. Even the difficulty depends to a large extent on the amount of autonomy the part has within the whole.

> KAD—Kodak's manufacturing arm that produces all of its products except film—converted to an internal market economy. The first problem it faced derived from the fact that the corporation of which it is a part did not convert to an internal market economy. As a result, KAD had to operate as a market-oriented economy within an economy that was centrally planned and controlled.
>
> The corporation continued its overhead assessment on KAD for corporately provided services, whether or not KAD used them. KAD could not break these charges down into those for services it used and those it didn't. Therefore, KAD had to develop surrogate costs. It treated the estimated cost of corporately provided services that it did not use as a tax. Furthermore, it had to continue reporting to the corporation as it had before it had converted to an internal market economy. Therefore, it had to maintain one set of books for the corporation and another for itself. It continues to evaluate itself as though it were operating within an internal market economy. It has been a bright spot in an often bleak environment.

Like KAD in Kodak, the R and D unit of Esso Petroleum Canada, a division of Imperial Oil, also converted to an internal market economy within a centrally controlled corporate economy, but in this case, the corporation tried to facilitate the conversion. It did so because it considered the R and D conversion to be a trial, which, if successful, would lead it to support similar conversions of other units and eventually of the whole corporation.

Fourth, another reason often given for not taking the idea of an internal market economy seriously is that certain internal service functions cannot "reasonably" be expected to obtain external customers. Accounting is often cited as an example. Nevertheless, one corporation headquartered in a small city in the Midwest converted its accounting department into a profitable business unit. Many local small- and medium-sized companies lacked access to high-quality professional accountants and wanted its services badly. This enabled the accounting department to sell its services externally at a very good price. One consequence of this was that the quality of the services it rendered improved significantly; it had to in order to retain external customers. It also led to the formation of several significant strategic alliances.

In the same corporation, the art department that prepared the corporation's displays for conventions, audiovisual presentations, and print illustrations remained in the corporation but became a profitable business.

Some Added Advantages of an Internal Market Economy

A number of the benefits of an internal market economy have already been discussed, in particular, increased responsiveness of internal suppliers, better quality and lower cost of internally supplied services and products, elimination of fluff, debureaucratization, and demonopolization. In addition, as we will see in Chapter 12, the need for drastic downsizing is also eliminated. A few other advantages are worth mentioning.

First, because virtually every corporate unit operating within an internal market economy becomes a profit center, the same measures of performance can be applied to each of them. This makes it possible to compare performances of units that were previously not comparable, for example, manufacturing and accounting.

Second, the manager of a profit center within an internal corporate market economy is necessarily a general manager of a semi-autonomous business unit. This provides all unit managers with opportunities to improve their general management skills and to display their ability. Therefore, it enables executives to evaluate the general management ability of their subordinates better than they can otherwise.

Third, when units are converted to profit centers and are given the autonomy that goes with it, their managers are in a much better position to obtain all the information they require to manage well. They become more concerned with providing themselves with the information they want than with providing their superiors with the information they want.

Fourth, a major advantage of an internal market economy is that it automatically takes care of potential outsourcing.

> A company that occupied a number of buildings in a suburb of a major metropolitan area converted its facilities-and-services department (buildings, grounds, and utilities) into a profit center that operated within a corporate internal market economy. All of its internal users shifted to outside agencies from which they obtained better services at a lower cost than had been provided by the internal unit. As a result the service department gradually shrank and was eventually eliminated at a considerable saving to the company.

As we will see in Chapter 12, a company involved in eliminating a department has a responsibility for finding productive employment for those displaced by this act.

Finally, it should be apparent that organizational units that have to compete with external suppliers are much more likely to adopt and adapt relevant innovations by others. They are also more likely to innovate themselves. There is no more effective way of competing than by developing a unique and superior service or product that can be offered at an attractive price.

Conclusions

Conversion to an internal market economy obviously raises a number of implementation problems. Therefore, it is not a task that attracts the fainthearted; it requires considerable courage. Moreover, conversion to an internal market economy is risky for those managers whose units either are unable to compete effectively in the open market or are no longer needed within the corporation. Such units are very likely to be eliminated in an internal market economy. The fact that they should be eliminated offers little solace to those who are affected. The possibility of creating activities that will use excess nonmanagerial personnel productively is seldom considered in such circumstances. (It should and can be, as we will see in Chapter 12.) Nevertheless, the managers who are responsible for the excesses and the layoffs that correct them are usually retained and rewarded for reducing costs, and most are moved to other jobs within the corporation.

A major obstruction to the conversion to an internal market economy is the reluctance of many higher-level managers to share with their subordinates information to which they alone have had access. To be sure, information is power, and many managers are not willing to share their power. Unfortunately, they fail to recognize that there are two kinds of power, power-over and power-to. Internal market economies may decrease managers' power-over, but they more than make up for this by increasing their power-to. Unfortunately, this is no consolation to those who value power-over for its own sake and value it over power-to. Those who want authority for its own sake do not fit into a democratic organization.

The conversion to internal market economies by American corporations can provide them with an opportunity to increase their effectiveness by an order of magnitude. Such restructuring is as important to our country on the microeconomics level as it was to the Soviet Union on the macroeconomics level. Without it we will inevitably experience economic decline.

Further discussion and examples of the internal market economy can be found in Halal (1996) and Halal, Geranmayeh, and Pourdehand (1993).

11

The Permanently Structured
Multidimensional Organization

We trained hard—but it seemed that every time we were
beginning to form into teams, we would be reorganized. I
was to learn later in life that we tend to meet any new situation by reorganizing and what a wonderful method it can be
for creating the illusion of progress while producing confusion, inefficiency, and demoralization.

—Petronius Arbiter (210 B.C.)

Introduction

Because American corporations are in a rapidly changing and increasingly complex environment, they reorganize frequently. In fact, some
appear to reorganize continuously. A great deal of time, energy, money,
and morale are consumed in this process.

Among employees, the possibility of layoffs, often associated with
reorganization, is very unsettling and frequently leads to decreased
productivity and quality of output. In order to be inconspicuous when
further layoffs are believed to be in the offing, innovation comes to a
virtual halt; it is too risky.

At the organization level, most institutions and enterprises seek
what Donald Schon (1971) called a "stable state." Like a coiled spring,
their resistance to change tends to be proportional to the effort to
change them; the more turbulent their environment, the more stability
they seek. But the only equilibrium that can be obtained in a turbulent

environment is dynamic, like that of an airplane flying through a storm.

However, reorganization is only one possible way of adapting to change. If it were possible to design an organization that could adapt to change without reorganizing, with less disruptive interventions, then the resistance to change would likely be significantly reduced. Such an organizational design *is* possible and has, in fact, been used. It is called *multidimensional*.

The Multidimensional (MD) Design

The Multidimensional Design (MD) concept was originally developed at Dow Corning by chairman of its board and CEO, W. C. Goggin (1974). However, what is presented here is a variation on Goggin's theme. To understand how the design presented here eliminates the need to reorganize when faced with a significant internal or external change, it is first necessary to understand the nature of organization.

The need to organize derives from the need to divide labor. To organize is to divide labor among different individuals or groups and to coordinate their activities in such a way as to obtain a desired output. The more divided the labor, the more coordination is required. In a typical organization chart, the horizontal dimension shows how labor is divided at each level, that is, how responsibility is allocated. The vertical dimension shows how labor at different levels is coordinated and integrated, that is, how authority is allocated.

There are only three ways of dividing labor and, therefore, only three types of organizational unit:

1. *functionally defined (input) units,* the outputs of which are principally consumed or used internally, for example, purchasing, finance, legal, personnel, R and D, building and grounds, industrial relations, and parts manufacturing departments;
2. *product- or service-defined (output) units,* the outputs of which are principally consumed or used externally, for example, the beer, entertainment, and metal container parts of Anheuser-Busch Companies;
3. *market-, or user-defined units,* which are usually identified by the classification of external customers to whom the organization tries to sell the outputs of its product- and service-defined units, for example, units defined by the geographic areas they sell in—such as North and South America, Europe,

Asia, and African divisions—or units defined by categories of users—such as ultimate consumers, retailers, and wholesalers.

Most organizations, and corporations in particular, have all three types of unit. They are seldom taken to be equally important, and their importance is ordered in the structure of most organizations. Judgment of that importance is usually based on what is believed to be most essential for survival or success in the organization's current environment: monopolies do not rank user-defined units highly. If product uniqueness is most important, then product-defined units dominate. If costs are the primary concern or if there are very few products involved, functionally defined units are likely to be the most important. In a country that has all functions in each of a number of counties, it is very likely to be organized by regionally defined markets.

Organizations are normally designed from the top down, beginning with the chief executive officer (CEO) and sometimes a Chief Operating Officer (COO). In designing the first level at which labor is divided, the level below the CEO and COO, one or more of the three criteria for division are used. At each successively lower level, labor is again divided, with one or more criteria used at each level. The higher the level at which a criterion is used, the more importance is attributed to it. Therefore, the resulting organizational design always reflects the relative importance attributed to each criterion: function, product or service, and market.

Now it is possible to understand the nature of reorganizations. *All reorganizations involve changing the relative importance of the three criteria used in dividing labor,* that is, changing the organizational levels at which units of the three types appear.

A reorganization typically takes place when a corporation whose senior vice presidents are defined, say, by their functions have their functions changed to ones involving coordination of activities in market areas. The functionally defined units are moved down the organizational hierarchy and made to report to market-defined units, not the executive office or officer. This has happened in many globally expanding corporations. They begin by establishing small units in a foreign country that report back to functionally or product-defined units in the home country. As the units increase in size and number, it usually becomes necessary to coordinate them from a country's point of view. User-defined units are moved up and are made to dominate the other types.

Reordering the criteria used in an organization's design may be required by a change in either its environment, in the organization itself, or in its role or function in the larger system of which it is part. A change in AT&T's environment occurred when it was deregulated and for the first time had to deal with competitors such as MCI and Sprint. This increased the relative importance of marketing and reduced the importance of functions and products/services. An increase in the number of products and their differences, such as occurs in diversification programs—for example, when Pepsi-Cola acquired Frito-Lay and fast-food chains—may require elevating the importance of product-defined units. Then, *if units of all three types are established at a particular level of an organization, as their relative importance changes all that is required at that level is a reallocation of resources among them. Their reorganization is not required.*

Therefore, if the three types of unit are established at every level of an organization, the need to reorganize at any time is completely eliminated. Units of any of the three types can be added or subtracted without requiring reorganization; the organization's structure remains the same.

Figure 11.1 shows a simplified version of a multidimensional organization. The surface of each cube represents the interactions of two units of different types. Each cube represents the interactions, if any, of three units, one of each type. Not all units of an organization necessar-

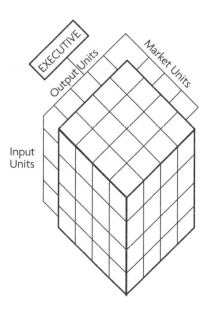

Figure 11.1   A simple multidimensional design

ily interact. Therefore, not every possible type of interaction would necessarily take place in a multidimensional organization.

Note that the three-dimensional representation of an organization makes it possible to show explicitly the interactions that should or do take place between units. Conventional representations of organizational structures do not indicate the interactions of units. Most of the interactions between units of a conventionally organized corporation take place between units that are not directly connected structurally. Therefore, their interactions are not shown on conventional organization charts and are frequently not in the mind of the lowest-level manager where the interacting units converge. Little wonder, then, that managers are more concerned with how their subordinate units act than on their interactions.

The three-dimensional representation of a multidimensional organization shown in Figure 11.1 is not one most organizations like to use. They prefer a representation such as is shown in Figure 11.2. A still more conventional but less commonly used representation is shown in Figure 11.3. It eliminates the ability to show interactions of units.

An example of a multidimensional organization is provided at the end of this chapter. It should be borne in mind that every application of the multidimensional design is a variation on the theme presented here; no two are exactly alike.

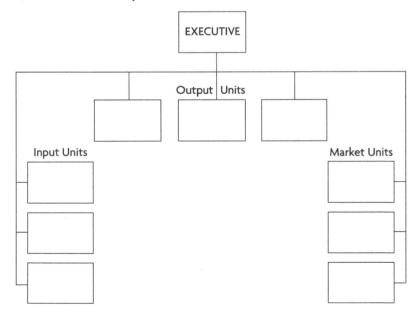

Figure 11.2   Usual representation of a multidimensional organization

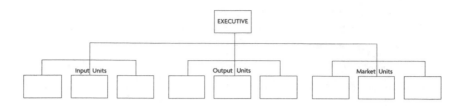

Figure 11.3   Conventional representation of a multidimensional organization

Descriptions of Types of Units

Although a multidimensional design can be used without an internal market economy, the value of each concept is greatly increased when the two are used together. Therefore, this combination is assumed in the descriptions provided here, but it is easy enough to separate the two concepts and conceptualize the multidimensional organization independently of the internal market economy.

Product- or Service-Defined (Output) Units

In a multidimensional organization, product- and service-defined (output) units consist of a management and only a small supporting staff, but no other personnel, and no facilities other than what is required to house this small number of people. There is an exception: if an output unit is the exclusive user of another internal unit—for example, a production facility—then that unit is made a part of the output unit it serves.

Notice the similarity of these units to brand-managed units in consumer-goods industries.

Output units make direct payments to all their internal or external suppliers for the services, facilities, and products they receive. Therefore, they usually require no investment since they have no fixed assets, but they do need operating capital. They receive all the income generated by the sale of their product(s) and service(s). They also receive income from lending their parent organization or organizational unit any excess capital they generate.

Product- and service-defined units are responsible for providing or arranging for all the activities required to make their products and services available to customers. In an internal market economy, all of them are profit centers. However, as discussed in Chapter 10, not all of them need be profitable. Some may deal with new products just being introduced and some may be used for products that serve as loss leaders. However, because they are operated as profit centers, their cost is known to the organization as a whole.

For example, at one university that operated with an internal market economy, any academic department that incurred a loss for three consecutive years came up before a faculty committee for possible discontinuation. Of the first three that came up for such consideration, two were discontinued because they were at best of mediocre quality. The third was retained because of its excellence and international reputation. In one department, each professor was also treated as a profit center. One who ended the year "in the red" was not eligible for a salary increase. This had a greater and better effect on professorial activity than anything else that had ever been tried; they were now all anxious to teach or do research.

Output units must buy all the inputs (goods and services) they require, and they are free to do so from any internal or external source they choose. This freedom is subject to an override by a higher authority such as was discussed in Chapter 10. Recall that the cost of an override is borne by the manager who is responsible for it, not the one(s) affected by it.

These units obtain income from sale of their products or services. If they require more capital than they generate or accumulate, they can apply for it from a higher level of the organization. They are expected to treat such funds as loans or investments. They must pay for their use, one way or another.

In an internal market economy, the profits that product- or service-defined units generate are subject to a tax levied by a higher level of management. The tax rate applied should be designated in advance of the relevant period. It should not be so large as to deprive profitable units of discretionary funds. Units should be able to use some of their profits as they see fit, for example, to improve old products, develop new ones, or open new markets. However, as discussed in Chapter 10, the accumulation of discretionary funds should be limited to the largest amount they can invest with an acceptable return rate. Excessive accumulation of profit reflects an inability to find profitable uses for it. Therefore, excesses should be passed up to a higher level at which they can be used profitably.

Product- and service-defined units are easy to add or subtract because they usually have no fixed assets and they involve only a relatively small number of people. It is more difficult to add or subtract an output unit when it contains an input unit of which it is the exclusive internal user.

Function-Defined Input Units

Units whose outputs are consumed primarily by other internal units are functionally defined, or input units. Examples are units that provide such services as manufacturing, transportation, warehousing, data processing, personnel, legal, and accounting. They may also supply or serve external customers, but this is a minor responsibility. However, if and when they begin to do more external than internal business, they should be converted to product- or service-defined units.

Functional units are often divided into two types, one defined as "operations" and the other as "service." Operation units are ones that have a direct effect on the output (operations) of the organization, for example, manufacturing, maintenance, and purchasing. Service units have no such effect; they affect the nonoperational behavior of other units, for example, accounting, data processing, and human resources. There is nothing absolute about the distinction between these types of unit. Any distinction may be used when the number of input units is too large to be coordinated by one manager.

Some functional units—for example, parts manufacturing and assembly—need facilities and equipment as well as personnel. Therefore, these units may require investment, as well as operating, capital. As is the case with product- and service-defined units, functional units can apply to a higher level of the organization for more capital than they can generate or retain. Such investments or loans must be treated as though they were externally provided, that is, they must be bought.

In an internal market economy, functional units are free both to purchase whatever they need and to sell whatever they produce or provide, either internally or externally. Their purchasing and selling decisions are subject to intervention from above and to compensation for such intervention when appropriate. They receive the income that their sales generate, and they pay the cost of whatever they purchase.

If the executive office observes that an important externally provided product or service is consumed heavily within the organization, it may vertically integrate by creating an appropriate functional unit or

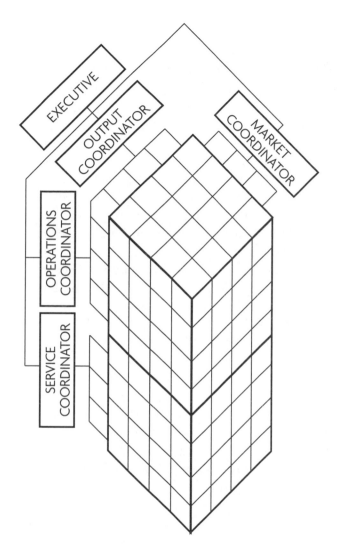

Figure 11.4   A multidimensional organization with a divided dimension

extend an existing one to provide that product or service. In general, it would do so only if it believes it can provide such a product or service with either a superior quality or lower cost than it can get externally. On the other hand, if the executive office observes that a product or service that can be obtained internally is usually procured externally by other units and then determines that this is because of a cost or quality advantage, it may eliminate the internal providing unit and outsource.

An organization's structure need not be changed to accommodate either the addition or deletion of a functional unit.

Market- or User-Defined Units

Market units—units that are defined by the users they serve—have two complementary functions. First, they sell the outputs of any other unit in the organization that wants to use their services. They are also free to sell their services externally, subject to the type of executive override discussed in Chapter 10; for example, the detail men of some large pharmaceutical companies who also sell the products of some smaller companies, for a fee, enable the companies to spread the cost of having professionally trained detail (sales) personnel calling on physicians. Second, market units also serve as advocates of the users in the markets for which they are responsible. They should not only represent the company in the market, but also the market in the company.

In an internal market economy, market units operate as profit centers. As such, they can generate discretionary funds. These can be used to initiate old-product improvements and new-product development. These developments may be sold internally or externally, subject to the usual executive override. Their income can be in the form of a commission on sales or fixed fees, or they may buy products from their internal or external producers and resell them at a profit. Where a company markets in foreign countries from which it is difficult to remove profits in cash, a trading company can be established as a marketing unit. It takes profit out in the form of products that it then sells in countries from which cash can be withdrawn. Such trading companies can be excellent hedges against devaluation of the currency in a foreign country. When the value of its currency goes down, the profit on sales of its product in other countries usually goes up.

In their advocacy role, market units evaluate the activities and outputs of other internal units from the point of view of potential and actual users of the organization's outputs, who are outside the corporation and are, or can be, affected by these outputs. This can help organizations identify unexploited opportunities and actual or potential threats. Therefore, market units can operate as consultants to the executive office and other unit heads. Market units should be paid for such service and be free to provide it to external noncompetitive organizations where doing so does not conflict with corporate objectives.

Because market units have few or no fixed assets, they can easily be added, subtracted, or otherwise modified.

Unit Designs

Many units in an MD organization can themselves be designed in three dimensions. Moreover, this can be done even where the organization as a whole or higher- or lower-level units have not been so designed. Figure 11.5 shows the type of variation of the MD design employed in the redesign of the Iranian Ministry of Health before the revolution in that country. (It was one of the few branches of the government that was not reorganized after the shah was dethroned.) The country was divided into regions (units), and each was given a multidimensional organization of the type described above. However, the headquarters, consisting of the minister, his deputy ministers, and the regional directors, was organized conventionally. In general, geographically distinct multidimensional units can be created where the regions are at least partially autonomous from a political point of view. For example, in a multinational corporation, national units may be organized multidimensionally even if the corporation isn't. Similarly, in a conglomerate, strategic business units can be organized multidimensionally even if the corporation itself is not.

In R and D organizations, programs consisting of two or more projects have been organized multidimensionally, with their projects set

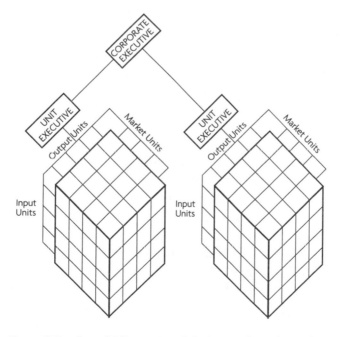

Figure 11.5   A multidimensional design at the subunit level

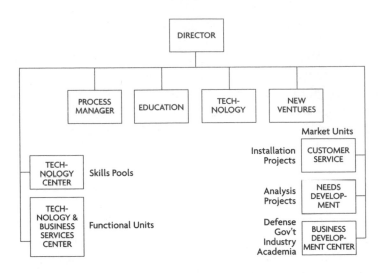

Figure 11.6   Multidimensional design of an R and D organization

up as output units and skill groups as input units. However, such programs have reported to conventionally organized top managements. For example, a software R and D unit that is part of a large research organization, which develops, installs, manages, services, and educates users and operators of large computer software systems, is organized, as shown on Figure 11.6.

A multidimensional structure can sometimes be used at even the lowest organizational level. For example, a graphic reproduction unit can assign purchasing and billing to some individuals, operation of different reproduction equipment to other individuals, and marketing of its services to other members. Several different functions can be assigned to a single individual.

Every unit in an MD organization can be organized as the organization as a whole is. This is most apparent in the case of functional units, particularly manufacturing. Functional subunits of a manufacturing unit might include purchasing, stores, maintenance, quality control, and so on. A manufacturing unit that sells parts and component production, subassembly, and assembly may organize service units accordingly. Its market subunits can be organized to match its internal or external customers or to match both. An example of a multidimensionally designed functional (manufacturing) unit of a large corporation is shown in Figure 11.7.

In the limiting case, two or more multidimensional units can share all or some of their subunits along any one dimension, as shown in

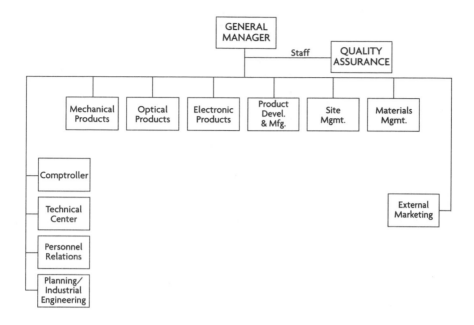

Figure 11.7   Multidimensional design of a manufacturing division

Figure 11.8. The input (functional) and user (market) dimensions are the ones most commonly shared. For example, two multidimensionally structured strategic business units may share their marketing because their products are complementary, or they may share such services as accounting, building and grounds, and data processing in order to obtain economies of scale.

Product and service units can be further divided into narrower product and service subunits using, say, brands, models, or sizes to define them. For example, each subbrand of Chevrolets or Fords could be set up as an output unit with the equivalent of a brand manager. Such subunits would be larger and as complex as many corporations.

Subunits of a market unit that is defined nationally can be defined by subdivisions of the nation involved, for example, states or regions of the country. Functional subunits might include market research, media purchasing, and special events specialists. Finally, since a marketing unit in an internal market economy can have external users, it may itself have a marketing activity that has responsibility for selling its services.

Although multidimensional design can be applied at any level of an organization, in practice it has tended to be employed mostly at the upper level of organizations or in semiautonomous business units.

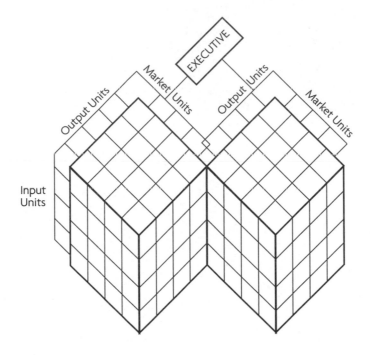

Figure 11.8   Two multidimensional units with a common dimension

Multidimensional Design of Large Organizations

If the number of units of any one type is too large to report directly to the chief executive, one or more coordinating executives can be used for each dimension, as shown in Figure 11.4. If the number of units in any one dimension is too large for one coordinator, more than one coordinator can be used, as is the case relative to input units in Figure 11.4. For example, functional units may be divided into two groups, operations (line) and services (staff), or into administrative services and human resources. Product units may be divided into broad product categories such as automobiles, trucks, buses, and tractors or research and technical planning, products and services, and information systems and processing center. Markets can be grouped geographically and marketing activities can be classified functionally, for example, into customer assistance center, account management, and customer service center.

Coordinating executives may be incorporated into the executive office.

Multidimensional Design Versus Matrix Organizations

Those familiar with matrix organizations will recognize their superficial resemblance to the multidimensional design presented here. Davis and Lawrence (1977), who are prominent proponents of the matrix, refer to multidimensional organizations as merely an expansion of a matrix organization (234). Not so.

Davis and Lawrence wrote:

> We believe that the most useful definition [of the matrix organization] is based on the feature of a matrix organization that most clearly distinguishes it from conventional organizations. That is its abandonment of the age-old precept of "1 man-1 boss" or a single chain of command in favor of a "2-boss" or multiple command system. So we define matrix as any organization that employs a multiple command system that includes not only a multiple command structure but also related support mechanisms and an associated organizational culture and behavior pattern. (3)

The principal difference between MD and matrix organizations lies precisely in the fact that in matrix organizations employees have two bosses. One is the head of the input unit of which they are a part, the other is the head of the output unit to which they are assigned. According to Jay Galbraith (1973), "They jointly determine his chances for promotion and his salary increase, and they determine performance goals with him," and later, "the matrix design institutionalizes an adversary system" (105). This property of the design produces what might be called "organizational schizophrenia." When an employee's bosses do not agree or have different value systems, the employee does not know how to behave. This can be very stressful. The decision on to whom to pay attention is usually made politically rather than in the best interests of the organization. The multidimensional design creates no such problem.

In a multidimensional organization, members of one unit whose services have been purchased by another unit are related to the head of the second unit in the same way they are to an external customer. They have only one boss, the head of the unit of which they are a part. The head of the unit for which they are working is their *client*, not their boss. Their boss may or may not use the client's evaluation of the server in evaluating the server. Those in one unit of an organization who work for another unit in that organization—for example, computer programmers who write programs for other parts of the organization—know who their bosses are and who their customers or clients are. Because it is much easier for a dissatisfied customer or clients to dismiss an unsatisfactory server than for a boss to dismiss an unsatisfactory subordinate, servers tend to be very responsive to their clients, particularly when the clients are paying the server's units for their work.

Furthermore, matrix organizations normally have only two dimensions, inputs and outputs, and no market units. If marketing is a separate function in a matrix organization, it is either incorporated in output units or set up as an input unit.

If marketing is organized as a functional unit rather than on a third dimension, the result is a two-dimensional organization, not a matrix, because employees do not have two bosses and most units are profit centers. The elimination of the market dimension may reduce organizational flexibility and sensitivity to the needs and desires of customers and consumers. In particular, it eliminates the role of marketing personnel as advocates of actual and potential customers and consumers. However, there are situations in which marketing is clearly best done by those who produce the product or service offered to the outside world. This was the case for ALAD (Armco's Latin American Division).

This metal-producing business unit, a subsidiary of Armco, a multinational company, operated in eight different countries. Its design was two dimensional because it incorporated marketing into its product (output) units. It did so because of the substantial amount of technical content of its products and the desire of its customers to have direct contact with the producers of the products they bought. ALAD's design is shown in Figure 11.9, which also shows the company's explanatory notes. This organization also adopted an internal market economy and circular organization.

Since matrix organizations are seldom endowed with internal market economies, their functional units are usually subsidized and therefore often tend to become bureaucratic monopolies that are more interested in their own survival than service to the organization of which they are part. Their users seldom have alternative sources of supply, and they seldom have users outside the organization. Furthermore, because product and service (output) units in a matrix organization can have large investments in facilities and equipment and large complements of personnel, they are much more difficult to add to and subtract from a matrix organization than output units from a multidimensional organization. Recall that the latter usually include little but management and operating capital.

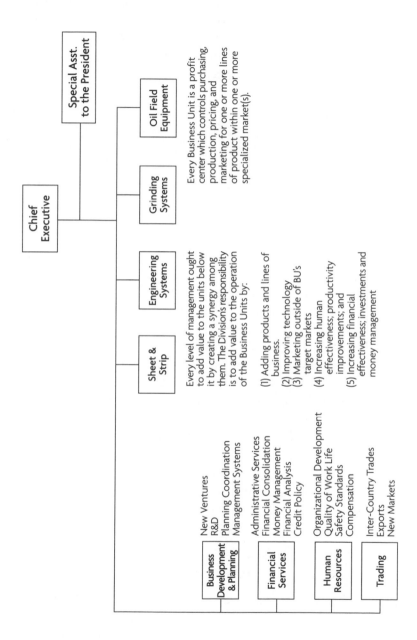

Figure 11.9 Multidimensional design of ALAD (ARMCO's Latin American Division)

Chief Executive

Special Asst. to the President

Sheet & Strip

Engineering Systems

Grinding Systems

Oil Field Equipment

Every level of management ought to add value to the units below it by creating a synergy among them. The Division's responsibility is to add value to the operation of the Business Units by:

(1) Adding products and lines of business.
(2) Improving technology
(3) Marketing outside of BU's target markets
(4) Increasing human effectiveness; productivity improvements; and
(5) Increasing financial effectiveness; investments and money management

Every Business Unit is a profit center which controls purchasing, production, pricing, and marketing for one or more lines of product within one or more specialized market(s).

Business Development & Planning
New Ventures
R&D
Planning Coordination
Management Systems

Financial Services
Administrative Services
Financial Consolidation
Money Management
Financial Analysis
Credit Policy

Human Resources
Organizational Development
Quality of Work Life
Safety Standards
Compensation

Trading
Inter-Country Trades
Exports
New Markets

Program and Zero-Based Budgeting

Program and zero-based budgeting is a way that managers can prepare budgets for subordinate input and output units that begins with the assumption that no financial obligations are carried from the past into the future. It starts from scratch. Programs are output units, hence program budgets are prepared initially only for them. These are then broken down into the costs for services or products required of input units. In this way, input-unit budgets are the result of aggregating the parts of output-unit budgets that are allocated to the input units. The intent of such budgeting is that programs be adequately financed and that supporting activities be no larger than required by the programs.

Program budgeting may be, but seldom is, associated with an internal market economy because in a multidimensional organization that has an internal market economy, managers do not prepare budgets for their subordinate units. As is currently the case with corporations as a whole, each unit in such an organization prepares its own budget. Higher levels invest in, lend money to, and extract money from lower-level units, but they do not prepare their budgets.

Program budgeting normally does not affect organizational design (although it is more compatible with matrix organizations than with traditional ones), and it has no effect on organizational flexibility. Such budgeting does make it easier to eliminate make-work and to estimate the financial requirements of both output and input units, assuming that the output units must use the input units as their sources of supply. Therefore, program budgeting does nothing by way of benchmarking input activities; it provides no comparison of internal costs with those that would be incurred by using external sources of supply. Internally provided support services may well be excessively costly without this being revealed by the budgeting procedure. In an MD organization with an internal market economy, every input unit competes against external sources of their outputs. Therefore, in such an organization, benchmarking is automatic and continuous.

An Example

The Great Atlantic and Pacific Tea Company (A&P) had been in trouble since the early 1970s. Mounting losses had resulted in several changes in management and ownership, and the number of stores had been cut from about thirty-five hundred in 1974 to about a thousand in March, 1982.

In the Philadelphia metropolitan area, the company had closed down about 60 out of 110 stores over a two-year period, two-thirds of them in early 1982. The company cited high labor costs as the major problem with its operations. As A&P's workforce was completely unionized, the layoffs were mostly among part-time, younger, and cheaper labor due to seniority clauses in the labor contracts. Therefore, A&P's labor costs were much higher than average (15 percent of operating revenues as compared with 10 percent for the industry) and the average length of employee service was twice that of other supermarket chains.

Early in 1982, Wendell Young, president of Local 1357 of the United Food and Commercial Workers (UFCW), contacted the Busch Center in the Wharton School of the University of Pennsylvania to discuss the imminent closing of Philadelphia area stores and what might be done about it. The outcome of these discussions, led by Jamshid Gharajedaghi of the Busch Center, was that the union organized its members to buy and operate some of the stores being shut down. The main question was how the union might succeed where the company had failed.

It was realized that the workers had invaluable knowledge about operations of the stores that management had never tapped. When collected, this knowledge led to innovative organizational forms, participative management, and some training. This was a radical departure from traditional union roles, which normally involved organizing, bargaining, pension administration, and so on. There was considerable skepticism about whether this would be a proper role for the union and whether it could make it work.

Despite serious reservations among its top A&P officers, the union made its bid to buy several stores in early March 1982. Two weeks later, it was announced that 600 members had pledged $5,000 each as seed money to build a purchase fund. This made the company rethink its position and consider alternatives to mass closings. Together with the union and its consultants, the company came up with what it called the "Quality-of-Work-Life Plan." Negotiations led to an agreement between A&P and locals 56 and 1357 of the UFCW based on the following principles:

1. A&P agreed to reopen at least twenty stores and give workers a chance to buy four more. This would be done under a new subsidiary of A&P called Super Fresh.
2. The locals accepted shorter vacations and pay cuts up to $2.00 per hour.
3. The workers would receive 1 percent of gross sales if the labor costs were held at 10 percent of operating revenues. This share was to be reduced if labor costs exceeded 10 percent and would be increased if they fell below 9 percent.
4. The company committed itself to the Quality-of-Work-Life Programs to be initiated immediately in the new stores.

The Busch Center was selected to work with the company and the unions on this program.

By mid-June, three design teams had been formed with a deep slice of the new organization, including the president of Super Fresh and workers down to the level of part-time checkers. Each team completed a design for the whole organization and a synthesized version was approved with few modifications by the whole group in mid-September. In the meantime, the first new stores were opened.

The design agreed to is reproduced in part below. It was published in December of 1985 in a booklet entitled *Quality of Work Life for United Food and Commercial Workers, Locals 27, 56, 1357, 1358, and 1360 with Super Fresh Food Markets.* A small but relevant portion is reproduced below without modification. Notice that it combines variations on the circular organization, the learning and adaptation support system, as well as the multidimensional structure. The outcome of its application will be described after the design itself is presented.

Overview

Super Fresh will be organized as a two/three level structure. The first level will be that of the corporation itself, which will incorporate five different dimensions.
- Output Units (stores)
- Input Units (service functions)
- Environmental Unit (marketing/advocacy)
- Planning Boards (policy making bodies)
- Management Support System (control)

The second level will be the internal structure of the store itself, which will be organized along the same concept as the corporation, having the five dimensions as does the larger system.

- Output Units (departments)
- Input Units (front end; receiving)
- Environmental Unit (local business development and advocacy)
- Planning Boards (policy making bodies)
- Management Support Systems (control)

As Super Fresh increases the number of stores it operates a three level structure will be created that groups the stores into regional units.

Output Units

Achievement of the organizational ends and objectives (outputs) will be the responsibility of the output units (stores) of the system. The other units are created in order to facilitate the operation of these units. These units will be self-sufficient and autonomous to the degree that the integrity of the whole system is not compromised.

Input Units

Inputs are the services required to support the output units. Because of economies of scale, technology and geographic dispersion inputs can best be realized at the corporate level. These units will also be semi-autonomous.

Environmental Units

The interaction of the system with its environment is facilitated by the environmental units. The two main functions of these units are marketing and advocacy, that is, attracting the customers, making contact with the external stakeholders and advocating their point of view within the system.

Planning Board

Planning is a process that provides the overall coordinating and integrating function for the input, output, and environmental units. Planning Boards are the main policy making body of the organization and at all levels serve as the

vehicle for the participative management style of Super
Fresh. This enables the information, judgments, and concerns of subordinates to influence the decisions that affect
them. One of the key functions of the planning boards is to
constantly re-assess the progress that the corporation, store,
or department is making towards its goals (via feedback from
the management support system) and to chart new objectives when necessary. Planning at the store level is directed
to those matters affecting the store. Planning affecting more
than one store is done at the corporate level.

(Gerald Good, president of Super Fresh, said the chain was operating with "an open, participative management style involving every person in the organization. . . . There will be planning boards in every
store and every person will be involved in one.")

Management Support System

The management support system is responsible for the
comparison of the actual outcomes versus expected outcomes based on the plans and policies set by the planning
boards. This provides the means for learning and adaptation.

In an article in the *Philadelphia Inquirer* on Sunday, April 3, 1983, Jan
Shaffer wrote:

When the first Super Fresh food market opened here $8^{1}/_{2}$ months
ago, it was hailed as a breakthrough in employee participation in
management.
    In fact, the reincarnated food chain, a subsidiary of A&P,
appears so promising that A&P is looking hard at the possibility
of expanding it nationwide. . . .
    The Super Fresh format, first used to reopen closed stores, now
is being used to convert existing A&P stores to Super Fresh
Markets. (1D–2D)

The agreement reached between management and labor during the
design process involved an exchange of higher hourly wage rates for a
share of the stores' profits and the opportunity to participate in decisions affecting store operations.
    Before the end of the year in which the design was completed Super
Fresh opened its twenty-ninth store. Its original goal was twenty stores
by that time. It hired 2,015 workers amidst the highest unemployment

rate since World War II. The very same stores that had been closed down only six months earlier because of their poor performance established record sales and profits almost every week. In June of 1983, A&P announced its first profitable quarter in two years. On June 17, 1985, *the Philadelphia Inquirer* reported that "as it gradually slices away at everyone else's share of the market, Super Fresh is accomplishing an enviable feat in the supermarket trade. It is making money."

Today Super Fresh has 128 stores in the United States. It has moved out of the Delaware Valley into other parts of Pennsylvania and into New Jersey, Delaware, Maryland, Virginia, and the District of Columbia. It also has opened some stores in Canada.

Conclusion

Many, if not most, of the obstructions to change are either removed or significantly diminished in a multidimensional organization operating within an internal market economy. First, in such an organization there is no need to reorganize in order to change the relative importance of criteria used in dividing work. Emphasis can be changed by reallocating resources and by the imposition of constraints by higher levels of management.

Second, units can be added, subtracted, or modified without serious dislocation of other units. The more internal and external customers an internal unit has, the more robust it is and the less dependent it tends to be on any one customer.

Third, lower-level managers are given as much autonomy and general management experience as higher-level managers because even low-level units are operated as complete businesses within a market economy. Because higher-level managers also manage profit centers, they must take full responsibility for the effects of their decisions on the performance of units they oversee and, hence, contribute to their profits. These managers' primary concern must be with how their subordinate units interact with each other and how they interact with other parts of the organization and its environment, not their actions taken separately.

Last, a uniform, explicit, and operationally unambiguous measure of performance—which incorporates some function of the amount of profit generated, for example, return on capital employed—can be applied to units at every level, including the executive office. This makes possible comparison of the performances of units at all levels and discourages make-work and bureaucracy. However, profit is by no means the only important performance characteristic. Recall that in a social-systemically conceived organization, development of the organization, its stakeholders, and its containing systems are its overriding objectives. Although profit is necessary for corporate development, it is not sufficient.

When every part of an organization is organized multidimensionally, the organization can be said to be a "fractal" (Barnsley, 1988). Fractals are entities whose structure is the same at each of its levels. In view of the fact that fractals are currently facilitating major advances in our understanding of nature, one would think that fractal organizations would attract the attention of social scientists, but not so. Because comprehensive MD organizations operating with internal market economies are fractals, every manager within them is a general manager, no matter how specialized his or her unit may be. Each manages a complete business. Their differences are largely of scale. This characteristic of MD organizations simplifies succession planning and contributes significantly to management development.

Finally, it should be noted that the circular organization, the internal market economy, and multidimensional design can all be combined in one organization. The power of each is significantly enhanced by its interactions with the others.

Part IV

CHANGE

Reformations and Transformations

12

Panaceas, Fads, and Quick Fixes

A shortcut is the longest distance between two points.

—Charles Issawi

Introduction

Reliance on panaceas, quick fixes, cure-alls, and fads is in sharp contrast to reliance on transformational leadership.

Currently, panacea-prone management is confronted by more panaceas than problems. For example, the following is a partial list (alphabetically arranged) of alleged panaceas-plus collected from a cursory scanning of the management literature and listening to gurus in good currency:

Activity-based costing
After action review
Agile manufacturing
Benchmarking
Cognitive therapy
Commitment management
Continuous improvement
Core competencies
Customer focus
Cycle-time reduction
Dialogue decision process
Downsizing—Rightsizing

Economic value added
Groupware
Information architecture
Learning organizations
Outsourcing
Process reengineering
Scenario planning
Self-directed teams
Sense and respond
Strategic alliances
System dynamics
Total quality management
Value chain analysis

The search for simple—if not simpleminded—solutions to complex problems is a consequence of the inability to deal effectively with complexity. This deficiency induces a simplification of reality and ways of dealing with it. Those who cannot cope with the complexity of life itself turn to fundamentalism; in corporations, they turn to panaceas. Fundamentalism and panaceas are retreats from complexity and the uncertainty that accompanies them. Both are types of absolutism—a doctrine that provides a simple, ready-made answer to the questions one is willing to consider and a complete disregard for any other questions. A fundamentalist's doctrine is one that can survive any amount of disconfirming evidence because that evidence is considered to be false, a priori.

I am reminded of a biological taxonomer who once told me he had developed an exhaustive classification of sea shells. When I asked him how he established its exhaustiveness, he told me he had walked beaches all over the world examining and classifying each shell he saw. "Of course," he added, "occasionally I have to step on one."

Popular panaceas and the gurus who produce them seldom deliver all they promise. A significant part of the management literature reflects this evaluation (for example, Altier, 1991 and 1994; Ernst and Young and the American Quality Foundation, 1992; Hamel and Prahalad, 1994; Kiely, 1993/94; Kling, 1994; Arthur D. Little, Inc., 1994; Rakstis, 1994; Shapiro, 1995; Huczynski, 1996; and Micklethwaite and Wooldridge, 1996).

The critics of panaceas have found a number of reasons for their frequent failures. Nevertheless, I believe there is one reason for most of them: *failure to "whole" the parts*. By "whole-ing" I mean manipulating parts of a whole with the primary focus on performance of the whole of which they are part, not on their own performance. What they do in effect is the opposite: they "part the whole"; in other words, they treat the whole as an aggregation of independent parts. Such manipulation usually fails because the performance of a system, recall, is not equal to the sum of the performances of its essential parts taken separately, but is the product of their interactions. Therefore, improvement of the essential parts of a system taken separately may not, and often does not, improve and may reduce the performance of the whole. Recall the example used in Chapter 1 involving selection of the best available of each part required for an automobile. Their assembly does not yield the best automobile; they don't even yield an automobile because the parts don't fit. The evaluation of any essential part of a system should be based on its effect on performance of the relevant whole. A Rolls Royce motor that performs wonderfully in a Rolls Royce may perform miserably or not at all in a different car.

Another common deficiency is the failure of some panaceas to take into account a social system's developmental responsibilities to its stakeholders and the larger systems of which it is a part.

To demonstrate their antisystemic character, I review a few of the most popular panaceas and quick fixes.

Downsizing

The most frequent approach to improving white collar productivity is the meat axe—indiscriminate, across-the-board staff cuts that can seriously weaken a division or department. Instead of going through a series of downsizings that yield no lasting cost reductions, companies need to manage internal operations and keep them under control. In turn, support units need to be made responsible for adapting their service functions to fit internal customer needs. They cannot be permitted to expand with few, if any, constraints on their growth. (Davis, 1991, 21)*

It is no longer necessary to argue that downsizing fails more often than it succeeds. Within a short time after it takes place, costs tend to rise and serious morale problems usually emerge. An extensive litera-

---

* Quotation of Tim R. V. Davis reprinted by permission of the publisher, from ORGA-NIZATIONAL DYNAMICS AUTUMN 1991 © 1991. American Management Association, New York. http: WWW.amanet.org. All Rights Reserved.

ture provides evidence to this effect (e.g., Drucker, 1991; Rakstis, 1994; Pourdehnad, Halal, and Rausch, 1995; and Wysocki, 1995). "Every employee marched before the firing squad signals the death of a possible innovation, the evaporation of another revenue stream or the abandonment of a new opportunity to serve customers. Downsizing encumbers tomorrow's growth for a quick fix today" (Petzinger, 1996).*

Despite its ineffectiveness, downsizing's popularity has persisted largely because of the enthusiastic reception it has received by stock market analysts. They have almost uniformly reacted positively to the stocks of companies that have downsized. From a very short-run perspective, they have been right in expecting performance to improve, but in the long run, they have almost always been completely wrong. They then retrofit their previous expectations so as to rescue their egos.

I argue here that: *Downsizing is irresponsible and ineffective because it treats symptoms rather than the disease that is responsible for them; it attacks effects, not causes.* Because downsizing leaves the cause of overemployment unaffected, more often than not, it requires repeating. "Downsizing tends to be repetitive: on average, two-thirds of the firms that cut jobs in a given calendar year do so again the following year" (American Management Association, 1995).

Why has it taken some companies the accumulation of more than 100,000 excess employees before they realize that they employ more people than they need? What generates such an oversupply of personnel as appears to require downsizing and how can it be stopped? And why have these questions so seldom been asked?

The Irresponsibility of Downsizing

A corporation is clearly a social system and as such has functions in the larger systems of which it is a part. As we saw in Chapter 2, from society's point of view corporations have two principal functions: to produce and distribute wealth. They distribute wealth through compensation for labor, paying interest on loans, providing dividends, paying taxes, purchasing goods and services. However, productive employment is the only means available to society that both produces and distributes wealth. All other ways of distributing wealth, whether good or

---

* Quotation of Thomas Petzinger reprinted by permission of *The Wall Street Journal*,
   © (1996) Dow Jones & Company, Inc. All Rights Reserved Worldwide.

evil, consume it. Therefore, *the creation and maintenance of productive employment is a major social responsibility of corporations.* It follows that the failure to do this—and downsizing is such a failure—is irresponsible, if not immoral, from society's point of view.

The failure of private enterprises to provide enough productive employment can become a major destabilizing force politically. Governments usually react either by nationalizing weak companies and industries, as was done in the United Kingdom and Mexico, or by subsidizing them, as the United States did to Chrysler and does to the tobacco and dairy industries. These measures are taken to maintain productive employment and, in some cases, other reasons as well. Nationalized industries are seldom as productive or profitable as their private counterparts. (In the 1970s, of the more than 300 companies nationalized in Mexico, only 17 were profitable.) When nationalized companies and industries consume more wealth than they produce— which they often do—they wind up distributing poverty, not wealth, and the nation's standard of living suffers. This was the case in the Soviet Union.

Communism and socialism have *not* demonstrated an ability to produce enough wealth to make possible an acceptable standard of living. On the other hand, some capitalistic societies, particularly those that are less developed, have not distributed wealth equitably enough to attain political stability. The maldistribution of wealth is the kind of threat to capitalism that the insufficient production of wealth has been to communism and socialism.

The natural reaction to the assertion that the creation and maintenance of productive employment is a responsibility of private-sector management goes something like this: "The primary responsibility of a corporation is to its stockholders, and this requires them to be profitable. An excess of employees reduces profit; therefore, the corporation has an obligation to eliminate excess employees." This argument might be valid if there were no other ways of maintaining or increasing profit than downsizing, but there are. Consider the following socially responsible alternatives, which, not incidentally, also benefited the stockholders.

Better Ways Than Downsizing

The first case involves the Clark Equipment Corporation, which, as previously discussed, was in serious financial difficulty in the 1980s.

The new CEO, James Rinehart, who was appointed to pull Clark out of its difficulties, found that transporting the company's products to distributors by its internal transportation department cost significantly more than would outsourcing. He calculated the cost to the corporation of eliminating the internal transportation department. Then he asked local banks how much they would be willing to lend for a leveraged buyout of that department by its employees if the company were to put up the amount of money required to eliminate the department. The banks were willing to lend enough to make the buyout possible. Rinehart then put this possibility to the employees, offering them a contract for all the company's transportation for two years, providing they met common-carrier prices. The employees accepted the offer and established what turned out to be a successful independent trucking company. Clark Equipment, the enabling company, enjoyed significantly reduced transportation costs. Both parties benefited.

The second case is of a large, diversified corporation that decided in the 1970s to discontinue one of its businesses.

The company had a relatively new factory devoted exclusively to that business, one that employed several hundred workers. The corporation offered the plant for sale at a price significantly less than its value to anyone who would buy it and retain the employees. A buyer was found in a relatively short time. The amount of write-off saved made up for the loss on the sale of the factory. Both parties benefited.

In a third case, one vice president of a large corporation received an order from a higher authority to reduce the number of managers under him by about half.

Rather than face the task, which was much too painful for the vice president, he called a meeting of the managers from whom the layoffs were to be selected and turned the problem over to them. He gave them a month to tell him how to handle it. In addition to formulating criteria for selecting who should go, the group focused on finding employment for whichever managers would be dismissed. It conducted

its search in other parts of the corporation and in its principal suppliers and customers. Enough jobs were found to
absorb the number that would have to be let go. They then
turned the criteria they had developed over to the vice president and monitored the use he made of them. The reduction
went smoothly, without resentment, and none of those dismissed went jobless for long.

(For a similar example, see Petzinger, B7, 1996.)

Toyota Motors, handicapped by an excess of employees,
assigned the excess to teams that were given the task of finding ways to reduce costs, raise productivity, and improve
morale. "In fact, through four years of recession, Toyota not
only upheld the tradition of lifetime employment in Japan, it
actually turned to its workforce of 70,000 for help." [Peter
Jennings, *World News Tonight*, EST edition, 24 June 1996]
The manager at Toyota's main city plant said the suggestions
he received when implemented increased productivity by 10
percent and more than justified the cost.

These cases make it clear that a management that *cares* and *takes seriously* its social responsibility for maintaining or increasing productive
employment can usually find a way of doing so, even if it involves going
outside the company. This can often be done without a cost to the
company—in fact, it can be done profitably.

How Does the Excess Come About?

In a market in which sales volume increases less than productivity,
excess production workers are generated. To maintain a work force
under these conditions requires generating new products or services
that can absorb the excess. This, of course, may require additional
training of those to be moved from the old to the new products.
Therefore, maintenance or increase of productive employment in a
low- or no-growth market requires effective planning; it does not happen by itself. The number of excess employees produced by increasing
productivity and mature markets is small, relative to those produced by
internal bureaucratic monopolies.

The need for most downsizing has been "explained" by most executives by referring to changed competitive conditions that require

"restructuring" to remain competitive. If this were the case, then how come so many companies that have downsized have done so more than once? The answer lies in the fact that the principal cause of excess employees is not external but internal, is not removed by downsizing and, therefore, continues to operate afterward. If the internal sources of excess employees were treated properly, adaptation to changing conditions would not require large, disruptive layoffs.

As suggested above, the principal sources of excess personnel are *bureaucratic monopolies* within the firm. These are units within a firm that are monopolistic providers of services or products to other parts of the organization (and usually to no one else). The units they serve are permitted no alternative source of supply or service. Some common examples are such services as accounting, human resources, data processing, legal, R and D, and purchasing departments.

Furthermore, the users of the services or products provided seldom pay for them directly, but do so through an overhead charge (a tax) imposed and collected by a higher level of management. The units providing services are then budgeted (a euphemism for "subsidized") out of the overhead funds collected by and accumulated at a higher level. Therefore, such supplying units are not nearly as concerned with satisfying those they serve as their subsidizers. In effect, many such internal units can survive no matter how poorly they perform relative to those they serve as long as they are perceived to perform satisfactorily by those who produce or authorize their budgets. Such units often perform poorly because they do not have to compete for business or satisfy their users.

There are no economic indicators of the performance of bureaucratic monopolies. Neither the value of their outputs nor their costs are generally known. Therefore, their importance is normally judged to be proportional to either or both the number of people they employ and the size of their budgets. As a result, they tend to grow as much as the subsidizer will allow, and the subsidizers are usually quite generous precisely because they cannot evaluate the monopolies' performance. To facilitate growth, the monopolistic servicing units *make work*. This is work that has no useful product; worse yet, it often creates unproductive work for others who are doing productive work, for example, red tape.

When it becomes apparent that a company is not as effective financially and competitively as it should be and is overemploying, downsizing is usually the first way out that is tried. But once it takes place, the bureaucratic monopolies continue to make work and grow as much as the system permits. Overemployment usually reoccurs later and downsizing is repeated.

How To Prevent Excessive Employment

It should be apparent that an internal market economy (Chapter 10) is the most effective way of preventing or eliminating internal bureaucratic monopolies. Such units are not evil in themselves; their obstructiveness derives from the organizational arrangements that create and sustain them. They would not exist within organizations if the other parts served by them were freed to select external sources of goods and services and the internal suppliers that are bureaucratic monopolies had to sell their services or products to external customers. This would also eliminate the need to benchmark performance of the supplying units.

An internal service unit that has to compete against external sources must stay lean; it must eliminate or minimize excess personnel if it is to keep costs down so as to be able to compete effectively.

Total Quality Management

In the 1980s, following the Japanese, Total Quality Management (TQM) was the most popular means by which managers in the United States pursued improvement of the performance of their businesses. Although its popularity is waning, it is still resorted to widely. This is the case despite revelations by Ernst and Young (1992) and Arthur D. Little, Inc. (1994) that most applications of TQM have not met the expectations of their customers.

Clearly, product and service quality are desirable. So the failures of TQM must be due to how it has been implemented, not in its objective. What have been the most common deficiencies in the way it has been used?

Consumers as Well as Customers

"Quality," as applied to products or services, has generally come to be accepted as meaning "meeting or exceeding the expectations of customers." "In time, all the time" is sometimes added. Those who define quality in terms of the expectations of customers assume incorrectly, but often unconsciously, that "customers" are the same as "consumers." This is seldom the case, for example, where the supplier sells a product to wholesalers who sell it to retailers who sell it to others who may purchase the product as a gift for yet another: the purchaser of a gift is the customer of the retailer; the recipient of the gift is its ultimate consumer unless he or she also gives it away. Most would agree that quality should be concerned at least as much with the consumers' expectations as with the customers. Both are necessary; neither is sufficient. If either is dissatisfied with the product or service offered, it will either not be bought or, if bought, not be used.

Internal consumers of internally provided goods and services are usually taken into account in TQM programs. For example, the "miracle" produced by Jan Carlzon (1987) at SAS is attributed to his making all employees of the airline aware of the fact that every one of them had either internal or external consumers of their outputs and that they were responsible for meeting or exceeding their consumers' expectations. Note that, except in an internal market economy, internal consumers are seldom customers. They are seldom even willing consumers. Their monopolistic suppliers are imposed on them by higher-level authorities who allocate resources to sustain the internal service units.

The coverage of the concept "customer" as used in TQM has been enlarged over time. Total Quality Management has become increasingly total, but in most cases not nearly total enough. "Total" quality should apply to *all* those who are affected by what an organization does, all its stakeholders. This makes relevant the expectations of an organization's suppliers, employees, consultants and advisers, wholesalers, retailers, stockholders, bondholders, bankers, debtors, and so on. Only when it takes all these expectations into account does it deserve to be called a *total* quality organization, as distinct from a provider of a quality product or service. The objective of TQM should be the creation of total quality organizations, not merely quality products and services to its customers.

According to the *American Heritage Dictionary of the English Language* (1981), "expect" has two significantly different meanings: (1) "to consider reasonable or due," and (2) "to look forward to the probable occurrence of." It is in the first sense, not the second, that quality is defined with reference to the expectations of stakeholders. Expectations, in this sense, have to do with reasonable desires, not forecasts.

Determining What Consumers Expect

TQM is obviously concerned with providing the ultimate users of products or services with the quality they desire and those who purchase them with as low a price as possible Even where proponents of TQM differentiate customer and consumer expectations, they do not usually provide an effective way of determining what these expectations are. The relevant expectations are usually sought by use of conventional survey research: asking customers and consumers what they want.

Asking customers and consumers what they want often yields inaccurate and unreliable information. They frequently do not know what they want. Even if they do, they often give the inquirer answers that they think the inquirers want, rather than ones that reveal their preferences. Even when customers and consumers are aware of what they want and are willing to reveal it, their wants are likely to be strongly conditioned by what is available. They are not likely to reveal currently unrealizable desires, even when what is available is not very satisfying to them. It is apparent, of course, that necessity is the mother of invention, but what is not as apparent is that invention is the mother of necessity. There was no expression of expectations of handheld calculators, VCRs, or PCs before they appeared on the market. But once they did, the need for them became widespread.

There is an effective way of enabling customers, consumers, and other stakeholders to become aware of what they want and of encouraging them to reveal it as truthfully as they can. It requires involving them in the idealized design of the products or services in question.

Probing expectations using idealized design. Actual or potential customers and consumers of products or services can very productively be involved in preparing idealized designs of them. They have produced idealized designs of such diverse things as supermarkets, roofing materials, hospitals, drug treatment centers, schools, and men's stores.

In one example, five different stakeholder groups were used to design roofing for houses: architects, general contractors, roofing contractors, building material distributors, and those having houses built.

> A laboratory was constructed in which the subjects could design and build a section of roofing. The components provided were designed to permit the subjects to build sections of a wide variety of roofs. All the groups except the roofing

contractors converged on a type of roofing that differed from that all roofing manufacturers assumed customers and consumers wanted; they had incorrectly assumed that the roofs of houses should look like either wood shingles, slate shingles, or clay tile. They were wrong. Most of the other roofs produced in the laboratory were not monochromatic and plain, but colorful and contained designs. In contrast, the roofing contractors were not interested in the aesthetic properties of the roofs, only in the ease with which the materials could be applied.

The subjects, who had been expected to build only one roof, enjoyed it so much that they insisted on remaining late into the night in order to build at least three different sections. This suggested that a similar setup be created in the facilities of building material suppliers so that consumers could design and build a sample of the roofs they wanted.

Such design exercises always involve acts of discovery by both the subjects and the sponsors. Recall the chain of men's stores used in Chapter 6.

A design produced by potential customers revealed that, first of all, they wanted a store that offered the highest quality for the price they were willing to pay, not the lowest price for the quality they wanted. Discount prices, the chain's advertising message, turned them off because to them it implied lower quality.

Second, they wanted different articles of clothing of the same size to be grouped together in the store. They did not want grouping by type of clothing, which required their hunting all over the store, multiple checkouts, and so on.

Third, they wanted to examine clothing without a salesperson hovering over them. They suggested that call buttons be conveniently placed so they could call a salesperson when they wanted one. They also suggested women as salesclerks because they thought a woman's opinion of how they looked was likely to be more accurate than that of a man.

There are times when consumers cannot correctly articulate their expectations even through idealized design. This is most often the case when they have never experienced the product or service involved.

When they experience what they thought they wanted, they often discover that they don't want it. For example, Du Pont Fibers Division often finds that when companies that produce carpeting or rugs receive material that meets their specifications, these companies find it deficient in ways they had not previously considered. Then they often engage in a sequence of trials and errors before they obtain a valid formulation of their expectations, let alone a product that meets them. Architects know only too well that families that want to build a house seldom wind up wanting the house they described when they first met with the architect. As the design develops, their concept of what they want also develops. When they eventually occupy the house they thought they wanted, they almost always find ways by which the design could have been improved.

Even tests involving the actual product or service may yield misleading results unless they are designed to resemble normal usage as much as possible.

> We were once asked to conduct taste tests of a recently introduced beer to determine how its taste was thought to compare with competitive brands. We selected four competitive beers, each with a distinctive taste. We presented them to a sample of beer drinkers in five glasses, each identified by a letter (A, B, C, D, and E) and no identification of the brand. Two glasses, differently labeled, contained the same brand, the one in question. The testers did not know this. They were asked to rank the "five" brands by taste.
>
> The brand given to them twice was ranked as both the best and the worst, and the ranking of the others had no relation to their market shares. When we showed these puzzling results to a brew master, he said, "Of course; nobody ever tests beers that way. They drink one beer at a time and different beers on different occasions and then decide which they like best."
>
> We redesigned the test leaving an unmarked case of each brand, two of the brand in question, at the homes of a sample of beer drinkers for a month. At the end of the month, we asked for their preferences and received a consistent judgment of the beer in question and the preference ordering of the four beers was exactly the same as the ordering of their market shares.

It should also be noted that when long life is designed into products, it may preclude future options. For example, before its deregulation AT&T built so much life into its telephones that it withheld introduction of technological improvements in order to obtain as large a return as possible on the investment in them. It was only after deregulation and the invasion by competitors that AT&T introduced new technology and upgraded much of its equipment.

At best, TQM programs focus on trying to go from where one is to where one wants to be, to moving from a less preferred to a more preferred state. As we saw in Chapter 3, this is not nearly as effective as working backward from where one wants to be to where one is. This reversal of direction simplifies the process of getting what we want. It also provides greater assurance of getting it and expands our concept of what is feasible.

Quality of Work Life

There is a story that may not be true, but if not, it ought to be.

> A man who purchased a very expensive Cadillac picked it up at the dealership and drove only a few blocks when, on a bit of rough street, he heard a rattle. He turned around and brought it back to the dealer and complained bitterly about it. The dealer apologized and assured the customer that they would get the rattle out and would have the car ready by the next day. The dealer called the service manager and described the problem. The service manager put the car up on a rack but could find nothing that rattled. He did nothing, assuming the new owner imagined the rattle.
>
> The next day the owner picked up the car, drove it a short distance, and on the same stretch of rough street heard a rattle. Furious, he returned to the dealer and said he either wanted his money back or a different car. The dealer talked him into waiting one more day.
>
> The dealer then told the service manager to take the car out for a drive until he located the rattle. The service manager did so and found the rattle in the driver's side front door. He returned to the shop and removed and disassembled the door. At the bottom of the well into which the window was lowered was an empty Coke bottle, which contained a piece of paper. He withdrew the paper, on which

was crudely printed, "So you finally found it, you sons of bitches."

There is no way that an employee with such a negative attitude toward his work can be made to put quality into his product. His resentment of the quality of work life imposed on him dominates any consideration of the quality of his output.

My experience indicates that larger improvements can be obtained by focusing on quality of work life than on quality of products or services. It is not uncommon for those in a workforce to see TQM programs as another way of exploiting them, getting more out of them without giving them a larger share of the take. On the other hand, when a quality-of-work-life program that is designed and implemented by those whose work life is affected by it is installed and carried out without any strings attached, those whose work life benefits look for ways to express their appreciation for it. They naturally turn to increasing the quantity and quality of output. Then, if they are educated in quality improvement techniques, they take to them with enthusiasm.

Furthermore, I have found that both quality-of-work-life and quality-of-output programs that are designed by those who must implement them generally do a great deal better than programs designed by experts and imposed on those who must carry them out. (Recall that in the circular organization [Chapter 9], all employees have control over their quality of work life.) Experts can be made available to the workforce, but should be used only as the workforce sees fit. This results in a feeling of ownership of the program by those who must implement them.

Other Deficiencies and Omissions

TQM has its origin in statistical quality control, which was a very effective way of reducing defects in products or services. Over time, additional procedures and practices were added that contributed to the improvement of quality control, for example, quality circles and consensus decision making. These developments were based primarily on experience; little theory was involved. As a result, the various components of TQM do not hang together as a cohesive whole. The program tends to be an aggregation of independent procedures and practices rather than an interdependent systemic set of tools, techniques, and methods.

More importantly, TQM raises some issues it is not equipped to handle. For example, it tries to change management's activity from supervision, that is, controlling the actions of subordinates, to leadership, that is, guiding subordinates' interactions and encouraging and facilitating their development. But it has no theory to guide managers in efforts to create organizational structures that facilitate the management of interactions and the development of subordinates. Interactive and developmental management, leadership, is seriously obstructed in conventional hierarchies to which TQM does not provide an alternative. Such alternatives exist (e.g., the circular organization as presented in Chapter 9), but TQM does not deal with them.

Furthermore, TQM implicitly assumes a relatively stable structure in the organization over the time TQM is being installed and applied. The fact is that the time between reorganizations of most enterprises in the United States is less than the time required to install TQM. Can organizations be structured so that restructuring is not frequently required? The answer is "yes." The multidimensional organization (Chapter 11) eliminates the need for periodic reorganization.

TQM also assumes a management that learns and adapts rapidly and efficiently, but it provides no concept of the management-support system required to accomplish this. Learning and adaptation without certain kinds of support is slow at best and absent at worst. A Learning and Adaptation Support System (such as is described in Chapter 8) not only facilitates and accelerates learning and adaptation, but it also facilitates learning how to learn and adapt.

Nor does TQM deal with measures of performance and compensation systems that act as incentives for the type of behavior that it seeks to encourage. These have a very significant effect on organizational behavior. Therefore, if they are left unchanged, behavior will not change significantly and the changes that are made will not last long. The types of measures and compensation required are discussed by Gharajedaghi and Geranmayeh (1992).

The most serious consequence of focusing on continuous quality improvement is the failure to distinguish between efficiency and effectiveness. TQM can just as easily be applied to the production of poison gas as to a lifesaving pharmaceutical. In itself, this is not a defect, but the failure to consider whether or not poison gas is an appropriate product is a serious defect. For example, TQM has been used extensively by the Japanese to improve the quality of their automobiles. But it has not raised questions about the rationality or appropriateness of the automobile as it is currently conceived. It has become increasingly apparent that today's automobiles are creating monumental problems such as air pollution, excessive dependence on fossil fuels, and congestion. Automobiles that can avoid creating these problems have been designed and could be produced.

Put another way: TQM does not, but should, incorporate ethical and aesthetic evaluations of the products and services whose quality it attempts to improve.

Continuous Improvement

Continuous improvement programs are usually an important part of TQM but are also used separately. They usually begin by examining a current activity, process, product, or service to determine what is wrong with it. Then they focus on such weaknesses as clerical errors, product defects, and incorrect or late deliveries. Improvements are usually conceptualized as the removal of defects or deficiencies and this is assumed to move one incrementally from where one is to where one wants to be. As discussed above and in Chapter 3 in connection with reactive management and planning, this assumption is false. Getting rid of what one does not want provides no assurance of getting what one does want.

The solution to a problem conceptualized as removal of a defect or deficiency may be worse than the defect or deficiency that it removes. Recall Prohibition's effort to get rid of alcoholism and the current effort to get rid of crime. Improvement programs should be directed at getting what organizations and their stakeholders want, not at getting rid of what they do not want. Idealized design defines what is wanted.

Discontinuous Improvement

Continuous improvement involves relatively small incremental changes made close together in time. This precludes creative quantum leaps. Creative acts produce discontinuities, qualitative changes. They involve three steps: (1) identifying self-imposed constraints (assumptions), (2) removing them, and (3) exploring the consequences of their removal. This is why there is always an element of surprise when we are shown creative work: it embodies the denial of something we have (usually unconsciously) taken for granted. This is particularly apparent when we are exposed to the solution of a puzzle that we have been unable to solve. An unsolved puzzle is a problem precisely because of something we incorrectly assume, a self-imposed constraint, hence the "aha" experience we usually have when the solution is shown to us.

Creative but discontinuous improvements are usually worth much more than a string of small but continuous improvements. Nevertheless, creativity is often discouraged in organizations because it so frequently is destabilizing and disruptive. It is, as well, difficult to encourage, although it can be encouraged by open minds and a high tolerance for the errors that may result from creative acts.

There are a number of techniques for enhancing creativity (Ackoff and Vergara, 1981), for example, lateral thinking (de Bono, 1973), synectics (Gordon, 1961), brainstorming (Osborn, 1953), TKJ (Getzels and Csikszentmihalyi, 1971), conceptual block busting (Adams, 1974), and idealized design. Elsa Vergara (1976) compared these techniques experimentally and found that idealized design outperformed the others significantly. Recall that idealized design involves starting with the assumption that the thing to be improved was destroyed last night or never existed. When this assumption is adhered to, it leads to the removal of many self-imposed constraints and thereby enhances creativity.

Put another way: creative discontinuities are required to take the lead; continuous improvement is at best a way of getting closer to the leader. One cannot pass a leader by imitating him or her.

Analytic Versus Synthetic Improvement

In continuous improvement, the defects addressed are usually in parts of an organization and each is addressed separately. This flies in the face of the important systems principle discussed in Chapter 1: when every part of a system taken separately is made to perform as well as possible, the system as a whole will not perform as well as possible. The properties of the parts of a system should be derived from properties of the whole, not conversely.

Benchmarking

An organization's discovery of the need to benchmark is an indication that something is seriously wrong. Why should it take a crisis for an organization to inquire into its relative efficiency and to discover how inefficient it is? What keeps it from becoming aware of this when it begins to happen? This is clearly a situation in which an ounce of prevention is worth a pound of cure.

Moreover, in continuous improvement the improvements are internally generated; in benchmarking they come from external comparisons. But in both cases, a combination of the best practices by each part of a system taken separately does not yield the best system. We may not even get a good one.

> A company that has twelve facilities, each producing the same variations of the same type of beverage, had broken the production process down into fifteen steps. It produced a table showing each factory (a column) and each of the fifteen steps (rows). The company then carried out a study to determine the cost of each step at each factory (a costly study), which identified for each step the factory with the lowest cost. At each factory, the company tried to replace each of its steps that was not the lowest cost by the one used in the factory that had the lowest cost. Had this succeeded, each factory would be producing with steps that had each attained the lowest cost in any factory. It did not work! The lowest cost steps did not fit together. The result was only a few insignificant cosmetic changes that did not justify the cost of the exercise.

Management should focus on the interactions of parts and of the system with other systems, rather than the actions of parts taken separately. Practices selected by benchmarking seldom take interactions into account; it looks at isolated processes and actions. The only type of benchmarking that avoids such an error lies in competing for business; no business can survive without awareness of the relative performance of its competitors. This is why an internal market economy eliminates the need for benchmarking. In effect, it conducts benchmarking continuously and systemically.

Process Reengineering

"'Reengineering,' properly, is 'the fundamental rethinking and radical redesign of business processes to achieve dramatic improvements in critical, contemporary measures of performance, such as cost, quality, service, and speed.'" (Hammer and Champy, 1993, 32)

At least until recently, 75 percent of the applications of process reengineering were reported to be failures. There are two principal reasons for these failures, one of which was recently acknowledged by Hammer in the *Wall Street Journal* (White, 1996, A1).

The first cause of failure derives from the bias contained in the word "engineering." It implies the conscious manipulation of *things*; early application of process engineering did just that, but it also manipulated people *unconsciously*. It ignored people or treated them as though they were easily replaced machine parts. Those involved did not react as the engineers intended. People have a will of their own and resent not being consulted in the design of activities that they carry out. Having acknowledged the seriousness of this omission, it remains to be seen whether or not Hammer and other reengineers can adequately deal with human nature.

The connotation of the term "engineering" does not include ethical and aesthetic—that is, value—considerations, while the connotation of the term "design" does. Process reengineering is concerned with efficiency, not effectiveness. Therefore, it frequently results in doing the wrong thing righter, which makes it wronger.

The second deficiency of reengineering is also critical; it cannot be solved even by successfully humanizing the reengineering process. Reengineering addresses the problems created by the vertical segmentation of organizations, usually along functional lines into silos. As a result, coordination of horizontal interdependencies is difficult if not impossible. Process reengineering addresses the need for horizontal coordination by cutting the organization across rather than down. Unfortunately, this also results in a disassembly of the whole, even though it does so horizontally rather than vertically. Put another way, it may solve the coordination problem, but it creates an integration problem: management of vertical interactions. Once again, improvement of the parts of a system taken separately, whether vertically or horizontally defined, does not usually result in improved performance of the whole.

Idealized design avoids both problems incurred by process reengineering. It begins with the organization as a whole and moves to the parts rather than the reverse, as takes place in reengineering. And it deals with all the human and social aspects of the redesign as well as the mechanistic. It accomplishes what process reengineering hopes to accomplish but doesn't.

Conclusion

There are no simple solutions to complex problems. Furthermore, since problems are interdependent, their solutions should be. Interdependent problems constitute messes, systems of problems. Therefore, their solutions must also form a system. A system of solutions is a *plan*, and plans are complicated, not simple. It is not possible in a few minutes to find behavior that will resolve, solve, or dissolve a set of problems that took years to cultivate. Finally, as Einstein pointed out, it is not possible to find a plan that will handle the system of problems effectively without changing the pattern of thought that produced them.

13

Organizational Development and Transformational Leadership

Sooner or later some honking wannabe will lurch up to inform you that your choices are to lead, follow him, or get out of his way.

—Jack Gordon

The Nature of Development

In Chapter 2, I pointed out that the proper objective of a social system is self-development and development of its stakeholders and itself, and that quality of life is a more appropriate index of development than standard of living. Standard of living is an index of growth. Unfortunately, "development" and "growth" are commonly treated as synonyms. They are not the same thing. Either can take place without the other. Rubbish heaps grow, but do not develop, and Einstein continued to develop long after he stopped growing.

Growth is an increase in size or number. Therefore, corporations that equate development and growth focus on increasing their size and their market value, the amount of resources they have and can generate. This is reflected in acquisitions, joint ventures, mergers, strategic alliances, and other types of union.

Development is not a matter of how much one has, but of how much one can do with whatever one has. Therefore, Robinson Crusoe is a better model of development than J. Pierpont Morgan. Wealth by itself cannot produce development. Pouring resources on primitive peoples will not by itself develop them. Development is more a matter of *learning* than *earning. To develop is to increase one's desire and ability to satisfy one's own needs and legitimate desires, and those of others.*

Unfortunately, "need" and "desire" are also commonly used interchangeably. As I use these terms, a need is something that is necessary for survival, like oxygen and food. One may not desire what is needed—for example, calcium—largely because one is unaware of the need. On the other hand, one may want what is not needed—for example, addictive drugs or jewelry. *Satisfaction of a legitimate desire does not reduce, and may increase, the desire and ability of others to develop.* This concept exposes the ethical aspect of development.

Competence is the ability to satisfy needs and desires. Therefore, development is the pursuit of competence, not wealth. *Omnicompetence* is the unattainable but continuously approachable limit to development, its ideal. It is the ability to obtain whatever is needed or legitimately wanted. Omnicompetence differs significantly from omnipotence because it does not imply power over others, but it does imply power-to, the desire and ability to help them obtain what they need and legitimately want.

Development, in contrast to growth, is a mental rather than a material process. Because development is primarily a matter of learning and because one person or group cannot learn for another, one person or group cannot develop another. *The only kind of development possible is self-development,* but such social systems as governments and corporations can and should encourage and facilitate the development of all their stakeholders. This, together with producing and distributing wealth, is one of a corporation's principal reasons for being. *A corporation develops with increases in its desire and ability to facilitate and encourage the development of its stakeholders and the larger systems of which it is a part.*

This does not mean that wealth is irrelevant to a society's, a corporation's, or an individual's development, hence, to quality of life. To the contrary, it is very important, although it is neither necessary nor sufficient for development. Whatever one's level of development, the more wealth one has, the more additional development one can support.

Development, unlike growth, is value loaded. Growth may be either good or bad. Not so for development; it is necessarily good. Growth comes with efficiency; development, with effectiveness. Values that convert efficiency into effectiveness are the focus of ethics and aesthetics. But since effectiveness is a function of efficiency as well as value, development also requires data, information, knowledge, and understanding. These are primary products of science. Therefore, development has four aspects: scientific, economic, ethical, and aesthetic.

Aspects of Development

Ancient Greek philosophers identified the four primary aspects of development: truth, plenty, the good, and beauty/fun. Each aspect is necessary, but only when the four are taken together are they sufficient for continuous development.

Truth. The pursuit of truth is the function of science. Science produces information, knowledge, and understanding. Technology is the application of the products of science, and education is the principal means by which the outputs of science and technology are disseminated. Together, science, technology, and education enable people to pursue their ends more efficiently. They provide the *means* with which we pursue our ends and they try to improve these means continuously.

Plenty. The pursuit of plenty is the function of the economy, which is concerned with (1) producing and distributing the *resources* that make possible the pursuit of *ends* with the most efficient means available (the role of business and government); and (2) protecting the resources acquired against their appropriation, theft, or destruction by others or nature (the role of the justice system, the health system, the environmental protection agency, the military, and insurance).

The Good. The pursuit of the good involves the dissemination of ethical and moral principles. This is carried out primarily by religious and educational institutions, and more recently by psychiatry. It entails promoting cooperation to enable the attainment of objectives that would otherwise not be attained. This, in turn, requires eliminating conflict within individuals (peace of mind) and between individuals (peace on Earth) because conflict limits the number of objectives that can be attained or the number of people who can attain them. Therefore, ethics enables identification of the *ends* whose pursuit leads to development.

Beauty/Fun. The pursuits of beauty and fun—the products of creative and recreative activities—are inseparable aspects of aesthetics. Together they make possible the *continuous pursuit* of any ideal, including omnicompetence, and hence development, by providing the push and pull necessary for such pursuit.

Note that interactive planning (discussed in Part II) involves all four of these pursuits.

Politics is an aspect of ethics that is concerned with the way people interact and therefore with the way organizations are structured and managed. It deals with the distribution of authority and responsibility, hence power-over and power-to. It controls and distributes access to available physical and mental resources and therefore makes it possible or impossible for individuals and groups to obtain what they want.

The Role of Aesthetics

Aesthetics is the least understood aspect of development. The terms "management science," "management technology," "management education," "managerial economics," and "managerial ethics" convey at least some meaning to most managers. On the other hand, the "aesthetics of management" conveys little if any meaning to anyone, let alone managers.

In *The Republic*, Plato asserted that art—the product of creative activity—was a potentially dangerous stimulant that threatens the stability of a society. It stimulates visions of an allegedly better life than the one being experienced. Therefore, Plato saw art as a disruptive social influence. In contrast, Aristotle saw art as cathartic, a palliative for dissatisfaction, hence a producer of social stability and contentment. He saw art as *recreation*, something from which one extracts pleasure here and now.

These apparently contradictory views of art are actually complementary: they are two inseparable aspects of ideal-pursuit. Art produces beauty and beauty *inspires*: it not only produces visions of a better life, but also produces an unwillingness to settle for what we have and a desire for what is envisioned. It is the product and producer of creative activity, change, which is essential for continuous development.

Art also entertains, provides recreation, and produces *fun*, which is the satisfaction we derive from what we do regardless of what we do it for. It is the pleasure we derive from "going there" in contrast to the pleasure derived from "getting there." Recreation provides "the pauses that refresh," without which continuous pursuit of ideals would not be possible.

The Ethics of Management

Recall that the definition of development involves the desire and ability to enable others to satisfy their needs and desires. This is an ethical requirement. Ethics has to do with the way purposeful individuals and organizations affect each other, the way they interact. Clearly when management of a social system is said to have a responsibility to serve the interests of its stakeholders, this is an ethical requirement.

Since World War II, the number of interactions in which human beings, organizations, institutions, and societies are involved has increased dramatically with the explosive development of communication and transportation. Very recently, the development of the Internet has increased interactions and the potential for them by an order of magnitude. For this reason, among others, ethical issues have become increasingly important in corporate affairs.

Cooperation and Conflict

Recall that there are two basic types of interaction between animate beings: conflict and cooperation (Chapter 6). In conflict, the behavior of one party *decreases* the likelihood of another party getting what it needs or wants. In cooperation, the behavior of one party *increases* the likelihood of another party getting what it needs or wants. (Elsewhere, Fred Emery and I [1972] have shown that conflict and cooperation can be measured on a scale that runs from -1.0 to +1.0, where negative values designate conflict and positive values, cooperation.) *Competition* and *exploitation* are derivative types of interaction.

Competition

Recall also that competition consists of conflict that is imbedded in cooperation. For example, consider two friendly parties, A and B, who are opponents in a tennis match. Each has two objectives: (1) to win, and (2) to engage in recreation. They are in conflict with respect to winning the match, but in cooperation with respect to their recreational objective. The cooperative objective dominates. Most competitors would rather lose a hard match than win a very easy one. Evidence of this appeared in a statement by Ivan Lendl when he was ranked as number one among professional male tennis players; he expressed keen regret at winning a tennis tournament by default because his opponent had withdrawn due to illness. In general, the more intense the conflict over winning, the better served the cooperative objective of recreation.

The cooperative objective in competition may be one of a third party, for example, an audience. This is the case in many sporting events. The presence of a third party's objective does not preclude those competing from having a cooperative objective of their own, but there must be at least one cooperative objective that is served by the conflict imbedded in competition.

In economic competition, the cooperative objective is to serve the consumers' interests, but the companies involved are in conflict with respect to sales volume and market share. It can also be argued that such conflict between companies produces an economy that forces enterprises to operate more efficiently than they would otherwise. It also provides them with opportunities for growth and development that noncompetitive economies have never provided.

If the cooperation and conflict involved in competition are reversed—that is, if cooperation is imbedded in conflict and, hence, augments it—an immoral relationship results. For example, if two alleged competitors cooperate—for example, by price-fixing—they come into conflict with consumers. Exploitation of consumers becomes the dominant objective as seen from society's point of view, and this is against the rules.

The rules governing competition are intended to assure that the conflict serves the cooperative objective. In competitive sports, the rules are designed to keep conflict from getting out of hand, for example, to keep a boxing match from becoming a brawl. Mike Tyson was suspended from professional boxing for biting the ear of his opponent because this action broke a boxing rule.

Conflict imbedded in competition is not necessarily bad; it can be quite good. However, conflict that affects the desire or ability to attain legitimate objectives and is not imbedded in competition is considered bad. Recall that "legitimate" implies an objective that, when obtained, does not preclude anyone else obtaining their legitimate objectives.

Exploitation

Conflict and cooperation are not necessarily symmetrical; one party (A) may be in conflict with another (B), but B may be cooperating with A— as, for example, in a master-slave relationship—or A and B may be in unequal conflict or cooperation with each other. Such asymmetrical interactions constitute exploitation. It should be noted that one party can exploit another without intending to do so; for example, a sick person may unintentionally exploit someone providing him or her with care.

There are three types of exploitation:

1. *Benevolent.* Each party cooperates with the other, but they do so unequally. This is the type of exploitation that most colonial powers have claimed for themselves when they have admitted to benefiting more from their colonization than those who have been colonized. Many employer-employee relations are also characterized by this type of exploitation.

2. *Malevolent.* Each party conflicts with the other, but they do so unequally. The one who suffers least can be said to be the malevolent exploiter of the other. Such an exploiter is willing to suffer in order to make the opponent suffer more. This is usually the case when revenge is involved. Most wars are examples of malevolent exploitation.

3. *"Normal."* One party is in conflict with another who cooperates with the first. This characterizes the historic relationship between slave and master.

Now why is cooperation normally good and conflict normally bad? Before answering this question, consider the difference between ethics and morality.

Ethics and Morality

There is no generally accepted distinction between ethics and morality; therefore, they are often taken to be synonymous. This allows one to distinguish between them as one wants. I prefer to think of ethics as having the function of promoting cooperation and of morality, of reducing conflict. This makes ethics proscriptive—telling us what *should* be done—and morality, prescriptive—telling us what should *not* be done. Ethics is concerned with "thou shalt" and morality with "thou shalt not."

I think of "good" and "evil" as ethical concepts, and "right" and "wrong" as moral concepts. "Good and evil" and "right and wrong" are matters of degree; they are not dichotomies. To reduce conflict is usually right, but the amount by which it is reduced determines how right it is. Similarly, to increase cooperation is usually good, but the amount by which it is increased determines how good it is.

The eminent systems philosopher C. West Churchman wrote (1987):

Morality asks of any action or policy, is it right or wrong? But another thoughtful voice must ask, does "yes" or "no" exhaust the universe? Does the "answer" have to be "yes" or "no"? Is morality in a universe of discourse where "yes" or "no" are the only two possible answers? If the mind says "yes" then where does the mind find its authority? Surely systems research must find this question one of its fundamental ones, if systems research is seeking the design of a moral world.

Morality is an endless conversation of the living with our ances-
tors about how to design a good world for future generations.
And the conversation needs to be intelligent. . . . If one insists on a
"yes" or "no," the conversation ends. But it should not end. This
means that a definitive "yes" or "no" never occurs: morality is neither absolute nor relative. (257)

Nevertheless, ethicists and moralists have traditionally sought
absolute rules of conduct. The Ten Commandments, the Golden Rule,
and Immanuel Kant's Categorical Imperative are absolute. Those who
have produced such rules have attempted to reduce ethical-moral judgments to a determination of conformity to a rule or rules. This not
only makes such judgments dichotomous, but it invariably gives rise to
ethical-moral dilemmas. For example, who authenticates such rules?
God? Which God? What assurance do we have that those who claim
to speak in His name are authorized by Him to do so? How do we
account for the incompatibility of rules allegedly provided by different
gods? "Conscience" provides no better answers than "God." Whose
conscience? How can we deal with conflicting dictates of different con-
sciences? And so on.

As long as ethics depends on revelation for authentication, there will
be conflicting ethics. Consider all the genocide and wars justified by
such ethics. This, in a sense, is the ultimate conflict that we should seek
to eliminate.

I think a different approach to ethical-moral judgments is called for,
one based not on rules to be applied to the outcome of decisions, but *on
the way decisions are made*, on the decision-making process, not product.

Specification of an ethical-moral decision process must address two
questions: "Who should be involved in making a decision?" and "How
should they be involved?" The process principles that I propose are
ideal, not attainable but capable of being approached continuously.
The first such principle is:

**Decisions should be made by consensus of all those who are
directly affected by the decisions, the decision's stakeholders,
with the exceptions noted below.**

Application of this principle would assure decisions that serve the
interests of all the stakeholders in most situations and, therefore, their
cooperation with each other. I emphasize again that this is an *ideal* that
cannot be realized but can be approximated.

This ethical principle reveals why we consider criminal acts to be immoral. Criminals come into conflict with their victims, and they do so without the agreement of their victims. Criminals deprive their victims of their "right" to participate in decisions that directly affect them.

The second ethical principal, a corollary of the first, is based on the fact that there is only one desire that is and always will be universally shared: the desire for the ability to obtain whatever one needs or wants, omnicompetence. Put another way, no one would deliberately and knowingly deprive themselves of the ability and opportunity to develop. Therefore,

> No decision should be made that deprives another of the ability or opportunity to develop unless the one affected by the decision would otherwise deprive others of this ability or opportunity.

When criminals are apprehended, decisions must be made as to their treatment. Since they are directly affected by such decisions, should their agreement to it be required? No; this is an example to the first rule given above. How to treat one who behaves unethically should be a decision made by those affected by the unethical behavior or their representatives. However, that treatment should be directed at increasing the probability that the future acts of those who have acted unethically will be cooperative rather than conflicting. Increasing the probability of ethical behavior *is not the same* as decreasing the probability of unethical behavior. If *treatment-decisions are directed at reducing the probability of further unethical (conflicting) behavior by the guilty party, execution would be the most effective treatment.* But execution deprives the other of any possibility of development.

The treatment of criminals should focus on their reform, not punishment. Punishment should be used only when it can be demonstrated that reform is not possible without it. If reform is not possible with or without punishment, then the only appropriate punishment is separation of the criminal from his potential victims. This way of treating criminals would be in their best interests as well as in the best interests of their actual and potential victims. This concept of treatment applies to anyone who commits an immoral act, not only to criminals.

What about those whose immaturity, mental state, or ignorance prevent them from knowing what is in their own best interests? For example, should the agreement of children be required for all decisions made by their parents that affect them? Clearly not. It would be immoral to allow children or employees to harm themselves and others when enough is known to prevent such harm. The principle I suggest for such cases is as follows:

However unqualified individuals may be to participate in decisions
that affects them, they should be allowed to participate in making these decisions, but their agreement should not be required
if it can be demonstrated that they do not know what the consequences of these decisions are likely to be, and that the others
making the decision demonstrably know the consequences and
take the interests of the unqualified into account.

Who should decide who is qualified to make decisions on behalf of
others? The answer is the others. Recall that in the circular organization (Chapter 9) every manager's subordinates can remove their managers from their positions and therefore have a say in their selection.
This implies that experts who make decisions *for* others should be cer-
tified by those who are affected by them or representatives they have
selected. The authentication of experts is clearly a subject that requires
continuing discussion. (See Chafetz, 1996.)

Stakeholders

Corporate stakeholders are usually taken to include employees, shareholders, creditors, debtors, suppliers, distributing and retailing agents,
customers, consumers, government, and the relevant public. Competitors are excluded because they are not *directly* affected by what a
corporation does but indirectly, through the behavior of customers,
suppliers, or others.

Clearly, the number of stakeholders of some corporate decisions
runs into the millions, and there is no practical way of involving all of
them in every decision that affects them. This is the same problem that
the government of a democracy faces: it cannot conduct a referendum
on every issue to be decided. Therefore, it may be necessary in practice
to use *representatives* of various stakeholder groups. This, of course, is
what is currently done on corporate boards with respect to stockholders. Ideally, stakeholders should elect their representatives just as
stockholders do. This is possible for some of a corporation's stakeholders—for example, distributors—but not for others—for example, customers and the relevant public. In some cases, sample surveys could be
used to obtain the opinions that stakeholders have of those who have
been selected by others to represent them.

However, there is one very important group of stakeholders,
employees, who can either participate in decisions that directly affect

them or who can select their own representatives. A circular organizational design makes this—hence, ethical-moral decisions as I have defined them—possible.

The most overlooked group of stakeholders consists of future generations, born and unborn, none of whom can participate in current decisions, even through representatives they select. Of course, we cannot know what their specific interests will be, but we do know that whatever they will need and want, they will want the ability to pursue them effectively. Therefore, future stakeholders can be taken into account by making sure that nothing is done now to reduce their ability or desire to satisfy their needs and legitimate desires in the future. This implies, among other things, that the options available to future generations should not be reduced by decisions made now. Therefore, it is desirable for every organization, including governments, to designate individuals who will be responsible for identifying and evaluating the effects, if any, of current decisions on future generations' choices and the ability and desire to make them.

Now, how does all this relate to leadership?

The Nature of Leadership

Continuous development of a social system requires leadership. Unfortunately, there is a great deal of ambiguity associated with the concept of "leadership." It is often used interchangeably with "management" and "administration." What a waste! There are important differences between them. Without awareness of these differences, leadership is taken to be easier to attain than it actually is.

Administration consists of directing others in carrying out the will of a third party, using means specified by that party.

Management consists of directing others in the pursuit of ends using means, both of which have been selected by the manager. (*Executives* are managers who manage other managers.)

Leadership consists of guiding, encouraging, and facilitating the pursuit by others of ends using means, both of which they have personally selected or the selection of which they approve.

In this formulation, leadership requires an ability to bring the will of followers into consonance with that of the leader so they follow him or her *voluntarily*, with enthusiasm and dedication. Such voluntarism, enthusiasm, and dedication are not necessarily present in those who are managed or administered.

Leadership, Visions, and Strategies

According to Jan Carlzon (1987), who provided SAS Airlines with exceptional leadership, a leader must encourage and facilitate formulation of an organizational vision in which as many stakeholders as possible have participated. He must create

> an environment in which employees can accept and execute their responsibilities with confidence and finesse. He must communicate with his employees, imparting *the company's vision* and listening to what they need to make that vision a reality. To succeed . . . he must be a visionary, a strategist, an informer, a teacher, and an *inspirer.* (5, italics mine)

A organizational vision is a description of a state of that organization that is considered to be significantly more desirable than its current state. It is a state that cannot be approached without a *fundamental* change of direction, a change of the status quo. It takes courage to lead such a change, and it requires instilling the courage to make it in others. This involves more than persuasion; it requires the ability to *inspire.* Unlike persuasion, inspiration evokes a willingness to make sacrifices in the pursuit of long-run objectives or ideals. Therefore, visions that induce others to pursue ideals must be inspiring. An inspiring vision is the product of creative activity, of *design.* Inspiring visions are works of art. Effective leaders are artists.

Leadership may require the ability to encourage and facilitate the formulation of an inspiring vision, but it also requires the ability to implement pursuit of that vision. Inspiration without implementation is provocation, not leadership. Implementation without inspiration is management or administration, not leadership. Therefore, leaders must be creative in order to inspire and must inspire in order to evoke the courage required to pursue a vision. An inspiring, courage-evoking vision requires a *mobilizing idea* at its core. Such an idea need not appear to be realizable, as the Spanish philosopher, José Ortega y Gasset (1966), observed: "man has been able to grow enthusiastic over his vision of . . . unconvincing enterprises. He had put himself to work for the sake of an idea, seeking by magnificent exertions to arrive at the incredible. And in the end, he has arrived there" (1).

Summarizing this much, a leader is one who can either formulate an inspiring vision to facilitate the formulation of such a vision, or articulate and promote the acceptance of such a vision formulated by others. Realization of that vision may be unattainable, but it must be continuously approachable. The leader must also be able to encourage and facilitate (inspire) pursuit of that vision, that is, to invoke the courage required to do so even when short-term sacrifices are required. He must make the pursuit of the vision *fun as well as fulfilling*. Therefore, the major developmental aspect of leadership is aesthetic.

Why Leadership Cannot Be Taught

Teaching cannot produce great leaders precisely because leadership is primarily an aesthetic ability. The most schools can do is provide some of the tools and techniques usable in creative work required of leaders, but they cannot create creativity. For example, one can be taught to draw, sculpt, compose, or write better than one would without being taught, but one cannot be taught to do so creatively with excellence—to become an artist. There is a big difference between drawing well and creating a work of art. In fact, some great artists have not been able to draw particularly well.

In classes, students are given problems and taught to seek the solutions that their teachers expect; students' success depends on their ability to do so. This even carries over to corporate managers who, when presented with a problem, want to know what their bosses would expect or like. This approach to problems precludes creativity because creativity is the production of solutions that are unexpected. Leaders are driven by ideas, not by the expectations of others. They are skillful at finding ways to beat a system, not surrendering to it.

Beating a system is a creative act, an ability that is not sufficient for leadership but is necessary for it. It requires identifying, denying, and exploring the consequences of denying assumptions made by most managers. As Jose Ortega y Gasset pointed out, it is a way of arriving at the incredible. Almost every revolution appeared improbable at its outset, but those who led them found a way to beat the incumbent system—and usually with fewer resources than those available to the system they beat. The American Revolution was a good example.

The Nature of Systemic Transformations

A transformational leader must understand the nature of systems. They must also understand how transforming a system differs from reforming it. Transformations are discontinuous changes; reformations are continuous changes.

There are different kinds of transformations of an enterprise. For example, it may change the nature of its business by changing the nature of its output, as in changing from making horse-drawn carriages to making automobiles or in changing from making mechanical calculators to electronic computers. Or it may change the way the enterprise `s conceptualized. It is this latter type of change on which I focus here.

Recall that a system is a functioning whole that cannot be divided into independent parts. Recall also that four types of system were identified in Chapter 2:

Deterministic systems, in which neither the parts nor the whole are purposeful.

Animated systems, in which the whole is purposeful but the parts are not.

Social systems, in which both the parts and the whole are purposeful.

Ecological systems, in which some of the parts have purposes but not the whole.

Because of internally and externally applied pressures, some corporate managers are becoming aware of the fact that corporations are social systems and of what this implies. It implies the need to take into account the concerns, interests, and objectives (1) of the people who are part of the systems they manage and (2) of the larger systems that contain them—for example, society—and other systems and individuals who are parts of the same containing systems. In addition, these managers obviously have to (3) be concerned with the objectives of the organizations they manage. This preoccupation with the purposes of parts and containing wholes make it increasingly difficult for managers to think of their organizations as either mechanical or biological systems. Some have begun to think of them as systems in which people with purposes of their own play the major roles.

This social-systemic view maintains that executives have duties beyond maximizing value for shareholders. For example, Hicks B. Waldron, chairman of Avon Products, Inc., said:

> We have 40,000 employees and 1.3 million representatives around the world. . . . We have a number of suppliers, institutions, customers, communities. None of them have the same democratic freedom as shareholders do to buy or sell their shares. They have much deeper and much more important stakes in our company than our shareholders. ("The Battle for Corporate Control," 1987, 102)

Andrew C. Sigler, chairman of Champion International Corporation, said much the same thing:

What right does someone who owns the stock for an hour have to decide a company's fate? That's the law, and it's wrong. (p. 102)

Charles Handy articulated a transforming view of the corporation when he wrote:

A public corporation should now be regarded not as a piece of property but as a community—although a community created by a common purpose rather than by common place. No one owns a community. Communities, as democracies know them, have constitutions that recognize the rights of their different constituencies and that lay down the methods of governance. The core members of communities are more properly regarded as citizens rather than as employees or "human resources"—citizens with responsibilities as well as rights. (1997, 28)

A system is transformed when the type of system it is thought to be is changed, for example, when the concept of a corporation and the way it is managed and organized are changed from a deterministic or animate system to a social system. Therefore, a transformational leader is one who can encourage and facilitate the production and acceptance of a mobilizing (transformed) vision of a system. Equally important, the leader must be able to inspire and organize an effective pursuit of that vision and maintain it even when sacrifices are required.

The transformation to a social-systemically conceptualized and managed corporation requires a number of fundamental changes, including the following ones.

First, because today most employees in corporations can do their jobs better than their bosses can, the traditional notion of management as supervision of subordinates must be abandoned. Instead, managers have a responsibility for creating working conditions under which their subordinates can function as well as they know how. This requires that their subordinates have a great deal more freedom to work as they want than they have had up to now.

A study at Volvo AB revealed that employees are permitted to use only a very small portion of what they know that is relevant to their jobs. Pehr Gyllenhammar, then CEO, remarked at a meeting that if any other resource were used as poorly most companies would not survive.

Second, leaders have an obligation to enable their subordinates to do better tomorrow than the best they can do today, that is, to provide them with opportunities for continuous development through on- and off-the-job education and training. Leaders must be educators and encourage and facilitate education by others.

Boeing's program "Learning Together," which went into effect in January 1998, recognizes this obligation without reservations. The program has the following major characteristics:

Employees can study any subject offered by accredited colleges, universities, or trade schools.

Employees don't have to incur out-of-pocket expenses for tuition and many other fees.

Employees will receive up to $150 per class for books and other required materials. . . .

100 Boeing stock units, with a three-year vesting period, will be awarded to employees for each doctorate, master's, and initial bachelor's degree earned through the program. (Villiers, 1997)

Third, managers should manage the interactions (not the actions) of their subordinates and the interactions of the units they manage with other internal and external units so as to maximize their contribution to the organization as a whole.

These three requirements are best met in a democratic corporation (Chapter 9) in which (1) all stakeholders can participate directly or indirectly in making decisions that affect them, and (2) in which everyone with authority over others individually is subject to their collective authority. Without the support of one's subordinates, peers, and superiors, no one can manage effectively.

Fourth, internal units that supply products or provide service to other internal units must be as efficient and responsive as possible to those they serve. This can only be done by making internal sources compete against external sources of supply or service, that is, to operate within an internal market economy (Chapter 10). This precludes both internal bureaucratic monopolies and the need for benchmarking. It also eliminates the generation of make-work and the excess personnel associated with it that has led to downsizing.

Fifth, the organization's structure should be such that it is ready, willing, and able to change rapidly and effectively. Traditional treelike hierarchies cannot do this. There are several alternatives that can come closer to providing the flexibility required, including networks, heterarchies, and horizontal, matrix, and multidimensional organizations (Chapter 11).

Sixth, the organization must be capable of rapid and effective learning and adaptation. All learning derives from experience, our own and others'. Mistakes are the ultimate source of learning, which occurs when mistakes are identified, diagnosed, and corrected. Facilitation of these processes requires creation of a Learning and Adaptation Support System, such as was described in Chapter 8, one that identifies errors in expectations, assumptions, and predictions and corrects strategies, tactics, and operations appropriately.

Learning effectively from others requires creation of a culture in which constructive conversation and discussion is continuous. Jan Carlzon (1987) formulated much the same requirements of a transformational leader:

> A leader must have . . . a good business sense and a broad understanding of how things fit together—the relationships among individuals and groups inside and outside the company and the interplay among the various elements of the company's operations. . . .
>
> By defining clear goals and strategies and then communicating them to his employees and training them to take responsibility for reaching those goals, the leader can create a secure working environment that fosters flexibility and innovation. Thus, the new leader is a listener, communicator, and educator—an emotionally expressive and inspiring person who can create the right atmosphere rather than make all the decisions himself. (35–36)

The transformation of a corporation from one conceptualized as an animate system to a social system is only one kind of transformation that is possible. However, in our current environment—one characterized by an increasing rate of change; increasing complexity; and an increasing rate of production of understanding, knowledge, and information—there is no other type of transformation that can bring about the necessary focus on employees, customers, and the other corporate stakeholders. A corporation that fails to see itself as an instrument of all its stakeholders will probably fail to use them, and be used by them, effectively enough to survive in the emerging environment.

Conclusion

Development is not something that is done to an individual or group; it is something they do to themselves. It is an increase in the ability and desire to satisfy one's needs and legitimate desires and those of others. It is a matter of learning, not earning. No one can learn for another, but one can encourage and facilitate the learning of another. Development is not a matter of how much one has, but how much one can do with whatever one has and what resources one can create out of what is available.

An organization can develop without growing, but growth can provide the resources that facilitate development. Growth is primarily a matter of economics, but development also involves science, technology, and education; ethics and morality; and aesthetics. These four horses draw the development wagon, and this wagon can go no faster than the slowest horse.

Organizational development requires leadership, which is primarily an aesthetic activity. One who leads development must inspire pursuit of a vision in whose production the leader had a hand. A vision is a picture of a state more desirable than the one that the organization currently is in. Leadership must also facilitate development of the strategy, tactics, and operations by whose means the vision can be pursued. Since the vision is often one of an ideal that can never be attained, though it may be approached continuously, leadership must see to it that the pursuit itself is satisfying, that it is fun as well as meaningful and valuable. Effective pursuit of an ideal requires the leader to extract the best possible effort from those who follow. In a corporation, this requires providing nothing less than a very high quality of work life.

A vision that involves a radical change in the way an organization is conceptualized is a transforming vision. One who leads the pursuit of such a vision is a transformational leader. Transformations are primarily qualitative, rather than quantitative, and are large discontinuities, not merely reform or incremental improvements.

Development not only requires the ability to do things right—and thereby requiring information, knowledge, and understanding—but also the ability to do the right things—hence wisdom. Wisdom, in turn, is based on ethical and aesthetic value judgments. The function of ethics is to promote peace of mind and peace on earth; without such a state of mind and level of cooperation, continuous pursuit of an ideal is not possible. The ability to inspire is an aesthetic ability, as also is the ability to make the pursuit of a vision itself a major source of satisfaction. The leader is one who creates followers and re-creates them so as to maintain their continuous pursuit of the vision.

During the Renaissance, when everything, including life itself, was subjected to analysis, life itself was disassembled into what were considered fundamental but independent activities: work, play, learning, and inspiration. Institutions were created in which each activity could be carried out independently. Factories were designed for work, not play, learning, or inspiration. Theaters and arenas were designed for play, not work, learning, or inspiration. Schools were designed for learning, not work, play, or inspiration. Museums and churches were designed to provide inspiration, not for work, play, or learning. However, the transformation to systemic thinking has brought with it a growing awareness of the fact that the effectiveness with which any of these activities can be carried out depends on the extent to which they are integrated. Therefore, it has become apparent that a transformational leader must be able to integrate the various aspects of life in order to effectively pursue development. The transformational leader is one who can create an organization that reunifies life, who integrates work, play, learning, and inspiration.

Appendix A

A Short Bibliography on Systems

Ackoff, Russell L., and Fred E. Emery. 1981. *On purposeful systems.* Seaside, Calif.: Intersystems Publications.

Beer, Stafford. 1966. *Decision and control.* London: John Wiley & Sons.

———. 1994. *Brain of the firm.* 2d ed. Chichester, England: John Wiley & Sons.

Bertalanffy, Ludvig von. 1968. *General systems theory.* New York: Braziller.

Capra, Fritjof. 1982. *The turning point.* New York: Simon & Schuster.

———. 1996. *The web of life.* New York: Anchor Books.

Checkland, Peter. 1981. *Systems thinking, systems practice.* Chichester, England: John Wiley & Sons.

Churchman, C. West. 1968. *The systems approach.* New York: Delacorte Press.

———. 1979. *The systems approach and its enemies.* New York: Basic Books.

———. 1971. *Design of inquiring systems.* New York: Basic Books.

Emery, Fred E., ed. 1969. *Systems thinking: Selected readings,* Vols. 1 and 2. New York: Penguin.

Emery, Fred E., and Eric L. Trist. 1973. *Towards a social ecology.* London: Plenum Press.

Flood, Robert L., and Michael C. Jackson. 1991. *Creative problem-solving.* Chichester, England: John Wiley & Sons.

———, eds. 1991. *Critical systems theory.* Chichester, England: John Wiley & Sons.

Gharajedaghi, Jamshid. 1985. *Toward a systems theory of organizations.* Seaside, CA.: Intersystems Publications.

Gleick, James. 1987. *Chaos.* New York: Penguin.

Hutchins, C. Larry. 1998. *Systems thinking: Solving complex problems.* Aurora, Colo.: Professional Development Systems.

Jackson, Michael. 1991. *Systems methodology for the management sciences.* New York: Plenum Press.

Kauffman, Draper L., Jr. 1980. *Systems 1: An introduction to systems thinking.* Minneapolis, Minn.: Future Systems.

Kuhn, Thomas S. 1962. *The structure of scientific revolutions.* Chicago: University of Chicago Press.

Lazlo, Ervin. 1972. *The systems view of the world.* New York: Braziller.

Miller, James G. 1971. The nature of living systems; Living Systems: The
    group. *Behavioral Science* 16 (July): 277–398.
Schon, Donald A. 1971. *Beyond the stable state*. New York: Random House.
Senge, Peter. 1990. *The fifth discipline*. New York: Doubleday.

Appendix B

An Application of Interactive Planning

[Note: The account that follows is a portion of a report of an interactive planning project as described in Part II conducted on the DuPont Specialty Chemicals Safety, Health, and Environment (SHE) Function that was prepared by James E. Leemann, SHE Manager of Specialty Chemicals.

This account is a reduction by more than half of the original report. However, the writing is all Leemann's. The location of the deletions are indicated. I have made some format changes to make this account compatible with the rest of this book.

Leemann has seen this version and does not think it has distorted the original. Those who would like a copy of the original can obtain it from James E. Leemann, SHE Systems Manager, DuPont Specialty Chemicals, 800 Chapelle Street, New Orleans, LA 70124–3312.]

. . . In July 1994, DuPont took a giant step forward with the integrated development of a new safety, health, and environmental policy known as *The DuPont Commitment—Safety, Health, and Environment*. . . . From this commitment, the corporation adopted a new slogan, *The Goal Is ZERO*. The business units are striving to have zero injuries, illnesses, wastes and emissions, and incidents (e.g., environmental, process, and transportation incidents). For the Specialty Chemicals business unit to meet this new commitment and goal, the SBU's [Strategic Business Unit's] SHE function had to approach its work in a completely different fashion.

In March 1995, I presented a very high-level overview of the SHE system as it existed in Specialty Chemicals to the SBU's senior leadership. I characterized the current SHE system as being incompatible with the existing business system. Specialty Chemicals was home to twenty-three small independent businesses that manufacture, handle, and sell essentially all of DuPont's hazardous and toxic chemicals to almost *4,000* internal and external customers. The annual gross revenue of all these businesses together was $1.6 billion. The SBU was looking for growth opportunities in new products, new markets, and new regions of the world. In addition, the SBU was beginning to work on the development of a high-performing work culture.

At the time, the Specialty Chemicals SHE system was typical of most of those found in major manufacturing industries. The numerous disciplines of SHE were not integrated into the business decision making processes. The SHE function was a very centralized-hierarchical organization whose role was to ensure that the businesses complied with federal and state regulations and corporate policies and standards. Poor knowledge management that resulted in SHE professionals reinventing their SHE knowledge every two to three years hampered the SHE function. In addition, the business did not understand how to effectively use its SHE professionals' expertise, which resulted in SHE professionals performing very time-consuming clerk-type activities, reacting to operational crises, and having virtually no time or support for professional growth and development.

A sampling of the SHE trends that were evident in 1995 included federal and state government agencies beginning to experiment with more innovative ways to address industrial SHE issues rather than resorting to punitive enforcement measures. There was an increasing desire by U.S. EPA and environmental activist groups for industries to publicly disclose more data and information about their manufacturing operations, especially involving wastes and emissions. The use of independent third-party auditors to review SHE programs in corporations was expected by activist groups and local communities. Some attention was being given to the European-driven development of a new environmental management standard known as the ISO 14000 series.

In May 1995, Specialty Chemicals SBU senior leadership approved the redesign of the SBU SHE function project and committed to supporting the effort. The idealized redesign effort followed Ackoff's Interactive Planning methodology with some modifications based on advice provided by Dr. Ackoff.

Formulating the Mess

Normally, at this stage of the redesign process one would go through a systems analysis, conduct an obstruction analysis, and prepare reference projections followed by reference scenarios. . . . Dr. Ackoff advised us that, since DuPont is already recognized as the safest industrial manufacturing company in the world, there was no need to go through a full-blown mess formulation. Indeed, the reason the idealized redesign was so appealing to management centered on its desire to maintain a leadership position in the world and, if possible, to further develop its SHE functional excellence into a competitive advantage offering for its businesses. Since we had decided that the SHE function would have to transform itself in order to deliver the functioning capability necessary for the businesses to meet the new *DuPont SHE Commitment* and *The Goal Is ZERO* objective, a small team began to prepare for the idealized redesign process.

Ends Planning

The ends planning stage was divided into two distinct efforts. The first group involved consumers of SHE information. A second group would redesign the SHE system in accordance with the consumers' specifications.

The Consumer Group

The consumer group comprised a cross-section of participants from within Specialty Chemicals who were chosen based on the following criteria: (1) the participant uses SHE information; (2) the participant is responsible for implementation of SHE; (3) the participant has the ability to specify what he or she needs from a SHE system; (4) the participant represents diversity; (5) the participant is an "out-of-the-box" thinker; and (6) the participant understands the need for SHE and its role in the business. The seventeen participants who were chosen included manufacturing operators and mechanics, plant managers, manufacturing unit managers, product managers, business managers and directors, functional managers, and one SHE professional. The SHE professional was present to answer any questions related to SHE that might arise and to provide insights from the consumer group's work to the designers group.

The consumers' task was to identify the specifications they believed would be essential to creating an idealized SHE system that would meet their needs. Interestingly, many of my SHE professional colleagues were upset that this group of consumers was chosen to provide the specifications for a new SHE system that the SHE professionals were going to have to design in the next stage of the planning process. Several SHE professionals commented that "no consumers have any idea as to what they truly need to redesign a SHE system."

The consumer planning session consisted of a one-day meeting held off-site in Wilmington, Delaware. Past experience with DuPonters has shown that it is important to conduct these types of intensive thinking sessions away from the participants' work environment to limit the distractions. We began the session with a brief background on the planning process. The consumer group first identified the positive and negative output issues that they had with the current SHE system. Next, the consumers were asked to specify the properties that they believed were essential for an ideal SHE system if they could install the system today. The planning session was based on the assumption that the Specialty Chemicals SHE system had been destroyed the previous night, but that the remaining parts of Specialty Chemicals remained intact. The consumer group was given the challenge to specify the desired properties of a new redesigned SHE system. It was pointed out that these properties should not be constrained by considerations of feasibility. A distinction was made, however, between those properties on which a consensus was reached and those on which there were significant differences. As it turned out, there were no significant differences of opinion. To help specify the desired properties, a framework of questions was used.

The consumers proceeded to identify the output issues they believed characterized the current SHE system and subsequently used Peter Senge's multiple levels of explanation to divide these issues into three main categories: systemic structure, patterns of behavior, and events. As Senge (1990) points out in *The Fifth Discipline*, the systems perspective shows that there are multiple levels of explanation in any complex situation. Event explanations answer "who did what to whom" and are most common in contemporary culture. They are one of the reasons why reactive management prevails. Patterns of behavior explanations focus on seeing longer-term trends and assessing their implications. Systemic structural explanations focus on answering the question, "What causes the patterns of behavior?"

The *Systemic Structure* issues that were raised covered a wide variety of areas that had obviously been on these participants' minds. Several participants mentioned that they appreciated the opportunity to have a safe forum in which they could openly discuss these issues. . . .

The next step the consumer group participants took was to identify the ideal state specifications for a new SHE system. Recall that the SHE system was assumed to have been destroyed the night before, but that the remaining parts of the operating business systems were intact. . . .

The consumer group identified fifty-eight specifications it believed were necessary to create a new SHE system. These fifty-eight specifications were narrowed to nineteen and grouped into nine major categories. . . .

Several days later the consumer group participants were asked to review each specification one more time while applying the following test for each statement. First, they were asked to contradict the statement. Second, they were asked whether anyone would assert the contradiction. Finally, it was determined that no one would make the original statement meaningless. For example, stating that we are going into business to "not" make a profit would be nonsensical and thus should be dropped from the list of specifications. Satisfied with their specifications, the consumer group members were ready to hand them over to the designer group for the next step in the process.

The Designer Group

The designer group comprised another cross-section of participants from within Specialty Chemicals who were chosen based on the following criteria: (1) the participant has detailed knowledge of SHE; (2) the participant has progressive thinking capabilities (i.e., "out of-the-box" thinker); (3) the participant has a positive attitude; and (4) the participant represents diversity. The twenty-six participants chosen included thirteen SHE professionals, as well as functional managers, business and functional directors, business managers, manufacturing unit managers, and marketing managers.

The designer group's task was to develop an idealized redesign of the SHE system, again assuming that the existing SHE system had been completely destroyed the previous night, but that its environment remained exactly as it was. The redesigned SHE system would replace the existing system right now. In addition, the redesigned SHE system must reflect all the specifications identified by the consumer group and *dissolve* all the output issues raised by that group.

The designer planning session involved the use of an iterative design process that the designers would go through three times. . . . The process consisted of three two-day planning meetings held about two weeks apart from each other. At the first session all the materials (i.e., the SHE system's current state outputs and the specifications for an idealized redesigned SHE system) created by the consumer group were reviewed for the designers. A discussion for clarification followed. At this point in the planning session, it was interesting to note that the SHE professionals in the session did not disagree with the current state of SHE developed by the consumer group and were quite surprised and pleased by the specifications the consumers identified as necessary to an idealized SHE redesign. As mentioned earlier, the designers were tasked with having to create an idealized redesign of the SHE system that addressed all the current-state output issues and met all the specifications. The same assumption that the SHE system had been destroyed the night before but that the entire environment remained intact applied to these planning sessions also.

Before beginning the iterative design process, the designers were asked to identify which individuals and groups they would consider the SHE system's stakeholders. In other words, which individuals or groups will be affected by or affect the SHE system after it is redesigned? The designers identified the following stakeholders: customers, plant sites, employees, functions, government, businesses, local community, DuPont, the SHE Excellence Center. . . . They also prepared brief statements on what they believed each stakeholder's expectations would be regarding the redesigned SHE system. . . .

The iterative design process comprised four main parts that would be revisited three times. The parts included (1) the formulation of a mission statement; (2) the identification of the SHE system's functions; (3) the development of the SHE work processes; and (4) the design of the SHE organizational structure. A critically important aspect of the idealized design process centers on the designers focusing on the function and work processes of SHE first, then turning their attention to how the SHE structure should be organized to accomplish the work and achieve the mission. Rarely are all the individuals affected by a reorganization invited to participate in their own reorganization. Almost always, managers direct their attention to reorganizing their hierarchical structure first and rarely get around to redesigning the function or the work of the organization.

The designers used the . . . criteria developed by Ackoff [Chapter 5] to formulate the SHE mission statement. . . .

The next step in the iterative design process has the designers identifying the functions of the SHE system. The designers use the output issues identified by the consumer group and their own stakeholder expectations work to determine what the SHE system's functions need to be in order to serve the business needs. The key to this step of the process is defining the services and offerings the idealized redesigned SHE system will provide to its users (i.e., stakeholders). At this stage of the process, one significant barrier the designers ran into was trying to sort out opposing tendencies—for example, deciding whether a particular SHE function was going to be done by a central SHE staff group or by SHE professionals integrated in the businesses. To overcome this barrier we used [an] illustration . . . to move the designers from *resolving* conflict with solutions that are "good enough" to *dissolving* conflict by changing the nature of the system from an "Either/Or" relationship to an "And" relationship.

Once the functions had been defined, the designers' next step involved developing the SHE work processes. The processes on which the designers worked included organizational processes, throughput processes, and latent processes. Organizational processes deal with planning and decision making, the learning and control system, and the measurement and reward systems. Throughput processes are redesigned to reduce complexity and improve operational efficiency and quality. The objective is to produce an integrated solution (a single design) for all the critical throughput processes to achieve a reduction in cycle time, elimination of waste, increased flexibility, and total quality. In addition to throughput processes are the latent processes, which are aimed at creating potential for the SHE system. Latent processes capture and translate into the system the latent and implicit needs of the existing and potential users. They provide an ongoing basis for generating alternative products and services for existing and new markets. Latent processes help define the emerging competitive games and create readiness for a technological and organizational break with the past.

The final step in the iterative design process deals with the system's structure. This step defines how the major components of the SHE organization will be grouped together and determines the flow of responsibility and authority within the SHE organization. It determines what the relationships between units will be, the impact on internal communication, and how resources will flow between the units.

As I mentioned earlier, the designer group journeyed through each of these iterative steps three times. For most of the designer participants, the process at first seemed a somewhat torturous task. In fact, two participants dropped out of the process after the first two-day designer planning session, believing that what they had done was "good enough." As they passed through the steps of each cycle, the remaining participants began to see that their product was changing significantly and improving from one cycle to the next. By the end of the second two-day session, all of the participants were excited and extremely pleased with their work and wondered if they really needed to go through another cycle. After some discussion about meeting

again, everyone agreed to work through one more cycle. It was good
that they did, because the final planning session resulted in a more
refined and tighter mission statement, a clearer set of SHE functions,
better defined SHE work processes, and a completely new SHE structure that would dissolve the output issues identified by the consumer
group and meet the necessary specifications for an idealized redesigned
SHE system. . . .

Means Planning

After completing the idealized SHE system redesign, a team of SHE
professionals was chosen to close the gaps between the current SHE
state and the idealized redesign of the SHE system. As it turned out,
this step in the iterative planning process became one of the most difficult. To a great extent these SHE professionals began to realize for the
first time that they were being given the opportunity to redesign their
future SHE work by inventing ways to bring about the idealized
redesign. Another reason for the difficulty was the disparate opinions
and points of view as to how the team should approximate the idealized
redesign.

The team of SHE professionals comprised individuals who were
primarily located at our Specialty Chemicals plants. All these professionals had at least ten years of experience performing day-to-day SHE
work normally encountered at a chemical manufacturing plant. Some
were specialists in their field, such as industrial hygiene, safety, environmental issues, hazardous chemical handling, risk assessment,
process safety management, training, fire protection, and emergency
response, while others were generalists in the SHE fields.

During 1996, quarterly two-day meetings were held to scope the
overall project and raise the level of awareness and comfort for implementing of the idealized SHE redesign. The team spent the year identifying work projects, developing work practices, and learning the
Rummler-Brache Process Improvement Project approach to work-
process simplification and improvement (Rummler-Brache Group,
1988 and 1990).

The project's chosen included developing (1) a standardized SBU-
wide SHE training program to meet federally mandated training; (2) a
standardized "Safety How Manual" consisting of SBU-wide safety
standards and procedures; (3) an electronic tracking system to track
follow-up and completion of items identified during SHE audits and
incident investigations; (4) an electronic data management system to

serve as a "living memory" for all SHE-related reports; and (5) an electronic evergreen repository of federal SHE regulations and DuPont's Legal and Engineering interpretations and guidelines. The team selected these projects to serve as surrogates toward learning how to do work in a cross-SBU team network. Each project was evaluated for its overall business impact and feasibility (i.e., timing and costs). The intent of this exercise was to gain an appreciation for the means that would be used to undertake the work.

The evaluation concluded that the only project of this grouping that had a moderate business impact and could be implemented in a short time frame for significant cost savings was the electronic federal SHE regulations project. The regulatory interpretations and guidance portion of this project was placed on hold, based on concerns raised by DuPont's Legal Department. The team selected a commercial product that delivered all of the federal and states SHE regulations via the Internet. This decision led to the elimination of all paper subscriptions to regulatory services, such as BNA, Inc.; the *Federal Register*; and all state regulatory publications. The project was implemented within three weeks and the savings to the SBU were $47,000/year. The other two electronic projects (i.e., tracking and data management) were not pursued at this time, based on the lack of an electronic infrastructure across the SBU to support such projects. It was discovered that another group within the SBU was exploring the delivery of federally mandated training using computer-based methods. In light of this, the team elected to integrate the training project into the other group's work.

Despite a great deal of interest in tackling the development of a single standardized "Safety How Manual" that would apply to all Specialty Chemicals plant sites, there was a tremendous amount of apprehension among the team members in undertaking this project as one of its first. A main reason for the apprehension centered on the belief that because each plant has such a very high degree of ownership for its own "Safety How Manual," each plant would use whatever means possible to preserve the content of their own manual. History has shown that each plant has modified its own manual to address issues that surface as a result of an accident or injury, often at the plant location. For example, OSHA's standard for tying off [providing fall protection] a person starts at six feet off the ground. Most of our plants have a much tighter standard (e.g., tying off at three feet off the ground) because someone fell from an elevation less than six feet high and sustained a recordable injury. Recall that safety in the DuPont culture is valued as one of its highest operating principles.

Key Steps

It became quite apparent during the first Means Planning session that even though all the SHE professionals who had participated in the Designer Group's work were members of this team, there were enough new team members that additional work had to be done to bring everyone to the same point on the SHE redesign's progress. Although the better part of the year was spent aligning everyone, some key steps were taken that led to the success of this stage of the overall effort. [For example:]

- Providing a detailed grounding on the mission statement, functions, processes, and structure of the idealized SHE redesign and the specifications of the consumer group, as well as allowing time for interactive dialog and consensus building.
- Tying the idealized SHE redesign to the needs of the business in order for SHE professionals to understand why it was necessary to change the way SHE work would be done in the future.
- Defining the roles and responsibilities of the SHE professionals and ensuring that they understood and agreed to undertake the effort. . . .

Key Missteps

Some of the key missteps we experienced during the Means Planning stage in 1996 included the following:

- Everyone agreed to a 15 percent to 20 percent time commitment (approximately one day per week) to the SHE redesign effort; however, in reality participants were hard pressed to meet a 5 percent commitment primarily because of the pressing needs of the business. Many felt the effort was stealing parts of their at-work time; however, many believed in the effort so much that they worked on it during their off-hours.
- Most of 1996 was spent building the necessary energy in the network team leaders so that they would want to personally own the redesign of their work. This caused a significant delay in naming other SHE professionals to the various SHE knowledge network teams and establishing what the team roles would be in the effort.
- We assumed that the high level of management support

gained initially would be enough to encourage other levels of management support throughout the organization. The high-level support was primarily verbal with little action, which led to varying degrees of interpretation for actual support in other parts of the organization. In other words, a number of people believed that support for the effort was optional. . . .

Reflection on the first year. The first year's work on implementing the idealized SHE redesign actually turned out to be a year of working on the means by which the redesign would be implemented. The main areas of attention in the 1997 implementation included more visible and active support from management and their staffs, expanding participation, considering a full-time project manager and facilitator role, addressing information technology infrastructure issues, engaging a software developer, and determining how to increase contact time among team members without increasing travel costs.

Resource Planning

Toward the end of 1996 another organizational change took place involving the SBU SHE Manager position, which I had been in since 1991. I was placed on special assignment as the SBU SHE System Manager working full-time on the SHE redesign project, and a new SBU SHE Manager entered the position. After completing the transition of the day-to-day SBU SHE Manager's work, we focused on the SHE redesign project. Both of us realized that we needed to develop a plan that would identify the resources required to implement the idealized SHE redesign. The types of resources we addressed in the plan were personnel, money (financial planning), facilities and equipment (capital investments), and inputs (materials, supplies, and services).

Personnel Planning

Based on the magnitude of implementing the idealized SHE redesign, it was necessary to hire a full-time project manager and a new facilitator. It was estimated that these positions would be in place for approximately two years.

In order to deliver the idealized SHE redesign, it was determined that there would be eight SHE knowledge network teams, a core team of the network leaders and specific functional support staff members, and a steering team. The SHE knowledge network teams would cover

Safety, Health, Environmental Issues, Process Safety Management, Distribution, Community, Product Stewardship, and Fire Prevention/ Protection and Emergency Response. Each of these network teams would consist of ten to fifteen members drawn from Specialty Chemicals manufacturing plants and from some corporate SHE staff functions. The purpose of these network teams would be to undertake the tactical work of implementing the SHE redesign.

The core team membership would consist of the eight knowledge network team leaders, the project manager, the facilitator, the SBU SHE Manager, the SBU SHE Systems Manager, the project's Information Systems Manager, and the SBU Organization Learning Leader. The core team would also have functional support members from the corporation's Information Systems group. The purpose of the core team would be to address common tactical issues that surface during the implementation and to provide input on strategic issues.

The steering team would consist of the project manager, the SBU SHE Manager, the SBU SHE Systems Manager, the facilitator, the SBU Information Systems Manager, and the SBU Organization Learning Leader. In addition to these permanent members there would be a representative from the SHE knowledge network team leaders. The purpose of the steering team would be to address strategic issues involving implementation of the redesign.

Financial Planning

In addition to the network team leaders' difficulty in finding time to work on the redesign, issues of costs were always in the forefront of discussions with management. All during the second half of 1996, significant activities (e.g., downsizing, stop-spending programs, no travel, deferred training) were under way to reduce all costs in order to meet the SBU's profit objective. To get a better picture of the costs of doing SHE work in the current state of Specialty Chemicals, a comprehensive cost accounting project was conducted. The intent of this project was to establish an accurate accounting of these costs for the first time and to use the outcome as a basis to gain funding for the redesign work.

The work resulted in accounting for $106MM in annualized costs to do SHE work in Specialty Chemicals. This amounted to 7 percent of the SBU's total revenues (i.e., sales and transfers). Wastewater treatment costs accounted for 31 percent of the total. Operators, mechanics, and technicians spend approximately 15 percent of their time doing SHE activities, or about $17 million per year. Of these activities, about $11 million per year is spent on federally mandated training. . . .

To illustrate the cost savings that would be realized by implementing the redesign, an analysis was done of the costs to update standard operating procedures (SOPs) and develop monthly safety meetings. Currently, each year twenty plants review and update 10 SOPs per plant using a team of six people per plant for a total of 200 SOPs and 120 people. Each SOP takes about 10 hours per person to review and update, resulting in the expenditure of about 240,000 people hours per year for the entire SBU. By networking the plants and agreeing to more standardized and consistent SOPs for the entire SBU, a network of one representative person per plant (20 people) would work on reviewing and updating the 200 SOPs and spend 10 hours per SOP, resulting in 40,000 people hours per year. The cost savings would amount to 200,000 people hours per year. The representative person from each plant would not have to be the same person for each of the 200 SOPs.

Another example involved the design of one safety meeting topic per month per plant that is usually designed by a team of 6 people per plant. Each safety meeting topic takes about 3 hours per person to develop into a meaningful agenda for a total of 4,320 people hours per year for the entire SBU. By networking the plants and agreeing on twelve topics to be covered per year across the SBU, a network of one representative person per plant (20 people) would work on developing the twelve safety meetings, spending 3 hours per topic and resulting in 720 people hours per year. The cost savings would amount to *3,600* people hours per year for the entire SBU. Again, the representative person from each plant would not have to be the same person for each of the twelve topics.

By using the cost accounting work and these two cost savings examples, the redesign team succeeded in securing a three-year budget commitment for implementing the idealized SHE redesign. The total 1997 through 1999 implementation budget is $495,000 for network and computer software development expenditures. In addition, a commitment for 20 percent of network team members' time was agreed to by management.

Facilities and Equipment Planning

The facilities and equipment planning addressed computer equipment and the deployment of correctly configured hardware to all members of the network teams. In some cases, team members were in line to receive the equipment but were not scheduled to receive their upgraded equipment in the near future. The project manager and the SBU SHE Manager approached the businesses for which this was an issue and managed to rearrange the delivery schedule for those team members. There was some reluctance on the part of a few businesses because they had not anticipated these equipment costs during the current business cycle.

Inputs—Materials, Supplies, and Services Planning

The materials, supplies, and services planning focused on the need to deploy the software package that the team members would be using to collaborate on redesigning their work. It was decided that the team would use Lotus Notes 4.5 as the main software platform for the collaboration. Once the software was deployed there would be a need for training team members on how to effectively use the tool. The training of the team leaders would be accomplished by hiring a computer-training consultant. Thereafter, the team members would be trained at various plant sites by the facilitator with assistance from the SBU SHE Systems Manager.

In addition to these services, a Lotus Notes software developer was hired to design the templates for the computer database in which the SHE knowledge would reside. For the project to succeed, it would be important for the contractor to be able to do rapid application development of screens and templates as the project was progressing instead of waiting until a volume of material was developed and then inputted into the database.

Continuing cost-cutting pressure was being applied to everyone in the SBU. The team leaders realized that for the SHE redesign to be implemented more contact among the team leaders and network members had to occur. Agreement was reached with senior management to allow for quarterly face-to-face meetings in Wilmington, Delaware. To facilitate core team and network team meetings, everyone installed Microsoft's NetMeeting software from the Internet and began having meetings over the company's computer network, a move that significantly reduced travel costs. Within a matter of several meetings, everyone had become quite proficient in using NetMeeting and doing work.

Implementation

Implementation is about who is to do what, when, where, and how. As implementation milestones were achieved, the results of the work were monitored to ensure the idealized SHE redesign was being realized. During this stage of the interactive planning process, the overall effort had to exhibit a significant amount of flexibility and adapt to the ever-changing issues the businesses were addressing at the time. Some of the major issues included (1) continued pressure to reduce costs, (2) further downsizing, (3) increased integration of functional staff work into the various businesses, and (4) increased tension on making profit objectives.

The key factors that significantly influenced the successful implementation of the SHE redesign included:

- The Human Factor
- The Organizational Factor
- The Work Factor
- The Technology Factor
- The Commitment Factor

The Human Factor

The most important success factor involved the people who were tasked with realizing the idealized SHE redesign in Specialty Chemicals. Essentially, everyone in his or her career had experienced belonging to a committee or team. However, most would agree that their involvement had more to do with exchanging information and less to do with actually doing work that added direct value to the business.

To realize the full potential of the SHE redesign, the eight SHE Knowledge Network team leaders invited a cross section of Specialty Chemicals SHE professionals with expertise in their SHE knowledge arena to join the network team and help develop the SHE knowledge germane to Specialty Chemicals' businesses. Each team comprised ten to fifteen members. The SHE knowledge arenas covered by these network teams included safety, occupational health, environment protection, process safety management, distribution, community affairs, product stewardship, and fire prevention/protection and emergency response.

Prior to selecting network team members, the team leaders identified the attributes that would be essential for the networks to succeed. . . .

Once the network teams were established, the next challenge was to engage the team members, who were located at different plant sites across the country, to work in a virtual collaborative fashion. The use of Lotus Notes, Microsoft's NetMeeting, and e-mail certainly facilitated the virtual collaborative work. . . .

Within several months of meeting in a virtual fashion, the network team members became more acquainted with each other, some for the first time, and they began to undertake the task of identifying all the SHE work and prioritizing when, how, and who would be responsible for the work. . . .

All through the implementation stage it was critical to nurture the networks by helping the members realize the potential value they could deliver to the business and by identifying specific examples of where they had achieved success. . . .

The Organizational Factor

No effort of this magnitude would ever be allowed to occur unless management at all levels of the organization was fully supportive of the effort. The key to this success factor came in the form of engaging management in authentic participation as opposed to token participation. Often management will be supportive because it is politically correct to show support. The network leaders recognized that they needed highly visible active support from management in order to succeed. To gain active support each network team selected a member of management with a passion for its SHE knowledge area to serve as team sponsor.

For the purpose of the SHE redesign effort, the network leaders defined the attributes and expectations for sponsorship that they believed would lead to success. . . .

Early in the implementation stage, the SBU's plant managers and the Director of Operations were solicited for their insights on issues and any concerns they had with the SHE redesign effort. . . . Everyone agreed that . . . implementation of the SHE redesign would result in everyone's role and responsibilities changing in the future. The organization's leadership committed to personally taking the time to understand the details of the SHE redesign effort and to exhibit real involvement in their sponsorship roles. . . .

The Work Factor

In the beginning of the implementation stage many of the network team leaders and members were skeptical about redesigning their SHE work. Their skepticism ranged from how overwhelming the task would be to concern that the effort was merely a unique way to capture their SHE knowledge in an electronic fashion and further downsize their ranks. In dealing with the latter concern, we devoted time to developing the characteristics and expectations of the new SHE professionals' roles and responsibilities once the SHE redesign was implemented. . . . The personal benefits included having a better understanding of the businesses and their challenges, doing higher level work that is more interesting and challenging, and creating opportunities for advancement. The SBU benefits included more value-adding SHE work resulting in improved productivity, a better safety performance, and pollution prevention, along with development of a SHE learning organization.

Developing the SHE knowledge so that the ultimate users, the line organizations, would actually use it to make decisions during their daily work activities initially proved difficult. The SHE redesign networks realized early on that their work would need to reside in an electronic medium in order to allow easy access by the entire organization, including contractors. Eventually, the SHE knowledge would be available via the Internet to other SBUs in DuPont and to Specialty Chemicals' customers. . . .

After a module or application was developed and before any data were inputted into the knowledge database, a walk-through or heuristic evaluation was conducted. . . .Typically, a heuristic evaluation lasted one to two hours. . . .

The Technology Factor

Information technology has played a critically important role in providing an electronic mechanism to facilitate collaboration and retention of organizational memory during the SHE redesign implementation. Senior management in the SBU realized that entering the information age had the potential for accelerating the growth of and creating product differentiation for its commodity chemical businesses. Undertaking this task presented a number of challenges, including replacing essentially all computer hardware systems to PC hardware running on the Windows 95 operating system using Microsoft Office 95 or 97 software. Early in the implementation stage, the SBU leadership decided to migrate to Lotus Notes 4.5 and begin the migration from five e-mail systems to Lotus Notes e-mail. Fortunately, the SHE redesign network team members were among the first to be upgraded to the new computer systems. . . .

The key to our technology success can best be described as integrating the SHE redesign information technology requirements into the business's existing information system plans versus trying to drive the implementation of a totally separate information system. . . .

The Commitment Factor

Often the need for change and how change is brought about have been formulated by a small group of individuals and essentially forced upon the organization for implementation through hierarchical command and control measures. This popular approach to management will produce results; however, managers must continually apply command and control pressure to sustain the results. Those tasked with sustaining the results do so in a compliant fashion. Compliant employees range from those who see the benefit of the change and do what is expected, or even a little more, to those who do not see the benefit and do only enough of what is expected because they do not want to lose their jobs.

There is a significant difference between compliant employees and committed employees. Committed employees bring energy, passion, and excitement to their work. They have a belief in what it will take to bring about change and will do whatever it takes to get the job done even if it means changing the rules to accomplish the goal.

A main strength of interactive planning is the principle of participation by all those who will be affected by the planning process. . . .

By engaging a broad cross section of SHE professionals in the redesign process, the chances for achieving personal commitment for change from the SHE redesign network leaders and their team members were enhanced. . . . A new network leader who had joined the process well after it had started . . . commented that "the [SHE redesign] process is revolutionary, the outcome has the potential to change the fundamental way we do business. I believe the process will represent a step-change for the corporation because the outcome will be so compelling that everyone else in the corporation will be forced to defend why they are not doing the same thing. No other SBU is even close. . . ."

Design of Controls

The controls that were designed into the implementation process track the progress of each SHE Knowledge Team's work. At the beginning of the year each team selected critical operating tasks that would be accomplished by year-end. These tasks are directly connected to specific products identified for development in the consumer-idealized design. Progress on these critical operating tasks is reviewed at network meetings, the network leaders' meetings, and the steering team meetings. Deviations from the scheduled timing, financing, and/or resources are raised and addressed at these meetings. If issues cannot be addressed at the network team level, then they are raised to the next level for resolution.

Conclusion and Implications for Practitioners

The effort to redesign the SHE function in DuPont's Specialty Chemicals SBU represents a genuine application of the principles and methods of idealized redesign and interactive planning. In the past this type of effort would have limited its focus on the SHE function alone, without taking into account the numerous stakeholders the SHE function potentially affects. By embracing the principles of participation, continuity, and holism, we were able to overcome many of the obstacles traditionally faced by significant change efforts. In this case, redesigning the way we go about the task of doing safety, health, and environmental work in DuPont was tantamount to performing genetic engineering on the Corporation's DNA.

This effort set out to explore the application of systems thinking and interactive planning to a redesign of the work of SHE professionals to systemically deliver higher value adding results to the organization. Even though we could not draw on any literature written about the application of interactive planning to a SHE function, once the participants understood the theory and the practical application of the methods, they displayed a compelling sense of excitement, innovation, and creativity. For most participants, this was the first time in their careers that they had been given the opportunity to redesign their work and define their future roles and responsibilities to become contributors to the business's bottom line. By redesigning SHE work in a systemic fashion, we expected the following outcomes to occur.

The first outcome focuses on the proactive creation and development of a larger number of viable solutions to address SHE issues and problems. By establishing an environment that recognized the value of SHE professionals working together on common SHE issues and problems, we enhanced the creativity to explore a wider range of potential options and experiment with implementation. Becoming more informed on the business issue or problem, the SHE professional

could provide a variety of legal solutions, each carrying varying degrees
of risk. Providing a businessperson with a variety of solutions of varying degrees of risk allows him or her to make an informed business
decision suitable to the conditions of the business.

The second outcome deals with the ability of the SHE professional
to identify less expensive or cost-avoiding solutions. By first understanding the cost of doing SHE work and the impact of these costs on a
business, the SHE professional can find creative solutions to business
issues and problems.

The third outcome addresses the desire to have a step-change
improvement in SHE performance versus a continuous improvement
in performance. A step-change in performance requires a total rethinking of how one goes about improving performance. For SHE performance, we have had to recalibrate our belief system after introducing
the slogan "The Goal Is Zero." In addition, different approaches
involving more participation among employees and valuing their input
have helped significantly to achieve step-change in SHE performance.
One example involves the introduction of a behavior-based approach
to safety as opposed to the continuous use of the hierarchical com-
mand-and-control model for safety improvement. . . .The fourth outcome works on the conversion of a staff function from a cost-of-doing
business to a value-adding profit center whose services are in high
demand, both from the organization and its customers. All through the
implementation process, a mutual understanding between the SHE
professionals and the business professionals regarding each other's
issues and concerns has grown into a strong desire to make SHE a
competitive advantage feature of the business's product offerings.

The fifth outcome deals with the ability to create more time for
SHE professionals to do higher-value-adding work while trained line-
organization employees do the more routine work. Even though some
progress has been made toward this outcome, most SHE professionals
have difficulty transferring the routine work to trained line-organiza-
tion employees because many believe this work has made them successful to this point in their career. Emphasis is being placed on
redesigning the routine work and developing training programs to
help operators take an active role in doing SHE work. In my opinion,
this outcome is the most difficult to achieve but by far the most
rewarding for all involved.

The sixth outcome focuses on developing a more robust product
offering for customers. Throughout the implementation process and
beyond, the network teams are learning how to electronically docu-

ment their SHE work-experience memory so that it can be accessed in the future. Most of the products in Specialty Chemicals fall into the category of commodity chemicals. The competitive advantage for commodity chemical products comes in the form of price, quality, reliability, and service. Since most of our competitors can compete with us on price, quality, and reliability, the differentiator in the marketplace for us comes in the service we provide to our customers. As we continue to build our SHE knowledge database of experiences in doing SHE work and offer it to our customers, we believe this will provide a powerful differentiator in the marketplace for our product offering.

The seventh and final outcome involves SHE knowledge being made available to everyone in the organization so that they can make decisions that can lead to enhancing their SHE capability. As we begin to give all employees access to SHE knowledge, their desire to make their own decisions about their safety and health grows. An example of this came in giving operators access to DuPont's Global SHE Homepage on the corporation's intranet to look up the type of personal protective equipment (PPE) they needed when they encounter certain chemicals during their daily work. In addition, the operators were taught why they needed to wear the PPE. In the past this activity was accomplished by the operators seeking out the plant occupational health expert, who took his or her time to look up the information and identify the appropriate PPE. Now that the operators understand why they need to wear the PPE and how to find the PPE type, they have a much greater incentive to take personal ownership of their own occupational heath as opposed to relying on someone else.

. . . A great deal has been learned and continues to be learned as the implementation continues. Reflecting on the entire process, it would be easy to become seduced by the initial phases of the process since the consumer and designer approach to creating the idealized design is certainly unique compared to other planning processes. The real work, however, comes in sustaining the human energy and commitment to fully implement the idealized design.

References

Rummler, Geary A., and Alan P. Brache. 1988. *Developing organization maps: A handbook for understanding a business.* Warren, N.J.: Rummler-Brache Group.

———. 1990. *Improving performance: How to manage the white space on the organization chart.* San Francisco: Jossey-Bass Publishers.

Senge, Peter. 1990. *The fifth discipline.* 3rd ed. New York: Doubleday.

References and Sources

Ackoff, Russell L. 1962. *Scientific Method*. New York: John Wiley & Sons.

———. 1974. *Redesigning the future*. New York: John Wiley & Sons.

———. 1979. The future of operational research is past. *Journal of Operational Research Society* 30: 93–104.

———. 1981. *Creating the corporate future*. New York: John Wiley & Sons.

———. 1994. *The democratic corporation*. New York: Oxford University Press.

———. 1996. On learning and systems that facilitate it. *Center for Quality of Management Journal* 5 (fall): 27–35.

Ackoff, Russell L., Thomas A. Cowan, Peter Davis, Martin C. J. Euton, James C. Emery, Marybeth L. Meditz, and Wladimir M. Sachs. 1976. *The SCATT report: Designing a national scientific and technological communication system*. Philadelphia: University of Pennsylvania Press.

Ackoff, Russell L., and James R. Emshoff. 1975. Advertising research at Anheuser-Busch, Inc. (1963–68). *Sloan Management Review*, Winter, 1–15.

Ackoff, Russell L., and Miles M. Martin. 1963. The dissemination and use of recorded scientific information. *Management Science* 9: 322–36.

Ackoff, Russell L., and Elsa Vergara. 1981. Creativity in problem solving. *European Journal of Operational Research* 7: 1–13.

Adams, John L. 1974. *Conceptual Blockbusting*. Stanford: Stanford Alumni Association.

Altier, William. 1991. Benchmarking is a wonderful tool. . . . *the pa perspective* (December): 2.

———. 1994. Rightsizing = Wrongsizing. *the pa perspective* (June): 4–5.

American Management Association. 1995. 1994 AMA survey on downsizing. *Research Reports*, 20 July.

Argyris, C. 1993. *On organizational learning*. Cambridge, Mass.: Blackwell Publishers.

Argyris, C., and Donald A. Schon. 1974. *Theory in practice*. San Francisco: Jossey-Bass.

———. 1978. *Organizational learning: A theory of action perspective*. Reading, Mass.: Addison-Wesley.

Arthur D. Little, Inc. 1994. Companies continue to embrace quality programs, but TQM has generated more enthusiasm than results. 8 June press release.

Barnsley, Michael. 1988. *Fractals everywhere*. San Diego: Academic Press.

Bateson, Gregory. 1972. *Steps to an ecology of mind*. New York: Ballantine Books.

The battle for corporate control. 1987. *Business Week*, 18 May, 102–7.

Beer, Stafford. 1972. *The brain of the firm*. London: Allen Lane, Penguin Press.

Bertalanffy, Ludwig von. 1968. *General systems theory*. New York: George Braziller.

Bierce, Ambrose. 1967. *The enlarged devil's dictionary*. Harmondsworth, England: Penguin Books.

Burnham, James. 1941. *The managerial revolution*. New York: John Day.

Capra, Fritjof. 1983. *The turning point*. New York: Bantam Books.

Carlzon, Jan. 1987. *Moments of truth*. Cambridge, Mass.: Ballinger Publishing.

Chafetz, Morris. 1996. *The tyranny of experts*. Langham, N.Y.: Madison Books.

Checkland, Peter. 1981. *Systems thinking, systems practice*. Chichester, England: John Wiley & Sons.

Choo, Chun Wei. 1998. *The knowing organization*. New York: Oxford University Press.

Churchman, C. West. 1971. *The design of inquiring systems*. New York: Basic Books.

———. 1985. Churchman's conversations. *Systems Research* 2: 257–58.

Ciccantelli, Susan, and Jason Magidson. 1993. From experience: Consumer idealized design: Involving consumers in the product development process. *Journal of Product Innovation Management* 10: 341–47.

Davis, Stanley M., and Paul R. Lawrence. 1977. *Matrix*. Reading, Mass.: Addison-Wesley.

Davis, Tim R. V. 1991. Internal service operations. *Organizational Dynamics* (autumn): 5–22.

de Bono, E de. 1973. *Lateral thinking*. New York: Harper.

de Geus, Arie. 1988. Planning as learning. *Harvard Business Review* 66 (March–April): 70–74.

———. 1997. The Living Company. *Harvard Business Review* 75 (March–April): 51–59.

Department of Health, Education, and Welfare (HEW). 1973. *Work in America: Report of a special task force to the Secretary*. Cambridge, Mass.: MIT Press.

Drucker, Peter F. 1986. *The frontiers of management*. New York: E. P. Dutton.

———. 1991. Permanent cost cutting. *Wall Street Journal*, 11 January, A10.

———. 1994. The age of social transformation. *Atlantic Monthly*, November, 53–80.

Ernst and Young and the American Quality Foundation. 1992. Best practices report, October. Cleveland, Ohio.

Flood, Robert F. 1991. Implementing total quality management through total system intervention. *Systems Practice* 4 (December): 565–78.

Flower, E. F. 1942. Two applications of logic to biology. In *Philosophical Essays in Honor of Edgar Arthur Singer, Jr.*, edited by F. P. Clarke and M. Nahm, 69–85. Philadelphia: University of Pennsylvania Press.

Forrester, Jay W. 1961. *Industrial dynamics*. Cambridge: Wright-Allen Press.

———. 1971. *World dynamics*. Cambridge: Wright-Allen Press.

Friedman, Milton. 1970. The social responsibility of business is to increase its profits. *New York Times Magazine*, 13 September, 32f.

———. 1973. The voucher idea. *New York Times Magazine*, 23 September 23, 23f.

Galbraith, Jay. 1973. *Designing complex organizations*. Reading, Mass.: Addison-Wesley.

Gall, John. 1977. *Systemantics*. New York: Quadrangle/New York Times Book Co.

Geranmayeh, Ali. 1992. *Organizational learning through interactive planning: Design of learning systems for ideal-seeking organizations*. Ph.D. thesis in social systems sciences. Philadelphia: University of Pennsylvania.

Getzels, J. W., and M. Csikszentmihalyi. 1971. Discovery oriented behavior and originality of creative products. *Journal of Personality and Social Psychology* 19: 47–52.

Gharajedaghi, Jamshid. 1985. *Toward a systems theory of organization*. Seaside, Calif.: Intersystems Publications.

———. 1986. *A prologue to national development planning*. New York: Greenwood Press.

Gharajedaghi, Jamshid, and Ali Geranmayeh. 1992. Performance criteria as a means of social integration. In *Planning for Human Systems*, edited by Jean-Marc Choukroun and Roberta M. Snow. Philadelphia: University of Pennsylvania Press.

Goggin, William C. 1974. How the multidimensional structure works at Dow Corning. *Harvard Business Review* 52 (January–February): 54–65.

Goodman, Ted, ed. 1997. *The Forbes book of business quotations*. New York: Black Dog & Leventhal.

Gordon, Jack. 1996. A devil's dictionary of business buzzwords. *Training* (February): 33–37.

Gordon, W., 1972. *Synectics*. New York: Harper.

Halal, William E. 1986. *The new capitalism*. New York: John Wiley & Sons.

———. 1996. *The new management*. San Francisco: Berrett-Koehler Publishers.

Halal, William E., Ali Geranmayeh, and John Pourdehnad, eds. 1993. *Internal markets*. New York: John Wiley & Sons.

Hamel, Gary, and C. K. Prahalad. 1994. *Competing for the future*. Boston: Harvard Business School Press.

Hammer, Michael, and James Champy. 1993. *Reengineering the corporation*. New York: Harper Business.

Handy, Charles. 1997. The citizen corporation. *Harvard Business Review* (September–October): 27–28.

Huczynski, Andrej A. 1996. *Management gurus*. London and Boston: International Thomson Business Press.

Hussong, A. M. 1931. An analysis of the group mind. Ph.D. Dissertation. Philadelphia: University of Pennsylvania.

Hutchins, C. Larry. 1996. *Systems thinking*. Aurora, Colo.: Professional Development Systems.

Issawi, Charles. 1973. *Issawi's laws of social motion*. Princeton: Darwin Press.

Jenks, Christopher. 1970. Giving money for schooling: Educational vouchers. *Phi Delta Kappan* (September): 49–52.

Jennings, E. E. The world of the executive. *TWA Ambassador Magazine*, April, 28–30.

Kauffman, Draper L. 1980. *Systems one: An introduction to systems thinking*. Minneapolis, Minn.: S. A. Carlton.

Kiely, Thomas. 1993/94. Unconventional wisdom. *CIO*, 15 December/1 January, 24–28.

Kling, Julia. 1994. Re-engineering slammed. *Computerworld* (24), 13 June, 1, 14.

Laszlo, Ervin, and Alexander Laszlo. 1997. The contribution of the systems sciences to the humanities. *Systems Research and Behavioral Science* 14: 5–19.

Meier, Richard L. 1963. Communication overload: Proposals from the study of a university library. *Administrative Science Quarterly* 7: 521–44.

Micklethwaite, John, and Adrian Wooldridge. 1996. *The witch doctors*. New York: Times Books, Random House.

Miller, George A. 1956. The magical number seven, plus or minus two: Some limits on our capacity for processing information. *Psychological Review* 63: 81–97.

New encyclopedia britannica. 1974. 15th ed. *Macropaedia*, vol. 3, "s. v. Bureaucracy."

Nonaka, Ikujiro, and Hirotaka Takeuchi. 1995. *The knowledge-creating company*. New York: Oxford University Press.

Ortéga y Gasset, José. 1956. *Mission of the university*. New York: W. W. Norton.

Osborn, A. J. 1863. *Applied imagination*. New York: Scribner's.

Ozbekhan, Hasan. 1977. The future of Paris: A systems study in strategic urban planning. *Philosophical Transactions of the Royal Society of London*, A. 387: 523–44.

Peters, Tom. 1994. To forget is sublime. *Forbes ASAP Supplement*, 11 April, 128, 126.

Petzinger, Thomas, Jr. 1996. The front lines. *Wall Street Journal*, 10 May, B7.

Pourdehnad, John, William E. Halal, and Erwin Rausch. 1995. From downsizing to rightsizing to selfsizing. *Total Quality Review* (July/August): 43–50.

Rakstis, Ted, J. 1994. The downsizing myth. *Kiwanis*, April, 46ff.

Rapoport, Anatol. 1960. *Fights, games, and debates*. Ann Arbor: University of Michigan Press.

Raven, B. H., and H. T. Euchus. 1963. Cooperation and competition in means-independent trials. *Journal of Abnormal Psychology* 67: 307–16.

Rovin, Sheldon, Neville Jeharajah, Mark W. Dundon, Sherry Bright, Donald
    H. Wilson, Jason Magidson, and Russell L. Ackoff. 1994. *An idealized
    design of the U.S. healthcare system.* Bryn Mawr, Penn.: Interact.
Sachs, Wladimir. 1975. Man machine design: An inquiry into principles of
    normative planning for computer-based technical systems. Ph.D. the-
    sis in social systems sciences. Philadelphia: University of Pennsylvania.
Schon, Donald A. 1971. *Beyond the stable state.* New York: Random House.
Senge, P. 1990. *The fifth discipline.* 3rd ed. New York: Doubleday.
Shannon, Claude. 1952. Presentation of a maze-solving machine. *Conference
    proceedings of the Josiah Macy Foundation, eighth cybernetic transactions,*
    New York: Josiah Macy Foundation, 173–89.
Shapiro, Eileen C. 1995. *Fad surfing in the boardroom.* Reading, Mass.: Addi-
    son-Wesley.
Snow, C. P. 1964. *The two cultures: A second look.* New York: Mentor Books.
Sorokin, P. 1928. *Contemporary sociological theories.* New York: Harper &
    Brothers.
Stata, R. Organizational learning: The key to management innovation. *Sloan
    Management Review* 30: 63–74.
Toffler, Alvin. 1971. *Future shock.* New York: Bantam Books.
Vergara, Elsa. 1981. *Creativity in strategic planning.* A Ph.D. thesis in the social
    systems sciences. Philadelphia: University of Pennsylvania.
Villiers, Chris. 1997. Learning together. *Boeing News* (56), 3 October, 1.
Vogel, E. H., Jr. 1962. Creative marketing and management science. *Manage-
    ment Decision* (spring): 21–25.
White, Joseph B. 1996. Re-engineering gurus take steps to remodel their
    stalling vehicles. *Wall Street Journal,* 23 December, A1f.
Wysocki, Bernard Jr. 1995. Some companies cut costs too far, suffer "corpo-
    rate anorexia." *Wall Street Journal,* 5 July, 1f.
Zeleny, Milan, ed. 1981. *Autopoiesis: A theory of living organization.* New York:
    North Holland.

Index

Note: Page numbers in *italics* refer to illustrations or tables.